Figures of Dissent

Figures of Dissent
Critical Essays on Fish, Spivak, Žižek and Others

TERRY EAGLETON

VERSO

London • New York

First published by Verso 2003
© Terry Eagleton 2003 and the publications listed below
All rights reserved

The author and publishers would like to thank the *London Review of Books*, the
Independent on Sunday, the *Times Literary Supplement*, the *Times Higher Education Supplement*,
the *Guardian* and the *New Left Review* for permission to reproduce material for which they
hold the copyright.

1 3 5 7 9 10 8 6 4 2

Verso
UK: 6 Meard Street, London W1F 0EG
USA: 180 Varick Street, New York, NY 10014-4606
www.versobooks.com

Verso is the imprint of New Left Books

ISBN 1–85984–667–X

British Library Cataloguing in Publication Data
A catalogue record for this book is available from the British Library

Library of Congress Cataloging-in-Publication Data
A catalog record for this book is available from the Library of Congress

Typeset in Baskerville by YHT Ltd, London
Printed in USA by R.R. Donnelley & Sons

For John Barrell

Contents

Preface

The discerning reader may note that though some of these reviews sing the praises of their subjects, not all of them are uniformly enthusiastic. Perhaps this combative tone is among other things an heirloom of the Cambridge English school in which I was trained. I studied English at Cambridge in the last days of F.R. Leavis, so trenchancy seems to come naturally to me. I hope, even so, that some of these pieces are more humorous than Leavis ever was; and I am also conscious enough of how vindictive reviewing can sometimes be, having been regularly on the sticky end of it myself, to trust that though some of these essays may be polemical or satirical, they are not spiteful or unfair.

But that, of course, depends on where you happen to be standing. Liberals and conservatives really cannot complain when radicals take them to task. That is what we are in business for. Our political opponents should remember that there are many more of them than there are of us, and that they exchange quite enough plaudits among themselves to be able to dispense with ours. For every leftist voice which dares to suggest that W.B. Yeats could be remarkably silly, or that Isaiah Berlin was not the unqualified genius of liberal legend, there is a mass choir of commentators prepared to bawl out the alleluias.

I hope that these reviews, reprinted from various journals, may also bear witness to the fact that a kind of public sphere, in which one can try to write companionably about complex matters, lingers on among us in however vestigial a form. In Britain, such a forum has been provided in particular by the excellent *London Review of Books* under the imaginative editorship of Mary Kay Wilmers; and since many of these articles first appeared there, I feel a special gratitude to that periodical and its staff for allowing me to write so often at length on so many topics. I apologise in advance to those readers who, on perusing these pieces, feel unable to share that sense of gratitude.

Terry Eagleton
Dublin, 2002

Postmodern Savages

It is remarkable how many literary studies of so-called barbarians have appeared over the past couple of decades. Representations of Gypsies, cannibals, Aboriginals, wolfboys, noble savages: these, along with reflections on monsters, Mormons, cross-dressers and hairy Irish ape-men, have all flowed from postmodernism's enduring love-affair with otherness. One wonders what the Tuareg would think, if they ever got wind of it, about being classified with werewolves and fallen women. A flourishing industry in the study of travel writing can be traced to much the same sources. Criticism is becoming a minor offshoot of science fiction, even if it presents the exotic and outlandish only to upbraid such notions as imperialist. 'We are obsessed with "barbarians"', Claude Rawson remarks in this erudite, passionate book; but by 'we' he seems to be thinking of literary critics, not grapepickers or hairdressers.

The good news is that the Home Counties view of literature has now been decisively despatched. The native of the Southern hemisphere no longer appears in Anglo-Saxon culture only through the sights of a rifle or at the end of a sherry decanter. E.M. Forster had it both ways, allowing his bogusly emancipated reader to feel superiorly satirical about the redneck English while suddenly unmasking foreignness as a genuine threat, and so sending up liberals like himself into the bargain. But the days when any half-decent verse or prose emanating from the former Empire could be recruited as 'Commonwealth literature', ascribed a sort of country rather than town membership of the literary club, have vanished for ever. In cultural studies if in precious few other

First published as 'A Spot of Firm Government' (a review of *God, Gulliver and Genocide: Barbarism and the European Imagination 1492–1945* by Claude Rawson) in the *London Review of Books*, 23 August 2001.

places, what was once rejected has become the cornerstone, and centuries of insult and odious patronage are accordingly being made up for.

The bad news is that otherness is not the most fertile of intellectual furrows. Indeed, once you have observed that the other is typically portrayed as lazy, dirty, stupid, crafty, womanly, passive, rebellious, sexually rapacious, childlike, enigmatic and a number of other mutually contradictory epithets, it is hard to know what to do next apart from reaching for yet another textual illustration of the fact. The theme is as theoretically thin as it is politically pressing. Nothing is now more stereotyped in literary studies than the critique of stereotypes.

In any case, stereotypes are not always illusions. Many of them, to be sure, are both baseless and pernicious; but though it is not true, for example, that the Irish are lazy, it is true that the Irish immigrants who flooded from their small farms to the industrial cities of Victorian Britain in the wake of the Great Famine were accustomed to a less crippling work-discipline than their British counterparts, which could look to the latter much like indolence. Life as a small tenant farmer involved sporadic bursts of labour but a fair bit of leisure, too, and the Irish were fond of their fairs and feast-days. You could turn the muscles involved in planting potatoes to digging canals, but there seemed no point in overdoing it. How well you could live on an Irish farm was determined largely by its size, not by how hard you worked. And the puritan work-ethic of the British had few takers among pre-industrial Irish Catholics.

Not all stereotypes are pejorative or patronising. The Irish have been depicted by the British as feckless, bellicose and illogical, much given to guileful charm, rhetorical blather and deceitful deference; but they have also been seen as sensitive, congenial and gregarious, which is one reason they made such a signal contribution to the 18th-century cult of benevolence. When the English middle classes of the day desired a mode of sensibility less martial and frigid than that of their autistic rulers, it was often enough to the Celtic fringes that they turned, from which some semblance of pre-modern *Gemeinschaft* might still just about be salvaged. Richard Steele, Oliver Goldsmith, Laurence Sterne, Francis Hutcheson and Edmund Burke all made vital Irish contributions to this nouvelle vague of meekness, *tendresse*, womanliness, the glowing, melting sentiments, while David Hume, Adam Smith, Henry Mackenzie and

James Macpherson weighed in from North of the border. The Irish were never just gorillas with gelignite. Those Irish historians who play down the anti-Irishness of the British for their own political ends are right to that extent.

It would be surprising if people who have shared roughly the same cultural and material circumstances over long periods of time did not manifest some psychological traits in common. It would certainly be surprising to a materialist, which most scorners of stereotypes claim to be. Though stereotypes are sometimes purely fictional, they are not always so. The upper-class English are indeed for the most part more emotionally reserved than working-class Greeks or Italians, a fact which has more to do with their prep schools than their genes. Critics of stereotyping insist that the human subject is socially constructed, and end up endorsing the liberal banality that we're all individuals. They tend to believe, rightly, that men in general have some less than healthy attitudes to women, but not that Americans are on the whole more upbeat and affirmative than the English. Cultural traits exist, but not national characteristics.

Just as one of the customs most native to Ireland was getting out of the place, so nothing is more indigenously American these days than otherness. Openness to the other is a rebuke to the parochialism of a nation which finds it hard to distinguish between Brighton and Bogotá; but it is also a piece of parochialism in itself, rooted by and large in the intractable ethnic problems of the United States. These home-grown concerns are then projected onto the rest of the globe rather like a cultural version of nuclear missile bases, so that post-colonial others find themselves obediently adopting the agenda of a largely American-bred cult of otherness. Critics in, say, Sligo or Sri Lanka are to be found busily at work on the 'other', partly because it is an important question in its own right, but also because this is the programme peddled for its own private reasons, as it were, by the nation which sets the academic pace in these affairs. When American critics come to write about Ireland or Egypt, what tends to catch their eye are questions of margins and minorities which loom large on the intellectual menu of their own culture, rather than, say, educational policy or religious architecture, which are less glamorous concerns in their own backyard.

Much of this fascination with otherness involves the liberal assumption that there are no real aliens, just ways of seeing others as aliens. For conservatives, aliens are other people; for liberals, they are the fruit of false consciousness; for radicals, they are ourselves. There is indeed a monstrosity, an enigma resistant to understanding; it's just that it is a lot closer to home than the Dinka or Transylvanian aristocrats. The Yahoos, as Gulliver begins chillingly to realise, are as close to the bone as you can get. What we share with the allegedly impenetrable other is just this overlapping of strangenesses; and it is this, rather than some mutual mirror-imaging of egos, which has to become the basis of a genuine encounter. Always seeing the other as others is partly a way of avoiding this unnerving recognition, just as attending consistently to the margins is usually a way of implying that there are no conflicts or subversions to be found at the centre. In this assumption, post-modernists are rather more sanguine than the World Bank.

Claude Rawson, one imagines, would not in the least appreciate being mentioned in the same breath as postmodern otherness, even though his new book is all about genocide, barbarism, cannibalism, colonial conquest and mass extermination. For Rawson is essentially a conservative scholar, one of the finest 18th-century specialists, who unusually in such a traditionally stodgy area is also a critic of striking flair and delicacy. It is Swift, the Yahoos and the Anglo-Irish, stoutly traditional literary topics, which have led him to stray into the ethnic margins and domains of otherness, not some more modish pre-occupation with vampires or Vlad the Impaler. On the other hand, usually enough for someone working in such a traditionally stodgy area, he is testily hostile to literary theory and sports an English suburban distaste for political radicalism.

Rawson is thus keen not to be mistaken for Gayatri Spivak. With the air of a man fending off a fearful otherness with which he is covertly complicit, he writes scornfully of 'the indignant diatribes of self-righteous post-colonial censors', perhaps a necessary disowning of the voguish for a book which includes a chapter devoted to the protuberant buttocks and plump, pendulous or sagging breasts to be found in representations of female savages. Despite these dyspeptic disavowals, however, one can't avoid the impression that the transition from War-wick to Yale which Rawson underwent some years ago has left its mark on his intellectual interests. As probably the most accomplished Swift specialist in the business, he has now become rather more interested in the Anglo-Irish context as a whole, on which his book has an absorbing chapter; and Americans are generally more fascinated by Ireland than the English are, or indeed than the Irish are.

These interests may have been latent all along; but it can't be easy being a meticulously scholarly, politically right-of-centre critic whose current preoccupations happen by a remarkable stroke of ill luck to coincide with those of the post-colonial theoretical trendies one abhors. It's rather as though Roger Scruton were to find himself seized by a passionate zest for the minor details of the Marxist-feminist critique of housework.

God, Gulliver and Genocide is about ambiguity of motives—about those unstable mixtures of racism and anti-racism, collusion and rebellion, aversion and attraction, which, the book claims, defeat simplistic post-colonial polarities. It is about the half-joking yet half-serious desire to exterminate others, as well as about the way that authors like Swift and Montaigne are outraged by colonial brutality while being deep-dyed authoritarians themselves. Montaigne respected cultural difference except when he ran into a Huguenot, and denounced tribal cannibalism while turning a blind eye to the circulation of Huguenot body-parts on his own doorstep. Swift detested the Catholic Yahoos he obliquely championed. Both men recognise that the harmless native is neither harmless nor all that different from themselves; portraying him as gentle is usually a device to offset the viciousness of the colonialists rather than a judgment on how the natives actually are. Swift's Yahoos are both colonised wretches and humanity as a whole, which allows him to suggest that the imperialist is no better than the natives while continuing to promote a demeaning stereotype of the latter. Conrad pulls off much the same double-think in *Heart of Darkness*. If the Yahoos are all of us, then nobody deserves to lord it over anyone else; but if they are the lower orders, then they are brutish and belligerent enough to require a spot of firm government. Both authors also see that the colonialist partakes of the savagery he imputes to the barbarians, indeed outstrips them in it.

Swift's superior Houyhnhnms placidly debate whether the Yahoos should be exterminated from the face of the earth, which for Rawson prefigures in disconcerting detail much of what the Nazis actually did. He also thinks that Swift shows 'every sign of endorsing (or at least not disowning) the Houyhnhnm scheme', a statement which I should warn him is likely to get him into the newspapers. When I myself was as stern

as this about Swift in a review of a rather scrappy biography some time
ago, the enraged biographer took out a full page in the *Spectator* to
belabour my piece. Or so I am told; I don't read the *Spectator*. It is still
not acceptable, especially in certain genteel Anglo-Irish circles, to point
out what a deeply unpleasant bigot this stupendous satirist was. Only
Yahoos do that.

Rawson, however, who has a chapter impudently entitled 'Killing the
Poor: An Anglo-Irish Theme?', is clearly undaunted by the Ascendancy
literary mafia. Swift's *A Modest Proposal*, with its suggestion that the
famished Irish should cook and eat their own children, is in his view less
a satirical smack at the English than another of his intemperate digs at
so-called Irish self-destructiveness. The whole pamphlet, read by some
as magnificent anti-colonial polemic, is for Rawson 'an exasperated
version of the cannibal slur' on the Irish, a *canard* which its imagery
mischievously revives. Nor is Swift the only Anglo-Irishman to dream of
wiping out the underclass. Oscar Wilde poured scorn on sentimental
do-gooders who 'try to solve the problem of poverty ... by keeping the
poor alive', while Bernard Shaw declared that he hated the poor and
looked forward eagerly to their extermination. All this, as they say
earnestly, is only a joke; but it is part of this book's purpose to inquire
why we find phrases like 'They ought to shoot the lot of them' mildly
funny.

Shaw, who as Rawson points out has a good deal of sympathy for Saint
Joan's inquisitors, writes in his preface to *Major Barbara* that it would be
more sensible to put the poor in 'the lethal chamber' rather than in jail,
and advocated killing every adult who earned less than £365 a year.
Wilde rather less flamboyantly proposed what Rawson calls an 'aesthetic
cleansing' of the poor, as Swift had urged that beggars should wear
badges. Wilde and Shaw are being outrageous, of course, as the Irish in
Britain are expected to be; but this does not mean that they are not
being sincerely aggressive as well, and in Shaw's case autocratic. There
is a pathologically hygienic quality to his Fabianism, an anally retentive
horror of loose ends, which led him to some sinister political allegiances.

It's true that there is nothing peculiarly Anglo-Irish about this flip
heartlessness. One could find quite as many home-grown examples.
Even so, the book could have made more of what Roy Foster has called

the distinctive 'savagery of mind' of the Anglo-Irish Ascendancy, its semi-crazed pugnaciousness and crudity of spirit. Behind the vindictive rage of a Swift lies the unstable blend of arrogance and insecurity of a second-class governing class, one which, as Rawson comments of Swift, 'disliked the metropolitan masters not for their treatment of the native subjects but for an alleged betrayal of the *colons* themselves'. It is the *ressentiment* of the Ulster Unionists today. Boisterous, swashbuckling and uncouth, the more rapscallion wing of the landowning Ascendancy displayed a casual violence and cavalier disdain which can both be felt behind the more sadistic utterances of a Swift or Shaw, as well as in the *canaille*-hating superciliousness of a Yeats. In the case of the Anglo-Irish, then, the psychic ambiguities of racism and anti-racism, alienation and affinity, which Rawson traces from the conquest of the Americas to the end of the Second World War, take on a more concretely political form, one appropriate to a nation which the British Government treated sometimes like Kent and sometimes like Kamchatka.

There is, however, a more creditable reason for this Anglo-Irish savagery, which Rawson seems not to register. Much of the hardboiled irreverence of Wilde and Shaw is a covert smack at English moralism and sentimentalism, which the Irish have always found irresistibly amusing. Both men, confronted with the more edifying, lip-quivering discourse of the Victorian bourgeoisie, felt the outsider's compulsive urge to put their foot through it. This was partly because the Irish have been on the whole less sentimental than the English, having had less to be sentimental about. You do not go all gooey over children or animals when you see them primarily as labour-power, or over the family when most of its members have to emigrate. Love in such conditions is more a matter of dowries and land inheritance than of perfumed notepaper and candlelit dinners. Wilde and Shaw, as blow-ins in the English metropolis, were shrewd enough to see that sentimentalism is the lachrymose visage which power turns mournfully to the world. It is not at all surprising that hard-bitten politicians sob in public from time to time—not only because it might prove a vote-winner, but because sentimentalism is the kind of broad-brush caricature of feeling which strangers to emotional subtlety are able to pull off. It is the thick-skinned view of feeling, as the bohemian is the burgher's view of the artist.

*

Rawson misses this streak of colonial perversity, evident in Shaw's bumptious paradoxes and Wilde's witty inversions, which inspires the outsider to violate linguistic decorum, turn a truth on its head or rip a moral tag inside out. Both men, like the authorial persona of *A Modest Proposal*, betray an animus which is perversely deepened by being so clinically formulated. There may also be in their calculatedly murderous comments the hint of an Irish culture which was never perhaps much more violent than that of its metropolitan proprietors, but where violence, partly because most of it was political, was more acceptable and everyday. It was a culture of verbal belligerence, too: somewhere behind Swift's virulent invective lurks the ancient lineage of Irish cursing, when the local bard could wither your loins with a well-aimed imprecation.

Rawson's new book, despite some repetition and an excessive relish for the word 'erupt' in all of its grammatical forms, is learned, wide-ranging and acute. Because so much of the discussion is drawn from recondite works about images of the Hottentot or Nazi medical experiments, the kind of close literary readings which Rawson can do best are disappointingly squeezed out. But *God, Gulliver and Genocide* is bound to be greeted with acclaim, not least for all those protuberant buttocks, by just the sort of readership that its author most disapproves of.

Last Words

The story is told of an Irishman who appeared on *Mastermind* and took as his special subject modern Irish history. Who was the first female President of Ireland? he is asked. 'Pass', he replies instantly. Which neighbouring island once had sovereignty over the whole country? 'Pass', he responds unhesitatingly. Which crop failed in the Great Famine? 'Pass', flashes back the contestant. The embarrassment in the studio is growing palpable when an Irish voice shouts out from the audience: 'That's right, Mick—tell the bastards nothing!'

From the secret societies of 18th-century rural agitators to the interrogation centres of modern Derry and Belfast, the Irish have been well-practised at telling the bastards nothing. The custom is reflected in one of Seamus Heaney's most quoted lines: 'Whatever you say, say nothing.' The one place where you might as well cough, however, is the gallows, as is clear from this volume of last speeches edited by the indefatigable Irish historian James Kelly. The speech from the gallows, along with the sermon, the sectarian pamphlet, the tall tale, the statement from the dock, the denunciation from the church altar and the address from the hustings, are among the most venerable of Irish literary genres. They are performative rather than representational pieces of discourse, as befits a society where, from Swift and Sterne to Bram Stoker and James Joyce, literary realism never really took root, and where the frontier between art and politics was never exact.

An Irish scholar boasted in 1684 that his far-flung sector of County Galway, Iar Connacht, was so law-abiding that none of its inhabitants

First published as 'Larry kept his mouth shut' (a review of *Gallows Speeches From 18th-Century Ireland* edited by James Kelly) in the *London Review of Books*, 18 October 2001.

had been brought to the bar or executed for thirty years. He did not mention that the law in the region was so ill-defined it was hard to know how to break it. Irish bandits in the 17th century were known by the Gaelic-derived name of Tories, a word still associated with daylight robbery, which was then derisively applied to those in Britain who resisted the new Williamite political order. Picturesquely holed up in mountain, bog and forest, some Irish Tories were rumoured to be popular champions or Robin Hood figures, genteel Catholic Jacobites who had squandered or forfeited their estates and now robbed the rich to give to the poor. Most of them, however, made do more modestly with simply robbing the rich. Like many an Irish dissident, they had no ardent objection to particular laws, just to the law itself. What never fully managed to sell itself in Ireland was legality as such, redolent as it was of imperial rule. Recent moral outrage over the introduction of wheel-clamping in Dublin would suggest that old anti-colonial habits die hard.

Tories may not all have been the Zapata figures they have been cracked up to be, but Irish rebellion was not without its aura of romance. Agrarian secret societies such as the Whiteboys, Rightboys, Defenders, Dingers, Black Hens, Blackfeet, Rockites, Shanavests and Caravats were Hobsbawmian 'social bandits', midnight legislators seeking by organised violence to regulate lands, wages, rents and tithes in the countryside. But they also formed a whole counter-cultural underground, with their carnivalesque iconography of cross-dressing, exotic oaths, bizarre pseudonyms, mythologised leaders and esoteric initiation ceremonies. In the early 19th century there were Caravat and Shanavest pubs, wren-boys, mummers' teams, songs and dance tunes. Nicholas Hanley, chief of the Caravats, was a flamboyant dandy who strutted about with a blunderbuss and brace of pistols, returned to his plundered victims any items he thought it beneath his dignity to pocket, and ostentatiously threw his elegant cravat to the mob from the gallows. Another bandit chief, Captain Wheeler, was a devout adherent of matrimony, having wangled himself three simultaneous wives and murdered an entire family to gain a fourth.

These primitive rebels shaded into the illicit world of Tories, smugglers, faction fighters and poteen brewers; in some parts of the country, smuggling and poteen brewing were key economic activities, so that normality required its deviation just to stay alive. Every decade from 1760 to 1840 witnessed at least one major outbreak of rural discontent, though for much of this period Ireland was not a particularly belligerent place, perhaps less so than Britain. Non-agrarian crime was remarkably rare. Even in recent times the record has been in some ways impressive: only 12 police officers were murdered in the country between 1970 and 1990, a statistic which might interest the mayor of Miami. The felons whose last words are recorded here are robbers and murderers rather than rural militants, but that is because they were executed in Dublin. There is one Tory among them, whose heart, liver, lights and members were burned after his execution, and whose head was set on the gaol, 'two yards higher than any of the rest', complete with its hat and wig.

One modern Irish historian, eager in revisionist spirit to dismantle images of Irish barbarism, points out emolliently that in mid-Victorian Ireland only 45 per cent of those killed died of gunshot wounds, while 30 per cent died of head injuries, 11 per cent of less precisely specified injuries, and 7 per cent of stabs and cuts. It is gratifying to learn that the Irish were such a pacific bunch. The same historian adds that 'few landlords were fired at more than once', further testimony to the rural tenantry's high moral tone. Agitators' attitudes to their landlords could indeed be ambivalent: it was not unknown to read the squire a loyal address on the morning of his wedding while creeping out that very night to disembowel his cattle. Nineteenth-century Ireland still had twice as many policemen per head of population as Britain, along with garrisons of troops and yeomanry, and witnessed an average of one coercive Act a year. But things were at least not as dire as when a legal judgment of 1758 had declared that a Catholic existed in law only for the purpose of punishment. Threatening letters to landlords, which for some reason worthy of scholarly investigation tended to peak in March and slope off in April or May, continued unabated; but one such missive, after issuing a lurid death threat, concluded with impeccable courtesy: 'Hoping to find you in good health as this leaves me at present.' Deference was clearly not dead.

Something of the theatrical spirit of the secret societies pervaded the later insurrectionary Ireland of Yeats, Maud Gonne and James Connolly. Nationalism is an aesthetic sort of politics, in which fact and fiction easily interbreed. Connolly's Citizen Army staged an assault on Dublin Castle one foggy night without being sure whether the operation was real or simulated. The labour leader James Larkin was smuggled into a Dublin hotel disguised in a count's cloak and false beard, while Maud Gonne, who had played an old crone in Yeats's play *Cathleen ni Houlihan*, played one again to smuggle herself back into the country when banned from its shores. The printing press for the 1916 insurrection was installed in the Abbey Theatre, and the first man to be killed in the uprising was an Abbey actor who had been playing the lead role in a drama by James Connolly, who in turn played a leading role in the revolution. An Irish nurse attending wounded British soldiers in Dublin was rewarded with a bit part in a West End revue.

Rural militancy gathered steam in the mid-18th century; and it was around that time, so Kelly informs us, that the vogue for broadsides of last speeches began to wane. Of the 62 gallows speeches reprinted here, 58 fall in the period before 1740. Since the speeches were less spontaneous confessions than a stratagem of the state, dramatising the submission of miscreants to its august authority, it is hardly surprising that they should be less in fashion as social dissent became more clamorous. As the country slid towards the ethnic cleansing of the revolutionary 1790s, the populace were less likely to relish accounts of each other's mutilation at the hands of a brutally inequitable law, let alone derive moral admonishment from them. From the 1740s onwards, so the editor informs us, the Irish were also less likely to take capital punishment as such lying down. Mobs would lay the bodies of hanged men at the door of their prosecutors, hangmen were occasionally stoned and gallows pulled down, while bodies left dangling on gibbets were taken down for revival, waking or burial. (Incredulous non-Irish readers should recall the Irish meaning of 'wake'.) And there was always a minority of the condemned who chose to 'die hard' by avowing their innocence or just keeping their mouths shut. Among this intrepid company was Larry, felonious hero of the magnificent Irish ballad 'The Night before Larry Was Stretched', who perversely insists on regarding the gallows as an Ideological State Apparatus:

> When one of us asked could he die
> Without having truly repented,
> Says Larry, 'That's all in my eye,
> And first by the clergy invented,
> To get a fat bit for themselves.'

Just as a sadist requires the active response of his prey, so the law risks falling into disrepute if those whom it penalises fail to affirm it. Rather as there is no literary work without a reader, so power lives only in the response of its victims. Indeed, Hume held that 'force is always on the side of the governed', since it is impotent without assent. Power is the effect of obedience, rather than vice versa. There is no more effective resistance to authority than genuinely not giving a toss for it, which is not the same as despising or resenting it. Barnadine, the psychopathic convict of *Measure for Measure*, is so morally indolent that he objects to his impending execution only because it interferes with his sleep. The state must therefore defer his dying until he has been persuaded to embrace it, otherwise his punishment will lose much of its point. Unless he somehow performs his own death, appropriates it as authentically his own, it will fail to constitute an event in his life and thus lapse from the sphere of meaning to the domain of mere biology. At the point of death, the most rebarbatively real of all occurrences, one is called upon to be an actor, as the rapists and footpads of 18th-century Dublin were expected to speak to a prepared text with the rope around their necks, striking pious or remorseful poses on the edge of eternity.

The question of consent to law is especially relevant to Ireland, since its Anglo-Irish governors were able to practise power but not, by and large, to enjoy hegemony. It thus comes as no surprise that hege-mony—the notion that power thrives only on assent and affection—is the abiding theme of the greatest of all Irish political thinkers, Edmund Burke. The law for Burke was essentially male, but to work effectively it had to engage in a spot of strategic cross-dressing just like its agrarian antagonists, kitting itself out seductively as a woman. Kelly has his doubts about the hegemony thesis, since gallows speeches were beamed at different audiences with variable effects. But one of their intentions was doubtless to legitimate an authority increasingly uncertain of itself. They belonged to what one historian has called 'the theatre of the scaffold', an arena in which violence must not only be done but must be seen to be done. On this view, a private execution would be as pointless as an orgy of one. If rebels had their spectaculars, so did the sovereignty they challenged.

Gallows speeches involved the death of the author as well as of the miscreant. As Kelly comments, they drew on the combined output of offenders, clergy, printers, publishers, and possibly family members, jailers and fellow prisoners. They were heavily formulaic affairs, set moulds into which a convict could pour his or her own particular mix of autobiography and spiritual reflection; and this blending of art and reality was reflected in the proto-postmodern practice by which hawkers would sometimes sell broadsheets of last speeches at the execution itself, in time-warping, life-imitating-art style. If these texts were political acts, they were also commercial commodities. Moreover, they combined fact and fiction in their content as well as in their occasion and mode of production. Edward English, a butcher executed for robbery in 1707, tells us that he was 'Born at *South-Gate* in Cork, and lived there for the space of Fourteen Years; during which time my poor Parents endeavour'd to keep me to School; soon after I left *Cork*, and came for *Dublin* ... where [my father] did endeavour like an honest Man to get his Bread and did keep me at School full Two Years more, and then bound me Apprentice to one *William Carter*, Butcher in *New-street*.' Later, having fallen prey to 'Cursing, Swearing, and Lewd Women' (a remarkable number of these crooks claim to have been brought low by floozies), he turned to robbery. The passage could be lifted from an 18th-century picaresque novel, as could the perfunctory phrases of contrition with which the speech concludes.

In fact, gallows speeches as a literary genre betray a contradiction which is also built into the realist novel. Some of their readers, Kelly comments, consumed them for their narratives rather than their moral lessons; but this is also a problem with *Moll Flanders, Tom Jones* and *Clarissa*, where we are supposed to do both. The novel is born of the subversive, soap-opera-like recognition that routine reality, the sheer quotidian flow, can be endlessly captivating, and that the mere representation of this process can be an enthralling end in itself. But this pleasure in the real is ideologically suspect, since like most pleasure it appears to be amoral. Reality must have a point, and narrative must double-code the stuff of the world so that it is at once itself and symbolic, empirical and moral, individual and typical. Otherwise we are in danger of wallowing in our senses, becoming enmired in the material signifier, mistaking the trees for the wood. The basis of major realism is thus also the rationale behind tabloid exposures: from the Newgate novel to the *News of the World*, the sensational is in the service of the socially responsible.

The story, in short, must have a moral. This moral will not convince us unless it is fleshed out in grippingly particularised form; but the more this happens the more realism becomes a sensuous pleasure in itself and so threatens to undermine the moral truth it is meant to illustrate. If God resides in the moral whole, the devil lies in the realist detail, and as usual he has all the best tunes. The more fascinating the narrative, the more endangered is its exemplary status. Richardson wrote to a friend that he did not want to announce that *Clarissa* was fictional, but neither did he wish the reader to think that it was genuine. To disclose its fictional status would risk undercutting its realist impact, but readers who took it as real-life history might miss its allegorical import. In his later fiction, Richardson is still pretending that his story is genuine but taking no pains to make the pretence plausible; he is, so to speak, pretending to pretend.

The drunks, thieves and fornicators of these orations are expected, like the realist novel, to treat themselves as individual and exemplary at one and the same time. The symbolic space of the gallows, like that of the literary narrative, transposes them for the duration of their fifteen minutes of fame from the empirical to the ethical, the descriptive to the prescriptive. Dying as real men and women, they are reborn in the same moment, down where the hawkers are touting their broadsheets, as fictional or mythological figures, dead marks on paper which will nevertheless live a lot longer than they did themselves. In one of the most celebrated of Irish poems, 'Easter 1916', Yeats will do just the same by the performative force of his rhetoric to the executed leaders of the Dublin uprising, gathering them from the contingency of history into the artifice of eternity.

Yet it is not easy to be simultaneously oneself and something else, and most of these amateur orators make something of a hash of it. If the empirical bits of their narrative are too dully digressive, incongruously at odds with the high drama of the occasion, the ethical or exemplary bits ('I die a *Roman Catholick*, and the Lord have Mercy on my Poor Soul Amen') are too tritely tacked on. One does not expect those who are just about to be topped to rise to Ciceronian heights of expressiveness; but it is interesting even so that the way in which so many of these pieces are botched reflects some of the structural problems of a newly emergent realism. It is not, one presumes, a point which would have been foremost in the mind of the plundering butcher Edward English.

As a champion of the common life, the novel is a genuinely democratic form. We can now only dimly imagine the baffled excitement of readers reared on a diet of tragedy, elegy and pastoral on first perusing a page of Defoe, where the everyday has suddenly become alluring in its own right. It is not an unqualified advance, for now the most humble of men and women can serve as tragic protagonists. You no longer have to rise high in order to fall with a suitably eye-catching splash. In fact, the more down-at-heel your life, the more precarious and potentially tragic it is likely to be. This is one reason the new heroes of 18th-century writing are whores and orphans rather than knights and dowagers. The other symbolic space which proves particularly hospitable to the dispossessed is the gallows, where absolutely anybody can play the leading role, and where you do not need to rise all that high in order to drop.

The Nature of Gothic

All over the world, postgraduate students of English who might once have written on Wordsworth or Mrs Gaskell are now turning out theses on vampires, monsters, sado-masochism and mutilation. Most of this can be put down to postmodern faddishness, though vampires have a more venerable pedigree, as Richard Davenport-Hines notes in his agreeable romp through Gothic art from Salvator Rosa to Damien Hirst. Bram Stoker's *Dracula*, now translated into over forty languages, has exerted an enduring fascination since its publication in 1897, with Dracula himself the most filmed fictional character after Sherlock Holmes. An English film, made in 1962, was responsible for five thousand fainting cases in cinemas, 75 per cent of them male. Women presumably see more blood than men, and men no doubt saw even less of it before they were allowed to be present at births. The late Romanian dictator Ceausescu decreed one of Dracula's prototypes, Vlad the Impaler, a national hero, while 27 per cent of respondents to an American survey confessed to believing in vampires. There is a Santa Cruz Vampires Motor-Cycle and Scooter Club, and US vampires communicate by e-mail.

Postmodernism's obsession with the deviant, exotic and grotesque is partly an inheritance from modernism itself. Modernism tends to find ordinary life tediously suburban, and sees the truth as disclosing itself only at an extreme. A tragic hero is anyone scooped off the 8.15 to Paddington and pushed to the limit. The *acte gratuit*, the existential gesture, the commitment sustained into death, the word to end all

First published as 'Allergic to Depths' (a review of *Gothic: Four Hundred Years of Excess, Horror, Evil and* Ruin by Richard Davenport-Hines) in the *London Review of Books*, 18 March 1999.

words, the one action which will fix your identity for all eternity: these are among modernism's myths of extremity, along with the belief that language itself is in so dismally inauthentic a state that only by purging or cramming or dislocating it will you force it to yield up its secrets. It is what one might call, after George Orwell's *1984*, the Room 101 syndrome: what Orwell's protagonist says when a cageful of starved rats are about to burrow through his cheek and devour his tongue must undoubtedly be the truth. Since most of us who found ourselves in this situation would say anything at all, the strangeness of this doctrine should give us pause. Why should truth and extremity be thought to be bedfellows?

Part of the answer is that everyday life is now felt to be irredeemably alienated, so that only what violates or estranges it can be valid. For postmodern thought, the normative is inherently oppressive, as though there was something darkly autocratic about civil rights legislation or not spitting in the milk jug. Norms are just those aberrations we happen to endorse—in which case, since all aberrations are potential norms, they, too, ought to be suspect. And if consensus is the tyranny of the majority, as it seems to be for, say, Jean-François Lyotard, then there can be no radical consensus either. Since most purveyors of this wisdom pride themselves on their historicising cast of mind, it is ironic that they fail to see in it a reflection of the particular social conditions of modernity. For Samuel Johnson, it was the socially typical which was imaginatively enthralling, and aberration which was boring. Johnson had a proudly populist trust in the robustness of routine meanings, and saw language as embodying the common experience distilled from everyday practices. These days, it is not hard to find radicals who affirm the cause of the common people but dismiss their language as false consciousness. Postmodern celebrations of the off-beat, marginal and minoritarian belong, among other more positive things, to an age in which the notion of a radical mass movement has become, not least for those too young to remember one, a contradiction in terms.

Davenport-Hines sees the postmodern as the latest resurgence of Gothic—a self-confirming case to some extent, since he tends to read the latter in terms of the former. But he has a point even so. The speech of American youth—*weird, gross, bizarre, wicked, scary*—is certainly the discourse of Gothic, which before modernism arrived on the scene was the most resourceful antagonist of literary realism we could muster.

Malevolent barons, lascivious monks, victimised virgins, shaggy ruins, mouldering dungeons: if these gaudy pieces of theatre hardly seem the stuff of high art, they nevertheless played their part in an extravagant critique of Enlightenment reason, not least from the standpoint of the women who represented that reason's repressed underside. Gothic is the grotesque shadow thrown by its remorseless glare, the political unconscious of a middle-class society which has thrust its anxieties and persecutory fantasies into the safekeeping of its fiction. If we were to imagine that our daily social doings were all the time weaving a monstrously distorted subtext of themselves, an invisible verso to the recto of our waking life, then the guilt, horror and spectacular violence of Gothic might well be one place where this dreadful discourse could be uncovered.

There are other parallels between Gothic and the postmodern, which Davenport-Hines rather too tersely notes. If schlock has always been part of Gothic culture, much of which is terrible in more senses than one, kitsch plays an equivalent role in postmodern art. Television soap opera, which supplies 'shocks, facile emotional thrills and factitious intensity by manipulating stereotypical characters in mechanistic plots', is for Davenport-Hines the very essence of Gothic. But the two currents are also akin in their campness, their self-conscious theatricality and over-the-top artifice. This book's subtitle—'Four Hundred Years of Excess, Horror, Evil and Ruin'—belongs to that genre. Davenport-Hines sees 'Goths' as in revolt against the stable, cohesive bourgeois self, celebrating human identity instead as 'an improvised performance, discontinuous and incessantly redevised by stylised acts'. This is to read the Gothic too doctrinally through the lens of the postmodern, with Ann Radcliffe playing Kathy Acker; but the analogy is suggestive. Horace Walpole's *The Castle of Otranto* is convincingly read here as high camp.

But there are important differences, too. Gothic represents a ruined or fractured realism, excessive because its desire carries it beyond the ego and social convention; postmodern horror belongs to an epoch in which horror itself has become conventional, and so must be suitably self-ironising. It is the culture of an era too calloused and streetwise to be shocked, and so reaps its wry humour from the pointlessness of any such attempt. Gothic, by contrast, is funny in the way all excessive intensity is, as well as in the manner of an obscene joke. It allows us to indulge our repressed fantasies so unashamedly that we laugh at its very barefacedness, quite independently of its content.

Any terror put into an accomplished enough artistic form becomes enjoyable, and so self-contradictory. To this extent, Gothic is sado-masochistic in its form as well as in much of its content. We take pleasure in being terrified, not least when the terrors in question are those of others. As Schopenhauer knew, we reap pleasure from fictional frights partly because we relish our own immunity to the injury they threaten, and thus, as Freud might have added, we allow Eros its momentary triumph over Thanatos. But since the death wish means that we are gratified by destruction in real life, the enjoyment we gain from horror stories is also a heightened version of how we react to real-life alarms. Like the Freudian unconscious, Gothic is at once intense and mechanical, a realm of noble passion full of creaking machinery, hamfisted gambits and crude stereotypes. It is a world of trompe l'oeil, in which bookshelves conceal instruments of torture and nothing is as it appears; but if it distrusts appearances it is also allergic to depths, preferring to stage emotion and externalise its conflicts.

Just as Freud unmasks the bourgeois family as a cockpit of lusts and loathings, so the Gothic novel turns that sacrosanct community into a nightmare of incest, greed and lethal antagonism. One does not need to stray too far beyond the domestic hearth to find skeletons in cup-boards, murky inheritances and murderous violence. Burke wished to portray political society as a family: the Gothic writers reversed the analogy to devastating effect. Davenport-Hines recounts the story of the extraordinary Kingsborough family of Mitchelstown Castle in Ireland, whose history outstripped their ill-proportioned Gothic pile in gro-tesquerie and extravagance. One Kingsborough, having blown out the brains of his daughter's seducer, chose to be tried in the Irish House of Lords, after his daughter had given birth to a still-born child and lost her sanity. Dressed in deep mourning for the man he had murdered, and standing under the poised axe of the executioner, Kingsborough was found not guilty by every peer there. His son George, having commanded his tenants to assemble in his hall to explain why they had failed to vote for him at an election, went mad before their eyes. Committed to the care of a mad-doctor, he 'was unwilling to conform to any regulations, but ... could give an opinion on the value of cattle'. When it comes to the Anglo-Irish Ascendancy, of which the author of

Dracula was himself a member, Gothic is largely a question—to quote another Irish Gothicist—of life imitating art. Mary Wollstonecraft was governess to the Kingsborough daughters for a while, and an under-cook called Claridge later opened a hotel in London.

If the demonic, macabre stuff of Gothic proves alluring, it is partly because the devil has all the best tunes. But why? For traditional theology, virtue is a matter of energy and enjoyment, and evil mere deprivation. Evil may make a lot of noise, but the dust and heat it raises derive from an incapacity for life, which is why nobody could actually be in hell. To be damned must mean to be dead. All this, however, is bound to look different when the middle classes are in the ascendancy. Once virtue becomes the deadly dull stuff of thrift, prudence, tem-perance, submissiveness and sexual repression, the devil has much less trouble in drumming up a fan club. Satanism is in this sense just the flipside of suburbia. As John Carey has observed, the grotesque freaks who populate the fringes of a Dickens novel represent the sadistic vengeance which the text wreaks on its own decorous middle-class story-line. Nobody would ask Oliver Twist to dinner if they could hook Fagin instead. Samuel Richardson must have known that the saintly Clarissa was a bore, just as the creator of Emma Woodhouse must have seen that the virtuous Fanny Price was hardly a bundle of fun; but both Richardson and Austen are challenging us to imagine how virtue, in such predatory social circumstances, could ever be anything else. The transgressions of Gothic are dependent on the sobrieties of realism, just as the 'bad' body of Gothic—monstrous, mutilated, libidinal—repre-sents the guilty yearning of the 'good', sanitised body of the suburbs.

A further parallel between the Gothic and the postmodern, though one which this study seems not to notice, lies in their political ambi-guity. Davenport-Hines points out that Gothic fiction 'is nothing if not hostile to progressive hopes'; for all its delight in excess and inversion, it is notably nervous of political upheaval. As he perceptively remarks, Gothic architecture evoked ideas of feudal hierarchy and stability which a good deal of Gothic literature took pains to subvert. But Gothic writing is more a revolution of the subject than a transformation of society, and much the same could be said of the politics of post-modernism. Much Gothic literature is sexually audacious for its time, and so, if the word 'audacious' still had any meaning, would a lot of postmodernist culture be. But in both cases sexuality can come to stand in for other political conflicts, in a process of displacement which is of interest to the psychoanalytical theory that reinvented sexuality for our time. In the case of late 18th-century Gothic novelists like 'Monk' Lewis and Ann Radcliffe, this was largely because of a conservative stance towards the revolutionary events of their day, whereas for the post-modernists it is largely because there seem to be no revolutionary events around. If working-class militancy is dead, Marxism discredited and revolutionary nationalism on its uppers, then the field of sexuality can provide the forms of power-struggle, symbolism and solidarity which are less and less available elsewhere, along with a greater chance of political gains.

Gothic, as this book recognises, is all about power and domination: the fiction of the Brontë sisters, in which there is hardly a human relationship that does not involve a sado-masochistic power-struggle, is Gothic in just this sense. The Gothic is one of the first great imaginative ventures into what we would nowadays call sexual politics, boldly pursuing the business of power into the very folds and crevices of human subjectivity. To this extent, Foucault is a thoroughly Gothic theorist. But like a good deal of postmodern thought, the sexual radicalism of Gothic doesn't imply a revolutionary politics in general. If sado-masochism can unmask sexuality as a political affair, it can also urge the delights of deference. Not every 'Goth' was a Sade (a social revolutionary to whom this book devotes some fascinating pages).

This is clear enough from Davenport-Hines's inclusion among his Goths of Alexander Pope, the Earl of Shaftesbury and the architect William Kent. The dominant culture of 18th-century England was not averse to a spot of wild irregularity, not least when it came to gardening. Or indeed to the heroic couplet, which combines symmetry with freedom, the regular tapping of the metre with the curvings and flexings of the speaking voice. The sublime, an aesthetic notion much touted by postmodernists as subversive, becomes in Burke's hands the intimidatory aura by which political authority secures our compliance. English ideology has always been canny enough to incorporate a fair amount of fancy and freewheeling, of that stubborn contingency which resists the high-rationalist schemes of the inhuman French.

Even so, quite what Pope, Kent and Shaftesbury are doing in a study of Gothic is a question worth raising. Davenport-Hines's Goths are an oddly assorted bunch, including among others Goya, Piranesi, Fuseli,

William Shenstone, Byron, Hawthorne, Faulkner, Evelyn Waugh, Poppy Z. Brite and David Lynch. 'Gothic' is no doubt as variable in definition as it is in quality, but one can't avoid the sense of a certain arbitrariness of selection. It is not so much that any obvious authors have been left out; it is rather that there are a few queer-looking gatecrashers, along with some unpredictable swerving between art-forms. One of the greatest accounts of Gothic, Ruskin's essay 'The Nature of Gothic', is passed over in silence. Nor does Davenport-Hines seem to spend much time actually thinking about his subject. A brief theoretical prologue, which concludes rather rashly with a flourish about the undying 'Gothic imagination', is followed for the most part by plot summaries and potted histories. Pitched adroitly in style between academia and the general reader, *Gothic* stitches together the topics of women, sexuality, the body, mystery, sensationalism and enigma. In today's cultural climate, it is hard to see how it could fail to win a wide readership—just what it was surely constructed to achieve.

Utopias 1

Utopia is the most self-undermining of literary forms. If an ideal society can be portrayed only in the language of the present, it risks being betrayed as soon as we speak of it. Anything we can speak of must fall short of the otherness we desire. Utopias rebel against the unimaginativeness of the present, and in doing so find themselves simply reproducing it. All utopian writing is also dystopian, since, like Kant's sublime, it cannot help reminding us of our mental limits in the act of striving to go beyond them.

The same problem is evident in descriptions of aliens, almost all of which are absurdly anthropomorphic. Beings who must have set out for Earth millions of years ago turn out to look pretty much like Paddy Ashdown apart from their dwarfish stature and sinisterly monotone voices. Spacecraft capable of negotiating black holes crash in the Nevada desert, while their occupants display an excited interest in human dentures and genitals. Their speech and bodies are inconceivably different from ours, except for the fact that they speak and have bodies. There can be no alien abductions, since any aliens who bothered to abduct us would not be aliens. UFOs, like utopias, are epiphanies of the beyond which bear witness to the fact that we can never attain it. The most mind-bending of literary genres provide evidence of our incurable straightness.

Utopias from the 18th and early 19th centuries, of the kind which Gregory Claeys has assembled in this handsome set of volumes, are outlandish precisely because of their ordinariness. What seems 'utopian', in

---

First published as 'Pretty Much like Ourselves' (a review of *Modern British Utopias 1700–1850*, 8 vols, edited by Gregory Claeys) in the *London Review of Books*, 4 September 1997.

the sense of extravagantly unreal, about them is precisely their incapacity to imagine a world significantly different from the one around them. In a bold-faced piece of bohemianism, the utopianists of Lady Mary Fox's *Account of an Expedition to the Interior of New Holland* (1837) hold casual buffets rather than dinner parties. In Sarah Scott's *A Description of Millennium Hall* (1778), utopia is a country mansion in Cornwall, an anodyne English pastoral in which female midgets play the harpsichord and tend the shrubberies. For the English, the ideal society needs to have an old orchard and a couple of herbaceous borders. *The Life and Adventures of Peter Wilkins* (1751) locates its perfect society in 'spacious vales and lofty mountains, pleasant verdure and groves of stately trees'.

This particular utopia smells good, whereas most of them are odourless, antiseptic places, intolerably streamlined and sensible, in which the natives will jaw on for hours about the efficiency of their sanitary arrangements or the ingenuity of their electoral system. Indeed, talk seems all that is left to a people whose history has come to an end, and who are dependent for diversion on some alien visitor dropping in to have their theological doctrines explained to him. Charles Rowcroft's ideal world in *The Triumph of Woman* (1848) is a drearily high-minded regime full of wholesome puddings, docile, state-funded artists and one pew per person in church. The space-travelling protagonist, who lands in Bavaria by meteorite, reports that there are no women in his world—a state of affairs which you suspect is the closest to perfection the patriarchal Rowcroft could get, even if his alien ends up falling for a female earthling. Douglas Jerrold's *The Chronicles of Clovernook* (1846)—an insufferably arch narrative which becomes peculiarly excited at the prospect of little boys rending their trousers while climbing for apples—enthuses over an imaginary society which still has taxes, prisons and poverty.

Whatever their radical content, the form of such utopias reflects back to us the actual world in mildly reformed guise, and so helps to reinforce it. They are end-of-history texts, fictional equivalents of Francis Fukuyama, which deny that reality could be transformed in the very act of proclaiming how it could be improved. *The Island of Liberty* (1848) shows an enlightened aristocrat carrying out an experiment in human equality on a South Sea island, a project which goes dismally wrong. The point of imagining an alternative society, not least in the year of European revolutions, is to reassure yourself that it isn't feasible.

Otherness turns out to be bogus: John Kirkby's *The Capacity and Extent of the Human Understanding* (1745) presents us with a noble savage on his paradisal island who has figured out more or less the whole of English 18th-century religion almost down to country parsonages, simply by attentively observing the natural world around him.

The paradigm of all such fiction is *Robinson Crusoe*, since what is so consoling about the book is the way its protagonist gets by in exotically unfamiliar circumstances by exercising a very English rationality. It is enheartening to see Crusoe briskly chopping wood and staking out his enclosure as if he were somewhere in the Home Counties. If you catch a sea monster in this kind of tale, it is in order to squeeze oil out of it. *Gulliver's Travels*, too, exploits this technique, introducing us to alien worlds whose natives turn out to be much more like us than their appearance would lead us to expect. Indeed, if this were not so the novel would not work—partly because Gulliver must share some cultural characteristics with the Lilliputians and Brobdingnagians if they are effectively to satirise his own society, partly because the truly other would be unintelligible.

That these freaks, microbeings, rational quadrupeds and immortal wrecks are not all that different from the citizens of Birmingham is in one sense a smack at the radical utopianists Swift detested: there can be nothing beyond the limits of what is already known. In another sense, however, it is a swipe at those Enlightenment philosophers who believed complacently in a universal human nature. The Lilliputians do indeed turn out to be pretty much like ourselves, more's the pity. Gulliver himself can never achieve a proper balance between standing superiorly aloof from these other cultures, and going pathetically overboard for their way of seeing. If he subjects the King of Brobdingnag to a blast of chuckle-headed English chauvinism, he is also foolishly proud of the title the Lilliputians bestow on him, and indignantly rebuts a charge of having had sex with a female only a few inches high. To embrace cultural otherness too eagerly is to betray a flaw in one's own identity; and Gulliver, who ends up believing that he is a horse, finally loses his precarious hold on selfhood and collapses into madness and despair.

The trick of *Gulliver's Travels* is to use imaginary cultures to estrange and unsettle our own. This means laying aside our own assumptions in just the way that the lesser writings collected here seem to find impossible. For all their supposed idealism, these utopian flights of fancy are doggedly realist works, displaying a world which is reassuringly familiar even as they clamour for it to be changed. This contradiction between form and content was to have a long after-history: Bernard Shaw's plays may issue subversive messages, but the loving precision with which their stage directions detail the furniture or the colour of the maid's stockings suggests a reality too massively solid to be more than tinkered with.

These 18th-century utopias exist on the margins of space rather than of time. They are more often set in the South Seas than in some era to come, since their authors have no particular concept of historical progress; and their function is to comment on the present rather than to project a desirable future. They are not particularly interested in how the transition from the actual to the utopian is made, in contrast with William Morris's *News from Nowhere*, which, as Perry Anderson has noted, is that rarest of socialist utopias, one which describes in some detail how the revolution actually came about. Nor are they especially interested in what their utopias look like. The stage-setting is generally accomplished in purely formulaic style, pressed to extremes in *Great Britain in 1841; or, the Results of the Reform Bill* (1831), which begins with its narrator blandly announcing that 'It so happened, that at the close of the year 1831, I fell into a profound slumber, which continued undisturbed till the end of the year 1841.' We are no more meant to ask how he came to sleep for ten years than we are supposed to find a pantomime horse anato-mically convincing. On awakening from his slumber, the narrator of this anonymous tract finds his brother bending benevolently over him, looking forty rather than ten years older than when he saw him last. This premature ageing is the result of the 1832 Reform Bill, which has allowed the state to confiscate their father's property and forced him into exile in the south of France. The funds of the universities of Oxford and Cambridge have likewise been grabbed by the Govern-ment, their Fellows reduced to beggary and their lecture halls thrown impiously open to religious doctrines other than those of the Estab-lished Church. England and Ireland have been dissevered, the King has fled to Hanover, the rioting populace is carrying out summary execu-tions and the brothers' mother has died of a broken heart.

The last thing such works are concerned with is a world beyond. Alternative universes are simply devices for embarrassing the one we have: the point is not to go elsewhere, but to use elsewhere as a reflection on where you are. The more relevant to our own concerns utopia is, the less utopian it becomes. William Thomson's *The Man in the Moon* (1783) whisks Charles James Fox into space to hang him from a wart on the moon's nose, but the political discussion which follows could have taken place in any London coffee house. The seditious republican satire *A Voyage to the Moon* (1793), which contains a savage libel of the Prince of Wales, imagines a society in which big snakes oppress little ones; but everything else about England is perfectly familiar, and even the snakes have to be supplied with arms to allow them to engage in amorous embraces.

Amorous embraces have their place in these countries of the mind, even though English utopias are typically rational rather than carnivalesque, more preoccupied with the constitutional than the carnal. The narrator of *The Adventures of James Dubourdieu* (1719) finds himself in a primitive vegetarian paradise in which inhabitants bereft of all body-hair leap naked into fountains. James Lawrence's *The Empire of the Nairs, or, the Rights of Woman* (1811), set among the nobility of the Malabar coast, portrays a libertine community in which women are free to choose their own lovers and children are tended only by their mothers. Both features are meant to be feminist, though the latter is no doubt more the sort of feminism that would appeal to a male author. The liberal-minded protagonist is pleased to see hordes of naked young women disporting themselves unashamed, though whether his pleasure is entirely ideological remains unclear. In *The Life and Adventures of Peter Wilkins*, the enlightened hero marries an inhabitant of the imaginary realm of Swangea only to discover on his wedding night that her body is entirely encased in an artificial skin. Anxious that he may be deprived of his conjugal rights 'either to my own Gratification, or the Increase of our Species', the fumbling Wilkins lights upon 'divers fat broad ledges, like Whalebone, seemingly under her Covering, which closely enfolded her Body'. Surmising that her second skin 'might all be laced on together, somewhat like Stays', he 'felt behind for the Lacing'. To his chagrin he discovers no way in, but the woman suddenly throws off her encasement by some mysterious device and gives herself up to his embraces. This book is a cautionary tale for liberals: those who think that cultural differences can be casually set aside might end up with a lifetime of enforced celibacy.

Claeys reprints a few well-known (anti-) utopian pieces like Johnson's *Rasselas* and Burke's spoof *A Vindication of Natural Society* (1756), but most of his chosen texts are obscure, amateurish and drearily written. An exception is the American socialist John Francis Bray's *A Voyage from Utopia* (1842), a scorching liberation satire dedicated to John Wilkes, which inspects English politics and religion from the viewpoint of a visiting native of utopia. He finds 'Anglos' full of ill-clad, half-starved humans who worship Fe-fo-fum, a god who lives in Blesso and has a sworn enemy in Blacko-Jacko, an inhabitant of Blazo. The 1840s, like the closing decades of the 18th century, were awash with utopias for obvious political reasons; but in common with the political journalism they covertly are, utopias are the most ephemeral of literary forms, constructing their ideal kingdoms simply to promote some parochial obsession in the present. No form of fantasy could be more provincial and prosaic. By the end of the 19th century, after Morris's mighty classic, the task of imagining otherness would pass to science fiction, which performed it with a good deal more panache.

There are two kinds of starry-eyed idealist: those who believe in a perfect society, and those who hold that the future will be pretty much like the present. Wedged between them are the realists, who recognise that the future will be a lot different, though by no means necessarily better. To claim that human affairs might feasibly be much improved is a realist position; those with their heads truly in the clouds are the hard-nosed pragmatists who behave as though chocolate-chip cookies or the International Monetary Fund will still be with us in two thousand years' time. Such a view is simply an inversion of the television cartoon *The Flintstones*, for which the remote past is just American suburbia plus dinosaurs. The 18th-century fascination with utopia went hand-in-glove with imperial expeditions, as a spiritual equivalent of the colonising project. One of the functions of the genre was to bring cultural difference under the sway of Western identity without thereby abolishing the exoticism which made the Tartars or Tongans worth writing about in the first place.

The irony of colonialism is that it cannot help flirting with cultural relativism at just the point where it needs to affirm the superior worth of its own way of doing things. Since this includes plundering other cultures, it is unavoidably confronted with the scandalous truth that these cultures are at once profoundly alien and in ostensibly good working order. Indeed, in order to impose its political rule colonialism often enough relies on the fact that its underlings have their own coherent values and institutions. Genuine savages could not be governed, since they would lack all concept of authority and subjection. The fact that you can conquer another society suggests that you shouldn't, since for this to be possible the natives must be sufficiently like us to render it morally dubious. If, on the other hand, they are incapable of our own level of civility, you can use this fact to justify exploiting them, but will be forced to give up trying to rationalise that exploitation as a part of a civilising process.

Utopias, however, are not just the products of colonialism; they are also attempts to imagine a condition beyond it. But all such generous speculations must buy their virtual realities at a certain cost. For one thing, the energies invested in imagining a better world may help to sidetrack the energies devoted to its realisation. For another thing, projecting the future may just be an attempt to control it is efficiently as you do the present. The true clairvoyants of our epoch are those specialists hired to peer into the entrails of the economic system and assure its proprietors that their profits are safe for another thirty years. Their opposite numbers are the prophets, who, like their Old Testament forebears, have no interest in the future beyond warning that it is likely to be unpleasant if we do not change our ways.

Walter Benjamin thought that the Jewish prohibition of graven images included a refusal to make a fetish of the future. There is remarkably little utopian speculation in the work of the Jewish Marx, who viewed his task not as sketching a blueprint for the coming kingdom but as resolving the contradictions which forestalled its arrival. Once the just society has arrived, Marx and his ilk will have done themselves out of a job: there will be no radicals in the New Jerusalem, since their discourse belongs to the present as much as the language of man-management. Left-wing utopias which dream of a society beyond privilege are instances of the privileges they disown: as Oscar Wilde knew, there is something offensively idle and frivolous about thinking up other worlds, a pursuit in which anyone can engage as readily as they can boil an egg. But Wilde was also aware that we fleshly creatures stood in need of such images, which is why he offered himself as a person at once intolerably self-indulgent and the harbinger of a future in which nobody else would need to work either. This collection provides us with other images of utopia, though anyone who can afford it is already living in one.

Utopias 2

Russell Jacoby has a good line in gloomy titles. *Social Amnesia* and *Dialectic of Defeat* were followed by *The Last Intellectuals*, which has now been joined by *The End of Utopia*. There is, of course, a good deal for the left to be gloomy about, despite the comrade who sanguinely announced at the Socialist Workers Party summer school last year that there had 'never been more revolutionary opportunities'. Quite what it is the left should be glum about, however, needs closer specification. Has utopia come to an end because of apathy, as the book's subtitle suggests, or because the left is in retreat, or because history is going downhill, or because it has slithered to a halt? These grounds are not mutually exclusive, but the relations between them need examining. Is the left in retreat, for example, because history is going downhill, or is it the other way round?

Apathy would seem a dubious reason for pessimism. People may not currently think much of political elections or theories of surplus value, but if you try to drive a motorway through their back gardens, throw them on the breadline or close down their children's schools, they are likely to protest swiftly enough. It is irrational not to resist an unjust power if one may do so without too much risk and with a reasonable chance of success. Such protests may not be effective, but that is a different matter. People are also likely to be up in arms if you dump refugees on them or deprive them of their right to defend their property, which is hardly enlightened but certainly not apathetic. The evidence does not in general indicate that the citizenry is torpid or

First published as 'Defending Utopia' (a review of *The End of Utopia: Politics and Culture in an Age of Apathy* by Russell Jacoby) in *New Left Review* 4, July/August 2000.

complacent. On the contrary, it suggests that they are considerably alarmed about a number of key political issues, even if most of them would be about as likely to turn to socialism for solutions as they would to Theosophy. Moreover, the penitent ex-socialist intellectuals whom this book rightly upbraids for their adaptation to capitalism are not necessarily *apathetic*. In fact some of them are far too little so, pushing their reformist panaceas with exasperating zeal.

Nor is it very likely that a system as perilously unstable as capitalism will escape without a major crisis over the next few decades, which is no argument for a socialist future but is certainly a case against the end of history. *Pace* Francis Fukuyama, we are likely to have too much future rather than too little. What is to be feared is less that history will do nothing but repeat itself, than the prospect that it will begin to unravel at the seams at a time when the left is still dishevelled and disorganised, and thus incapable of steering spontaneous revolt into productive channels. A lot more people might then get hurt than would otherwise be the case. The really hard-headed pragmatists are those who recognise that, as the history books declare of almost every conceivable epoch, we are in a period of rapid change, and that for hard-headed pragmatic reasons their own ideologies will thus rapidly become obsolete. This book reminds us that the end of ideology, if not quite of history, was announced by Raymond Aron and Daniel Bell as long ago as the 1950s and, with Vietnam, Black power and the student movement just round the corner, proved a singularly inept prophecy. As Oscar Wilde might have observed, to be wrong about the death of history once is unfortunate, whereas to be wrong twice is sheer carelessness.

Anyway, has the whole of the political left acquiescently thrown in its hand, as Jacoby seems dolefully to consider? What of the Brazilian landless movement, French working-class militancy, the student anti-sweatshop agitation in the United States, anarchistic anti-capitalism and a good deal else? When Jacoby envisages the whole of the left as having shifted spinelessly over from revolutionary socialism to postmodern pluralism, he is thinking for the most part, with postmodern parochialism, of his own society. The cultural turn is not, to be sure, peculiarly American; but it has certainly been more dominant and doctrinal there than among, say, the Indonesian or South African left. And if the left is on the back foot, is this simply, as Jacoby seems to imply, because it has cravenly lost its nerve? *The End of Utopia*, in a familiar nitty-gritty, cut-the-crap North American style, is full of a mutedly macho discourse of 'soapy' liberals, 'genteel' waffling, 'chalky' language and 'toothless' concepts, by all of which the 'bone and muscle' of a more virile left has been fatally infected. But the left is not just in retreat because it has lost its manhood. It is in disarray because—for example—it is not sure whether democratic, participatory economic planning really would be workable, or whether some form of market would not be necessary instead. This is not just a matter of formerly steel-hard comrades going all soggy; it is a question of genuine problems of socialist construction which Jacoby's book passes over. These, to be sure, are not its concern; but the upshot is an unduly moralistic portrait of the treason of the clerks, and a non-materialist account of the difficulties of materialism. The problem would seem to come down to a loss of 'vision'—a category which, in the United States, is dangerously contaminated by the idealist rhetoric of everyday politics: the crisis of the left is a Vision Thing.

Even so, this is an admirably brave intervention. In an enjoyably abrasive chapter on multiculturalism, Jacoby demolishes a number of postmodern myths. For multiculturalism, 'the future looks like the present with more options', and to the degree that culture subsumes everything, politics loses meaning. Ethnic identities in the United States are still sociologically robust, in that Jews tend to hang out with Jews and African-Americans with African-Americans, but cultural identities are hardly as well defined, in that the cultural goals of such groups are fairly homogeneous. The United States is becoming a less rather than more multilingual society. Indeed, few nations are so ruthlessly monolinguistic. Multiculturalism basically means wanting access to the social mainstream, thus ruling out groups like the Amish, who have no such desires. Fashionable denunciations of Eurocentrism assume that 'Adolf Hitler and Anne Frank represent the same Europe', and turn out often enough to be coded pleas for the accolade of the Establishment. Native American studies, for example, post a potent challenge to Euro–American hegemony, and so must become a fully accredited discipline with departmental status. In US academia, there seems no weighty political issue which cannot be translated into squabbles over funding. Intellectuals whose 'marginality is more and more marginal' trumpet their minority status. Cultural populism represents a similar political betrayal, as the honourable tradition of a Dwight Macdonald, scourge of exploitative mass culture, gives way to Lacanian essays on MTV and wide-eyed semiotic analyses of the opening credit sequence of *The Cosby Show*.

Little of this commentary is grippingly original, but all of it is timely. Jacoby is not always the most subtly nuanced of thinkers: 'Nineteenth-century Marxism', he writes, 'was materialist and determinist; late-twentieth-century Marxism is idealist and incoherent'. It is partly a problem of style. There is little linguistic middle ground in the United States between the arcane jargon of academia and the commodified discourse of the media, so that the terrain which this book seeks to occupy, pitched somewhere between intellectual and common reader, the elevated and the earthy, is itself a casualty of the very processes it seeks to examine. Perry Anderson, who once identified this split between specialist and everyday discourse as one reason for the lack of a major contemporary literary realism, becomes here 'one of the left's savviest thinkers', in an uneasy conjuncture of the racy and the ratiocinative. Jacoby is the kind of self-consciously plain-minded American who, one feels, would find Henry James a mite effete; 'Pass the sherry' is his caustic comment on one particular piece of 'genteel-leftist' speculation, hardly the sort of argument you might find in the pages of a Lukács or Marcuse. But this aggressively transparent idiom is, at times, uncomfortably close to the marketplace it denounces; and it is hard to write in this medium with the degree of subtlety the subject-matter demands. Even so, *The End of Utopia* represents a blast of steely common sense in a narcissistic culture, briskly impatient with the solemn absurdities of academia, and one of several straws in a wind of anti-culturalist critique which ranges from Toril Moi's *What Is A Woman?* to Francis Mulhern's *Culture/Metaculture*.

In a brave final chapter, Jacoby speaks up for the continuing necessity of the utopian impulse. In the 1960s, he observes, even sober liberals pondered the possibility of a completely transformed society, and there were anxious reflections about how to deal with an increasing abundance of leisure. The contrast with the present, when 'no society on the horizon promises a world beyond work', is telling. The dangers of universal prosperity, Jacoby dryly remarks, no longer keep anyone awake at night. Even the most imaginative prophets of our age foretell a future with war, money, violence and inequality—a more pleasant, commodious version of the affluent enclaves of today.

The myth that utopian thought has been a prime force for violence in the modern age is briskly nailed: more blood has been shed in our time by bureaucratic calculation, myths of racial purity, nationalism or religious sectarianism than through utopian dreams, and the book is not afraid to provide a bloody inventory to support its claim. Defending the utopian impulse, it concludes, may seem quixotic or irrelevant; but in a world which can alter so unpredictably—who foretold the political explosion of the 1960s, or the demise of the Soviet bloc?—we can never know what surprises the future may hold. The final note of this passionate polemic, then, is far from pessimistic, and it is a credit to its author's courageous unfashionability that it should be so.

Romantic Poets

Writing of Wordsworth and Coleridge's growing disenchantment with radical politics, E.P. Thompson remarks in this book that they were 'caught in the vortex of contradictions which were both real and ideal. They were champions of the French Revolution and they were sickened by its course. They were isolated as Jacobins and they abominated Godwinian abstraction. They had broken out of the received culture and they were appalled by some features of the new.' It is not hard to read these remarks autobiographically. Thompson himself hints at such a possibility a few pages later in the essay. Substitute 'Bolshevik' for 'French', 'socialists' for 'Jacobins' and 'Marxist' (or, better, 'Althusserian') for 'Godwinian', and one has some sense of the conflicts of the ex-Communist Edward Thompson in the late 1960s. The essay, 'Disenchantment or Default?', was written in 1968, the year in which Soviet tanks rumbled into Prague, the year of the Parisian *événements*, of the student and civil rights movements, and thus an odd time for a leftist to feel isolated. While his fellow New Left intellectuals of the day made some kind of accommodation to the politics of a younger, more impetuous generation, Thompson remained, like the Wordsworth and Coleridge of *Lyrical Ballads* in his reading of them, trapped between commitment and disenchantment. Or, one might say, between Paris and Prague.

Disenchantment, however, is not the same as apostasy; and it is on the distinction between these two terms that a good many of these reviews and lectures on English Romanticism turn. The passage quoted above

First published as 'First and Last Romantics' (a review of *The Romantics: Wordsworth, Coleridge, Thelwall* by E.P. Thompson) in the *Times Higher Education Supplement*, 17 July 1998.

instantly goes on to cast the struggle between engagement and with-
drawal in a suspiciously idealising language, at least as far as the Lake
poets are concerned: 'There is a search for synthesis at a moment of
arrested dialectic; a coruscation of perceptions coming from this tension; a fiery alternating current passing backward and forward.' The
melodramatic imagery protests a little too much; but Thompson is right
to distinguish between the later, out-and-out political 'apostasy' of his
two writers, which will lead Coleridge at least to a 'medley of insights
and nonsense', and that cusped, perversely creative moment in which,
caught between Jacobinism and creeping conservatism, they could
conjure some major art out of precisely that tension.

Thompson is perhaps a little too inclined to assume that the post-
revolutionary Wordsworth's continuing poetic concern with the common life keeps him on the side of the angels. He is also too inclined to
make *The Prelude* sound more politically radical than it actually is,
claiming rather rashly that its vision of some inner, universal human
equality 'takes us altogether outside the paternalist framework'. This is
the kind of grandly emphatic judgment that Thompson, too often in
his career, had to return to and qualify. But these occasional pieces,
which range in date from 1968 to 1993, display on the whole a judicious
balance of sympathy and censure.

'Judicious' is not on the whole the first word one associates with
Thompson's writing. If he is incapable of writing a dull sentence, it is
partly because he is incapable of writing a dispassionate one. His lucid,
muscular prose is infused with a personality that is alternately generous,
curmudgeonly, lovable, headstrong, sardonic and polemical. He is a bit
of an intellectual bruiser, with a briskly dismissive way with theoretical
abstractions and a rather heavy-handed line in irony. The judiciousness,
however, has its lapses. 'I see little point in abusing the poets for their
later apostasy', Thompson writes eirenically in 1968, only to jump in
with both boots flailing in 1979. Reviewing some Coleridge essays in
that year, he declares himself sickened by their 'surfeit of pharisaism
and cliché', by the unctuousness with which this erstwhile Jacobin
smugly travesties political positions that he himself had not long
abandoned. If the ingredients of his later thought were rich, the results
were 'always half-baked'.

In the first two decades of the 19th century, Thompson considers,
Coleridge pulled off the difficult feat of being wrong about almost

everything. Thompson reminds us, for example, that Coleridge opposed Catholic emancipation in Ireland, viewing the Irish as a 'wild and barbaric race'. Hazlitt, he rightly insists, was by far the greater political essayist. Fortunately for the historical truth, Thompson forgets for the length of an essay about laying aside his abuse. He insists, even so, that in the closing years of the 18th century Wordsworth and Coleridge are still in some sense criticising the French Revolution from the 'left'. Had he not retired to Stowey, Thompson believes, Coleridge's political trajectory at the time would almost certainly have retired him to prison. An essay on the poet's revolutionary youth vividly recreates his seditious leanings. But as the couple shuffle increasingly to the right, it is Coleridge who becomes in Thompson's eyes the unacceptable apostate and Wordsworth the just forgivable one.

In one sense, the renegation of both men is plainly intolerable: the England they were guiltily 'rejoining' was one that was 'suppressing Irish rebellion with a ferocity which outdistances the French Terror: an England of soaring bread prices and near starvation'. Wordsworth gets off much more lightly. 'How far is it possible', Thompson asks of him with himself well in mind, 'for men to hold on to aspirations long after there appears to be no hope of inserting them into the real world?' He does not ask the same question about Coleridge. He perceptively links Wordsworth's inner retreat to a slackening in his detailed observation of nature, though he does not seem to notice that his observation of nature was never particularly sensuous in the first place.

Wordsworth's rejection of Godwinian utopianism, Thompson argues, need not have been launched from the right because there was more to radical politics than Godwin. Instead, Wordsworth 'could perfectly well have been moving back to a more engaged sympathy with the poor and with the victims of war'. Godwin indeed figures in this book as the Louis Althusser of the late 18th century, an icy theoreticist to be contrasted with warm-hearted Thompsonian humanists like the Jacobin John Thelwall. There is even an implication that it was some kind of moral failing on Godwin's part that he never got himself imprisoned or transported.

Wordsworth's apostasy is tersely described as 'abject', but Thompson invites us to admire the steadfast faith in human potential that preceded it. He also claims that Wordsworth at least argued the matter honestly through with himself in the shape of *The Prelude*, rather than, like Coleridge, swinging instantly into vindictive lampoons of his former comrades.

The distinction between creative disenchantment and sterile apostasy that runs throughout these robust pieces is a shade too emphatic. It is as though the author needs to remind himself, or us, that his own growing distance from classical Marxism implies no abandonment of socialist principles. He may have felt the need to remind himself, but there was really no need to remind us. Thompson kept his political faith when all around him were losing it and blaming the loss on the likes of him. In a typically scathing aside, he observes that in our own era it has proved possible to enter the stage of utter disenchantment without having undergone 'the tedium and intellectual vulgarity of a prior enchantment' in the first place. Few snappier summaries of post-modernism could be imagined, long before the term was in currency.

There is something rather too convenient, however, in regarding the Lake poets' apostasy as an 'imaginative' as well as a moral failure, thus allowing Thompson to posit a suspiciously direct relationship between their political renegation and their aesthetic falling-off. Even he is forced to admit that Coleridge was at his critical acme as a Tory Anglican. 'Disenchantment', Thompson insists, is not inimical to art, and these essays certainly bear witness to the fact that it is by no means inimical to superb historical writing. Apostasy, however, involves the denial of 'aspiration', and so is to be roundly condemned. There is a touch of Leavisian moralism in this high-minded judgment, which fails among other things to account for why W.B. Yeats wrote most of his finest poetry after he had relinquished his Irish nationalist hopes.

Like Yeats, E.P. Thompson was one of the last Romantics. If his first major work was on William Morris, it was because Morris represented the point at which the English Romantic heritage finally intersected with the European materialist one. Thompson's generous trust in human capacities, his emotional and imaginative recklessness, his suspicion of the disembodied intellect, his self-dramatising flamboyance and hatred of the non-dynamic, all put him squarely in the camp of the Romantic poets he loved.

But the last essay in this collection is devoted to the Jacobin John Thelwall—a man who, as Robert Southey remarked, 'was once as near as possible being hanged, and there is great merit in that'. Thelwall, the non-apostate par excellence, represents the practical, workaday, 'materialist' radicalism that was the other face of Thompson, as a man finally so notorious that his former friends Wordsworth and Coleridge had to put some prudent daylight between him and themselves.

If E.P. Thompson never got round to the big book on Romanticism that he had been planning throughout the whole of his working life, it was partly because he was labouring away for some of that time to save Europe from nuclear catastrophe. It is a pity that instead of that major work we have only these scattered essays and a briefish 1993 study of William Blake. But to have a Europe in which to read them seems a reasonable exchange.

Branwell Brontë

In August 1845, Branwell Brontë, ill-starred drug-addict brother of the celebrated trio, took a trip from the Haworth family home to Liverpool. It was on the very eve of the Irish famine, and the city was soon to be thronged with its hungry victims. Many of them would have been Irish speakers, since it was the Irish-speaking poorer classes that the famine hit hardest. As Winifred Gerin comments in her biography of Emily Brontë: 'Their image, and especially that of the children, was unforgettably depicted in the *Illustrated London News*—starving scarecrows with a few rags on them and an animal growth of black hair almost obscuring their features.' A few months after Branwell's visit to Liverpool, Emily began writing *Wuthering Heights*—a novel whose male protagonist, Heathcliff, is picked up starving off the streets of Liverpool by old Earnshaw. Earnshaw unwraps his greatcoat to reveal to his family a 'dirty, ragged, black-haired child' who speaks a kind of 'gibberish', and who will later be variously labelled beast, savage, demon and lunatic. It's clear that this little Caliban has a nature on which nurture will never stick; and that's merely an English way of saying that he's quite possibly Irish.

Later in the novel, Heathcliff will stage a mysterious disappearance and re-enter the narrative as an English gentleman. It's a transformation with a venerable Irish history, all the way from Oliver Goldsmith to Oscar Wilde. Unlike Goldsmith and Wilde, however, Heathcliff doesn't make too impressive a job of impersonating the English upper class. You can take Heathcliff out of the Heights, but you can't take the

First published as 'Angry 'Un' (a review of *The Hand of the Arch-Sinner: Two Angrian Chronicles of Branwell Brontë* edited by Robert Collins) in the *London Review of Books*, 8 July 1993.

Heights out of Heathcliff. The Brontës' father, Patrick, had pulled off the trick rather better. Born Patrick Brunty into a poor peasant family in County Down (still 'Brontë country' for the Irish today), he frenchified his surname and made it to Cambridge, right-wing Toryism and a Yorkshire parsonage. But the Brontës' Englishness never entirely stuck. When Branwell, enraged at hearing his father shouted down on the Haworth hustings, intervened loyally on his behalf, the local people burnt an effigy of him with a potato in one hand and a herring in the other. And Branwell, whose first name was actually Patrick, lived a flamboyant stage-Irish existence all his life, obediently reinforcing the English stereotype of the feckless Mick.

Of course Heathcliff may not be Irish at all. He may be a gypsy, or a lascar, or (like Bertha Mason in *Jane Eyre*) a creole. It is hard to know how black he is, or rather how much of the blackness is grime and bile and how much pigmentation. As for the famine, the dates don't quite fit; the blight didn't strike until the autumn of 1845, so that August, the time of Branwell's visit to Liverpool, would have been too early for him to encounter its victims. There would, however, have been a good few impoverished Irish immigrants hanging around the city, since Irish emigration by no means began with the Great Hunger, and it is possible that Branwell ran into some of them and relayed the tale to his sister. In any case, there would be something symbolically apt in Branwell, the Luciferian rebel of the outfit, presenting Emily with the disruptive element of her novel. There are certainly strong parallels between the brother and Emily's Byronic villain. Earnshaw's ambiguous gift of a sullen urchin to his family is also, perhaps, an imaginative reworking of an actual present of twelve toy soldiers which Patrick Brontë bestowed on the children after a trip to Bradford. It was these figures around which they spun their earliest mythologies, so that the paternal gift burst open their fantasy world as Heathcliff unleashes the drama of the Heights.

It can't have been easy to have been the brother of those sisters, but Branwell made a more spectacular hash of it than was strictly necessary. Born in 1817, he was a nervous, violent, undersized child who was already glowering and teeth-grinding at an early age, and had to be withdrawn from his brief bout of schooling. Since school helped to kill off two of his sisters, this was not perhaps a wholly unwise move. Educated at home, he proved a remarkably precocious Classical scholar and became the fond hope of his doting father, who in traditional Irish-peasant fashion favoured the boy over the girls. At the age of eight he was bitten by a mad dog, as Emily was to be bitten by another somewhat later; the improbable coincidence seems grotesquely typical of the family's ill luck. Branwell revealed an early gift for art, music and literature, dreamed of becoming a great writer, and between the ages of twelve and seventeen penned around thirty assorted tales, poems, dramas, journals and histories, all written at fever pitch. He wrote more than the sum total of his sisters' output, though without a particle of the talent. But he was already slipping out of the parsonage to the Black Bull pub rather too regularly, a youth of sizeable personality and minuscule character who had developed a curious obsession with boxing. Packed off to London as an art student, he wandered around the capital in a dream, realised how shabby and provincial he looked among the metropolitan crowd, and kept his letters of introduction to distinguished painters firmly in his pocket. He washed up instead in a Holborn pub run by one of his pugilist heroes, drank away his money, and returned to Haworth with an implausible tale of having been mugged. London had confirmed what he already suspected: that he had megalomaniacal ambitions and no practical interest whatsoever in achieving them.

Back home with a flea in his ear, he wrote florid, fruitless letters to Wordsworth and *Blackwood's Magazine*, cadged gin money from his pals and became, improbably enough, secretary of the local Temperance Society. Though a confirmed atheist, he also taught in Sunday school, savaging his pupils in befuddled vengeance for his misfortunes. A second stab at an artistic future, this time as a portrait painter in Bradford, proved equally abortive: it was characteristic of Branwell's blighted career that he took up portrait painting at just the point when the industry was being killed off by the daguerreotype. In any case, he spent most of his time engaged in raffish carousals with louche artists in Bradford's George Hotel. To blot out this latest debacle he mixed opium-taking with his already well-entrenched alcoholism, and began to run up some alarming debts. There was now no avoiding a mundane job, and the prodigy of the parsonage was reduced to the ignominious role of assistant clerical secretary at Sowerby Bridge railway station. A year later, he was fired from the job for embezzling £11 1s 7d, an offence compounded by the lurid fantasies he had sketched and scribbled all over the company's accounts. He was particularly keen on pen portraits of himself hanged, stabbed or plunged into eternal perdition.

Broken in health, permanently boozed and blackly despairing though Branwell now was, the President of the Immortals still had a nasty surprise or two in store for him. When a post was swung for him as tutor in a respectable middle-class family, Branwell promptly fell in love with his pupil's mother and was pitched out on his ear by her irate husband. The pains of opium addiction were now compounded by the pangs of thwarted love; the husband died soon after, but his will threatened to cut his wife off if she married Branwell, and any insane thought of wedlock she might conceivably have entertained was quickly laid to rest. With the law breathing down his neck for unpaid debts, Branwell took to his bed, scrawled his final document (a begging note for gin), and died in his father's arms of wasting sickness and chronic bronchitis in September 1848. Profligate and preposterous though he was, an entirely fictional character in a world he couldn't handle, he had doggedly sprung back like his beloved pugilists from every cynical blow the fates had seen fit to deal him. He may have been disastrously bereft of the reality principle, but he certainly had guts.

The place where one can wreak vengeance on reality is known as art; and if Branwell wrote as compulsively as he did, it is because he was determined to give a malicious destiny a run for its money. So it was that at the age of seventeen he created the kingdom of Angria, and roped Charlotte into writing chronicles about it. Emily and Anne, distressed by the macho militarism of Branwell's fables, created the more peaceable kingdom of Gondal in a separatist gesture. The hero of the Angrian myths is Alexander Percy, anarchist and aristocrat, a Branwell in everything but the dope, spinelessness and pen-pushing in a railway station. Like his creator, Percy is a dissolute, self-destructive figure given to grotesque fits of passion; unlike him he is beautiful, powerful and prodigiously gifted, a haughty, arch-revolutionary *Übermensch* who—like Branwell himself before he ran out of drink money—arrogantly refuses to serve.

The Hand of the Arch-Sinner, lovingly reconstructed by Robert Collins from Branwell's preternaturally minute handwriting, contains two of the Percy stories, 'The Life of Northangerland' and 'Real Life in Verdopolis'. ('Northangerland' is Percy's aristocratic title, but also an apt

term for Brontë country.) Like the rest of Branwell's work, the tales are
of indifferent literary value, a slipshod brand of Gothic replete with
fiendish sneers, vengefully knitted brows and vindictively curled lips.
'The Life of Northangerland' is a murderous Oedipal fantasy of a kind
unsurprising to anyone acquainted with the character of Patrick Brontë
Senior. Percy is in hock to the tune of £300,000, a suitably glamorised
version of his author's slate at the Black Bull, and is egged on by his
rebel comrades to commit parricide to relieve his debts. Prominent in
this persuasion is Mr R.P. King, otherwise known as S'Death, or occasionally as R.P. S'Death, a revoltingly evil old retainer who speaks the
Yorkshire dialect despite the fact that the tale is set in Africa, and who is
clearly the prototype for old Joseph in *Wuthering Heights*. In the second
story, Percy is now called Rougue (Branwell himself got through a
bewildering array of extravagant pseudonyms), and is to be found
spearheading a political coup against the Angrian government, flanked
by his trusty companions Naughty and Lawless. He and his men have
bound themselves to atheism and revolution by a sacred oath, though
Percy, a stickler for political correctness, concludes the oath with the
words 'So help me, my mind.'

The Angrian myths, as Robert Collins points out, revolve on a conflict
between anarchy and order, republicans and royalists, individual ego
and social responsibility. But so does the Brontë sisters' mature fiction,
one might add. What fires that writing is a hunger for culture and
gentility edged with a smouldering animus against those who represent
it. It is the paradox of the Victorian governess, who is at once servant
and gentlewoman, socially inferior to her employers but a spiritual cut
above them, outwardly subservient while inwardly disdainful of their
Philistine habits and pampered brats. Or the paradox of the ending of
Jane Eyre—'pornographic', D.H. Lawrence typically called it—in which
the novel finally unleashes its repressed female fury by maiming and
blinding the aristocratic Rochester, but thereby reverses the power-
relation between him and the petty-bourgeois Jane and clears the path
for a fulfilling relationship between them. (It has, of course, first top-
pled mad Bertha Rochester conveniently off the rooftop, thus removing
another awkward obstacle to their wedlock.) Alexander Percy, the
gentleman rebel, unites in a single character Branwell's pathetic desire
for worldly power, and his revolutionary spurning of that very goal. In
this schizoid division between conformity and dissent, Anglican Tory

father and the Nonconformist aunt who brought them up, the Brontës faithfully lived up to Marx's description of the lower middle class they belonged to as 'contradiction incarnate'.

It is also, one might hazard, a conflict between imperial Britain and rebellious Ireland. Perhaps Heathcliff is not Irish after all. But it is interesting that several of Alexander Percy's rebellious comrades have Irish names; and one of his closest confidants, formerly a lawyer, is the son of one William Daniel Henry Montmorency of Derrinane Abbey. Derrynane, one of the most beautiful spots in County Kerry, was the ancestral seat of the lawyer Daniel O'Connell, the greatest of all Irish radicals during Branwell's lifetime. In 1829, when Branwell was twelve years old and in the process of launching his 'Branwell's Blackwood's Magazine', O'Connell victoriously concluded his campaign for Catholic Emancipation in Ireland; throughout the 1840s, when Branwell, now on his uppers, was still furiously scribbling, O'Connell was waging his struggle for the repeal of the Union, which the famine brought slithering to a halt. Alexander Percy is a supremely well-practised demagogue, able to stir crowds to insurrection; Daniel O'Connell, specialist in the 'monster meeting', led the greatest mass movement in 19th-century Europe. When the good people of Haworth, stung by Branwell's defence of the father he loved and hated, fashioned an effigy of 't' parson's Patrick' with a potato in his hand, they may not have been quite as off-target as it might appear.

Oscar Wilde

From time to time, the English need reminding that Oscar Wilde was an Irishman, just as Wilde did himself. Over the centuries, the Irish not only supplied Britain with its cattle and grain; they were also called upon to write much of its great literature for it. Declan Kiberd, in a lively essay in *Wilde: The Irishman*, shrewdly relates this to the fact that English was not the native tongue of the Irish. Because, as Wilde remarked, they were 'condemned to express themselves in a language not their own', they could reinvent it with a brio and boldness less marked in the metropolitan nation. Like J.M. Synge, they could stamp it with their native speech patterns to create an alluring new idiom. Wilde's son recalls his father singing him a lullaby in Irish, as befits a writer whose mother was an Irish nationalist rebel and folklorist, and whose father was a great Irish antiquarian.

Wilde was caught between languages as he was caught between sexual identities, a doubleness that was ethnically reflected in his Anglo-Irishness. To cap it all, as Owen Dudley Edwards reminds us in an erudite, elegant essay, Wilde was probably baptised a Roman Catholic, given his mother's political allegiances. If he was, socially speaking, an upper-middle-class Protestant, he was also the producer of a series of revolutionary tracts thinly disguised as fairy stories for children. In a fascinating piece, Angela Bourke sketches a parallel between those Irishwomen who were persecuted as possessed by evil spirits and those like Wilde enthralled by another type of fairy.

First published as 'Irish walk on the Wilde side' (a review of *Wilde: The Irishman* by Jerusha McCormack and *Decolonisation and Criticism: The Construction of Irish Literature* by Gerry Smyth) in the *Times Higher Education Supplement*, 20 November 1998.

Wilde was an upper-class parasite whose political sympathies were Catholic, anarchist and republican, a socialite who was also a socialist, a Victorian patriarch who disported himself with rent boys in cheap hotels. If he hobnobbed with the Lady Bracknells, he also moved freely in radical circles, befriending William Morris and Prince Kropotkin. It is not altogether surprising that he sprang from the city that his compatriot James Joyce, conscious of the oxymoronic status of a colonial metropolis, spelt as 'Doublin'. His drama is all about secret selves, ghostly doubles, tainted origins, split identities. Jerusha McCormack's brilliantly suggestive contribution to the volume she has edited sees him as parodying both the stereotypical Irishman (wild, anarchic, imaginative, witty, passionate and self-destructive) and the stage Englishman (cool, elegant, contemptuous, manipulative). What is laziness in the former becomes leisureliness in the latter. McCormack also sees how Wilde 'performed' his role as Englishman with such scrupulous fidelity that he succeeded only in ironising it, laying bare the constructed nature of all social identity and so implicitly challenging imperial images of the Irish.

Much the same can be said of his celebrated shafts of wit, those exquisitely studied Irish bulls that, as McCormack claims, can best be seen as the colonial's revenge on the imperial father-tongue. (By the time of *Finnegans Wake*, the English language would be lying in ruins, pummelled into pieces by another disaffected Irishman.) Deirdre Toomey reminds us in a powerful essay of how Wilde's aphorisms belong, like so much else in his writing, to an Irish oral tradition that prefers the voice to the printed sign, rather as he himself preferred an ephemeral identity to a fixed one. Wilde's epigrams are subversive deconstructions of English clichés, taking some stale piece of conventional wisdom and, by altering a word or two, standing it on its head or pressing it to an absurd extreme. Wilde was a devotee of inversion in much more than a sexual sense, and his Irish vein of humour is typically perverse and debunking, a subaltern's strike at the bland heartiness of his English betters. If antithesis is characteristic of orthodox habits of thought, the Irish colonial's customary tropes are those of paradox, irony, oxymoron—'two thinks at a time', Joyce called it.

As a proto-post-structuralist, Wilde knew that nothing—not least sexual identity—is ever entirely itself, and that the point where it becomes so is known as death. He inherited much of his mother's militant feminism: as Kiberd points out, it is the women in *The Impor-tance of Being Earnest* who read heavy works of philosophy, while the men lounge around eating dainty cucumber sandwiches. A colonial invert-edness is evident here too. But Wilde's feminism was laced with more than a dash of misogyny, as Victoria White argues in a splendidly written piece that indulges in that most unvoguish of activities, voicing criti-cisms of Wilde. Indeed, one of the few criticisms one can voice of this intricately intelligent collection is that it is too uncritical of its revered subject.

Wilde's fellow Protestant Dubliner Bernard Shaw, another licensed Irish jester to the English, observed that nothing in the world is quite as exquisitely comic to the Irish as the Englishman's seriousness. Wilde's dandyism, his disdain for high-toned moralism and metaphysical depth, his love-affair with style, mask, surface, appearance, is a politics in itself, deflating the ideological portentousness of late-Victorian England in the name of a very Irish compact with failure, marginality, disposses-sion. It is true that his obsession with scapegoating and martyr-dom—another distinctively Irish motif—has some dubious implications, as Bernard O'Donoghue points out in a strikingly thoughtful essay. Like the Anglo-Irish Ascendancy of which he was so doggedly disloyal a son, Wilde finally brought the roof down on his own head, and the extended act of self-immolation that goes by the name of his life corresponds with intriguing exactness to the final downfall of that class in Ireland. W.J. McCormack writes perceptively on the affinities between Wilde and Charles Stewart Parnell, that other celebrated Irish transgressor of English sexual mores, whose fall from grace seems to have touched Wilde so deeply that, as McCormack argues, his writing is eloquently, stridently silent about it. But both men fell only to rise again. Today, a flamboyant statue of Wilde sits composedly on a rock in Dublin's Merrion Square, known to the locals (as the Irish art historian Paula Murphy remarks in her essay) as the 'Quare on the Square', or alter-natively as the 'Fag on the Crag'.

Since post-colonialism is the fastest-growing corner of literary criti-cism, and since Ireland is now one of the most fashionable nations, the two were bound to converge. Gerry Smyth's *Decolonisation and Criticism* begins with a judicious, well-informed survey of what various post-colonial theories have to say about nationalism and decolonisation, before examining how Irish literary criticism has coped with the business of national autonomy. The book, written in the usual flat-footed style of the cultural left, seems reluctant to acknowledge the fact that culture and politics, however intimately interwoven, are different sorts of activities. It also agonises a little too much over the question of how anti-colonial revolutions are to escape the governing logic of the regimes they oppose—a conundrum that rests on the false assumption that everything in those governing regimes is unequivocally hostile to emancipation.

But there are some genuinely illuminating chapters on the politics of Irish anthologies and periodicals, along with a useful, well-researched account of some key critical encounters in Irish history. Unlike much in contemporary Irish studies, Smyth's study looks at institutions rather than isolated texts, and is all the more informative for it. If it had borrowed a touch of Wilde's elegance along with his engagement, it would be truer to the spirit of a culture for which form has generally been more than a mere container of content.

W.B. Yeats

'I dreamed last night I was hanged,' W.B. Yeats once announced, 'but was the life and soul of the party.' It is impossible with such oracular Yeatsian pronouncements to separate mask from reality, the *poseur* from the sincere eccentric. Auden called Yeats 'silly like us', but he was really just being polite; this table-rapping, spirit-summoning Rosicrucian was a lot sillier than most of us. Few major modern writers have been, in terms of their intellectual interests, so completely off the wall. But Yeats was one of the last great self-fashioners, and it is never quite possible to know how far he credited his own scrupulously cultivated absurdities, or even what 'credited' there would actually mean. On the one hand, there was the Celtic visionary who when he lived in Oxford couldn't cross Broad Street without taking his life in his hands. On the other hand, there was the hard-headed Protestant with (as his father told him) the virtues of an analytic mind, the crafty operator who could launch a theatre and help organise a political rally. Writing of the way leprechauns spin on their pointed hats, he inserts the scholarly reservation: 'but only in the north-eastern counties'. Is Yeats here sending up the reader, the folklorists, or mocking his own relentlessly mythopoeic mind? Or is he sending up nobody at all? A poet who literally lives in one of his own symbols, a half-ruined tower in County Galway, is either peculiarly self-mythologising or unusually self-ironising, and the question with this posturing, passionate man is sometimes undecidable.

It was Yeats's good fortune to have lived in a historical era—that of Irish nationalism—when it seemed possible to reinvent a public role for

First published as 'Spooky' (a review of *The Collected Letters of W.B. Yeats. Vol. III: 1901–1904* edited by John Kelly and Robert Schuchard) in the *London Review of Books*, 7 July 1994.

the poet. In England, the poetic imagination had ceased to act as a political force in the transition from Shelley to Tennyson: in fact, poetry and politics had now come to be constituted as each other's opposites, in a way which might have come as a surprise to Milton or Blake. Yeats will reach back over the head of this late Romanticism to its early forebears, to the Blake and Shelley who, writing in revolutionary conditions, can speak across the century to his own very different political moment in Ireland. English and Irish literary histories are out of sync; Yeats knocked around for a while with the fag-end of the English Romantics, the poetasters of the London Cheshire Cheese Club, but they couldn't yield him what he needed any more than could the English novel. Indeed, that novel summed up for him all that was awry with English culture—empiricist, sentimental, moralistic, slavishly mimetic—in contrast to an art that was lavish, extravagant, reckless, ceremonial and fantastic. Even so, in another curious hesitation between myth and irony, he will solemnly immortalise his Cheshire Cheese companions in the knowledge that they were a bunch of dopeheads and deadlegs.

Just as the theatre of Bertolt Brecht was made possible by the existence of a mass socialist movement, so Yeats's poetic enterprise was enabled by the tide of revolutionary nationalism in Ireland, of which he was the self-appointed mythologer. Whatever his doubts about the philistine middle-class Gaels who made the revolution, one of whom compounded the offence by stealing his sweetheart as well as his political thunder, his poetry remains on terms with politics in a way that much English modernism does not. In these volatile conditions, the poet could remake himself as hero, activist, rhetorician, cultural gauleiter, man of affairs, in a way no longer possible over the water. Yeats could draw here on the collective, impersonal nature of Irish art, all the way from the ancient bards or *filí* to the collaborative projects of the Young Irelanders, in a society where the symbolic remained locked into the social. And since the modernist movement in Europe was straining beyond the clapped-out ego of high Victorianism for some more transindividual culture, Yeats's Irish inheritance allowed him to loop time around him, uniting the archaic and the avant garde, the primitive and the progressive, in the manner of the great modernist artists. If he could do this so effectively, it was partly because Ireland had never enjoyed any very vigorous tradition of liberal individualism, given its clerical repressiveness, the marginal status of its industrial middle class and the communal emphasis of its Catholicism.

The Anglo-Irish Ascendancy into which Yeats was born had dismally failed to give political leadership to the Irish people, and was now, at the very point of its historical demise, trying to atone for this oversight by lending them cultural direction instead. A displaced, self-divided élite was now eagerly offering itself as a bunch of cultural commissars, intent on reviving the Gaelic culture that their ancestors had been intent on suppressing. Before Yeats's patron Lady Gregory came to collect folklore in the West of Ireland, her future husband William had been busy drafting the notorious Gregory clause in the depths of the Great Famine, which deprived thousands of relief-seeking small farmers of their paltry piece of land and was no doubt responsible for a fair number of unnecessary deaths. Steadily stripped of their political and economic power, the more enlightened of the Anglo-Irish sought to turn their uncomfortably hyphenated status to creative use. Perhaps the hyphen could become bridge rather than obstacle, as those caught between Dublin and London, cabin and big house, could set themselves up as the disinterested mediators between Ireland's clashing cultures. Perhaps culture itself could displace the rancour of Irish politics, providing a common terrain of symbol and archetype on which all the Irish could assemble. Since those ancient myths and symbols long predated the Reformation, they were conveniently absolved of sectarian animus. The enemy of the more patrician sort of conservative is not just radical politics but the category of politics as such, and from Burke to Scruton (if small things may be compared with great) they seek to oust it with instinct, tradition, unreflective habit. Yeats was the major architect of this project in fin-de-siècle Ireland, a kind of Hibernian Arnoldianism which is still alive if unwell today among the liberal intelligentsia of Northern Ireland. In the poeticised nationalism of the Celtic Revival, the Romantic idealism of a marginal sector of the Protestant upper class fused momentarily with the very different Romanticism of the Gaelic Catholic nationalists who were energetically digging their graves. Two dying cultures briefly intersected, as an Anglo-Irishry on the wane raked over the fading embers of a failing Gaelic heritage. Like most disinterested standpoints, however, this one was too palpably self-serving to survive long. If the Celtic Revivalists aimed to deepen and enrich a philistine Irish middle class, they were also out to displace their politics with an aristocratic paternalism which had never been much in evidence among the Irish landlords. It was a noble, generous, deviously self-interested piece of opportunism, which was to end up in the burning of the big houses, the decimation of the sons of Ascendancy in the First World War, and the fleeing of their relatives to the Home Counties.

As the *Collected Letters of W.B. Yeats* edge their snail-like path into the 20th century, this project is still on the boil, but Yeats's disillusionment with it is mounting apace. We watch him, in these seven hundred pages of correspondence, on the turn between early symbolism and later oratory, dream and drama, feminine languor and masculine hardness, imagination and will, populism and élitism. Innisfree is gradually giving way to Nietzsche, but in curiously paradoxical style: the aloof, self-delighting autonomy of the *Übermensch* is at once Yeats's retreat from a history which isn't going his way, and a displacement onto the individual life of an ideal of the free, self-determining nation. Just as the Irish dramatic renaissance is about to become materialised in the bricks and mortar of the Abbey Theatre, it is being pushed to the wall, howled down as immoral and unpatriotic by the nationalist press. 'I have an advantage over you', Yeats writes in 1901 to a minor poet, 'in having a very fierce nation to write for. I have to make everything very hard and clear, as it were. It is like riding a wild horse.' It doesn't sound like much of an advantage in some of the glum, dispirited letters here, but Yeats believed in keeping his chin up and his mask on, in facing down the impossible and dancing on the brink of the abyss with a very Anglo-Irish *hauteur*.

That arrogance is epistemological as well as moral. Yeats spurned English empiricism for the Irish idealism of Bishop Berkeley, which allowed him to believe that if you didn't like the world you could always invent another one. His art is a performative one, conjuring, mythifying, erasing, memorialising, invoking; 'Easter 1916' promulgates the Dublin uprising into authentic historical existence, gathers it into the artifice of eternity, even as it registers its own marginality to the event it records. Yeats's Nietzschean celebration of will and the creative mind has a streak of cavalier Anglo-Irish violence about it, as that class asserts a last defiant edge over a history from which it is being expelled. If that history is now opaque and untotalisable, Yeats and his colleagues will discover alternative totalities in ancient mythology, the obsessive systematisations of magic, the universal soul of Theosophy and the cobbling together of an Irish anti-Enlightenment 'tradition' which never really existed as such. The Anglo-Irish had always been a spooky lot, despite their contempt for Catholic superstition, and spectres throng their fiction from Sheridan Lefanu to Oscar Wilde. Dracula, the creation of a Dublin civil servant, is an Ascendancy sort of ghoul, wistfully poring over maps of London in his mouldering castle and finally deprived, like the Irish landlords, of his life-sustaining soil. The crazed precision of magic and occultism, beliefs which are systematic rather than nebulous, could provide Irish Protestants with a substitute for Catholic doctrine and ritual. Some of the letters in this volume are concerned with squabbles in the ranks of the Order of the Golden Dawn, a mystical outfit in which Yeats played a key role; and it is intriguing to see him arguing the toss over the Order's power-structure, committees and constitution, exercising the virtues of the toughly analytic mind in the cause of a lot of high-toned nonsense. Bathos is one of the most familiar tropes of Irish literary life, and Yeats's veerings from boardroom to Byzantium display it to the full.

There is a good deal of dross here, with only the occasional nugget; Yeats is more often to be found worrying about page proofs or his poor eyesight or how to spell Cathleen ni Houlihan than laying bare his soul or tossing off a dazzling essay on aesthetics. The arrival of a parcel of underwear is gratefully acknowledged. It is hardly surprising that he has trouble over the spelling of Cathleen ni Houlihan, given that he can't spell 'feel' or 'sleep'. Legend has it that he was turned down for a chair of English at Trinity College, Dublin because he misspelt 'professor' in his application. One or two historic moments nonetheless stand out. Hearing that the young James Joyce is about to soar on his Icarus-like wings from Dublin to Paris, Yeats writes him a kindly note on the advice of Lady Gregory, treats him to breakfast during his London stopover and offers to march him around the odd literary editor. It is a characteristically courteous gesture on Yeats's part, and an unwittingly ironic one too, since Yeats represented a major part of what Joyce was fleeing from. The arrogant young Joyce was predictably stroppy with the literary editors. He asked one of them whether he might review a particular book, and when the editor replied that he could put his head out of the window and get a hundred people to review it, Joyce asked: 'Review what? Your head?' Another historic moment is Yeats's dishev-

elled plea to his sweetheart Maud Gonne not to marry the loutish John
MacBride, who was to become one of the executed rebels of the Easter
Rising. Here, under intense emotional pressure, Yeats's spelling packs
up almost completely, along with his grammar and syntax, collapsing
into a garbled semiosis which Julia Kristeva would doubtless find of
interest. Maud must not marry MacBride because he is 'one of the
people'—pretty rich from a man who made a living out of idealising the
folk. Years later, Yeats will big-heartedly include MacBride in 'Easter
1916', though with the faintest hint that he might always have left him
out.

In these early years of the Irish theatre movement, Yeats is besieged
on all sides—by choleric priests, philistine nationalists, outraged Irish
Irelanders, journalistic hacks and yahoos. It is remarkable how he keeps
his cool, unfailingly generous, large-spirited and self-composed as these
letters are. Shuttling incessantly from Dublin to London, with the
occasional touchdown for a spot of fine living in Lady Gregory's Coole
Park, he snatches time to drop gracious notes to unknown authors who
have sent him their work, usually just when his eyesight is playing him
up. The latter part of the volume records his trip to the United States,
where like his compatriot Oscar Wilde before him he swapped his
poetic trinkets for the natives' hospitality and charmed them into Cel-
ticist fervour. John Kelly, general editor of the *Letters*, probably knows
more about this literary period in Ireland than anyone alive, and with
the capable assistance of Ronald Schuchard has produced another
scholarly masterpiece, deploying his immense erudition with tact and
verve in a marvel of intricate cross-referencing and annotation. This is
one of the great works of literary scholarship of our time, devoted to a
man of such towering stature that he can begin a letter by remarking: 'I
return Tables of the Law, corrected in pencil.' If we did not know that
Tables of the Law was a literary work, we might well suspect that here was
one greater than Moses.

Vivian Mercier, one of the leading luminaries of Anglo-Irish literature,
died in 1989, and his widow, the novelist Eilís Dillon, has assembled
Modern Irish Literature: Sources and Founders from some of his essays. Most
students these days tend to stick to Yeats and Joyce, Heaney and Friel,
rather than launch out into Moore, Morgan, Maturin and Mangan, to
stay only with that letter of the alphabet. The generous range of Mercier's pieces, from 18th-century Gaelic antiquarianism to 'Samuel

Beckett and the Bible', thus comes as a timely reminder of the limits of fashion. As Declan Kiberd remarks in an affectionate Introduction, Mercier was one of the last of the gentleman scholars, and one does not turn to his work for path-breaking concepts or supersubtle analysis. What one gets instead is the presence of a genial, well-stocked, humane mind lovingly immersed in its subject-matter, unbuttoned and anecdotal but painstaking in its scholarship. Mercier taught himself Irish in his mid-thirties, and some of the fruits of that labour are evident here in his authoritative discussion of translations of Gaelic texts. The volume is crammed with minor delights: Synge's scientific background, Yeats's humour, the influence of Racine on Beckett or of Flaubert's *Bouvard et Pécuchet* on Joyce's *Portrait of the Artist*. It also contains Mercier's seminal essay on the influence of evangelical Protestantism on the Celtic Revival, and a weighty centrepiece on Bernard Shaw. Of all Irish authors, Shaw, with his Dublin Southside accent, has perhaps been the one most thoroughly appropriated by the English literary canon; so it is refreshing to be reminded of just how profoundly Irish a writer he was.

I.A. Richards

Of all the great 20th-century critics, I.A. Richards is perhaps the most neglected. There is a crankish, hobbyhorsical quality to his work, an air of taxonomies and technical agendas which befits the son of a chemical engineer. His transatlantic counterpart in this respect is Kenneth Burke. Some of Richards's work smacks of the laboratory, and isn't helped by his charmless, bloodless prose style, laced as it is with briskly self-satisfied flourishes which his opponents saw as insufferable arrogance. An ardent propagandist for so-called Basic English, a project which reduced the language to a mere 850 words, Richards was also a precursor of today's global industry of English-language teaching. He published some founding, now forgotten texts in modern methods of language teaching, and once worked with cartoonists in the Disney studios, drawing up simplified language instruction manuals for the US Navy. He also conducted seminars with leading North American educators, and was hired by the Rockefeller Foundation to draw up a statement on the practice of reading. Some of his late works of the 1960s are described by the editor of this superb selection of his writings, a man not averse to rapping his author smartly over the knuckles, as 'febrile', 'unbalanced' and 'salvationist'.

It wasn't only the sojourn in Hollywood that marked Richards out from the average Cambridge don. One of the founding fathers of the Cambridge English School in the early 1920s, he was nonetheless deeply sceptical of the value of English as a distinct discipline, and at one point contemplated going off to train as a mountain guide. (He was

First published as 'A Good Reason to Murder Your Landlady' (a review of *I.A. Richards: Selected Works 1919–38*, 10 vols, edited by John Constable) in the *London Review of Books*, 25 April 2002.

a highly skilled mountaineer, and on one climb had his hair set on fire by lightning.) In the event, he went off instead to teach in China, as his most celebrated pupil William Empson was also to do, dropping in on Russia, where he met Eisenstein, and later on Japan and Korea. It is hard to imagine his piously parochial Cambridge colleague F.R. Leavis accompanying him on the Trans-Siberian railway. He also taught for a while at Harvard.

Richards was an unabashed system-builder, an enquirer after foundations and first principles in a field which, then as now, was scandalised by such anti-empiricist bad manners. (The editor of the TLS tells us in the centenary issue of the paper that he automatically deletes theoretical words like 'discourse' from his reviewers' copy, as some of his predecessors no doubt deleted words like 'montage' and 'neurosis'.) How can literary criticism be a system when literature itself is the acme of the anti-systemic, the home of the vividly contingent and sensuously particular? How can it submit to doctrine when doctrine, above all, is what it repudiates? It is true that this view of the literary would have come as something of a surprise to Dante, Pope, Voltaire, Austen, Goethe, Stendhal and Tolstoy; but most of these authors were foreigners, and though other nations may speak of a literary science, the English prefer to define the timeless essence of the literary in terms that have been current only for about two hundred years in a smallish corner of the globe.

The first theorist of academic English in Britain, Richards saw from the start that the discipline was stumbling along without stopping to examine its presuppositions, disastrously unable to justify its ways of talking. His aim was to substitute scientific rigour for belletristic waffle. Academic criticism he thought 'pernicious', and he wrote in 1933 that 'the worst threat to the world's critical standards comes just now from the universities'. Even Leavis, for whom 'academic' was usually a pejorative term, accused him of being 'anti-academic'. When Richards sent Leavis a note to congratulate him on becoming a Companion of Honour, he received back an unsigned note which read: 'We repudiate with contempt any approach from you.'

Richards is commonly thought to have invented 'practical criticism', which provides the title of one of his best-known books; but practical criticism had in fact been practised in Cambridge English well before Richards came over to it from the History faculty. (History, he remarked with glum accuracy, was simply a record of 'things which ought not to have happened'.) Practical criticism might have lent criticism some analytic edge, but Richards, as a theorist *avant la lettre*, was not a champion of it for this reason. Indeed, he was hardly a champion of it at all. What interested him about close reading, and the characteristic blunders it involved, was the material it could provide for a fully-fledged theory of communication. He described *Practical Criticism* as 'a piece of fieldwork in comparative ideology', and the book has a latent radical edge, recording as it does some remarkably obtuse critical comments from Cambridge students who, as Richards mischievously remarks, are 'products of the most expensive kind of education'.

To understand how communication functions was not, he insisted, the same as understanding how grammar or philology work. Richards was a discourse theorist before the title was invented (though the broader senses of 'rhetoric' came close to it), a scholar for whom the basic unit was the utterance, not the word. In *Coleridge on Imagination*, he describes Coleridge as a 'semasiologist' and proclaims that semasiology will constitute the critical science of the future. As it happened, the word to emerge was 'semiology'; but Richards was familiar with this term too, and makes use of it in *The Meaning of Meaning*. He also calls for a theory of interpretation, which later generations would dub 'hermeneutics'. There is even a dash of post-structuralist prophecy about him: bewitched by the propositional form, so he argues in *The Philosophy of Rhetoric*, we have failed to grasp that 'the world—so far from being a solid matter of fact—is rather a fabric of conventions ... and that sometimes is a dismaying rediscovery which seems to unsettle our foundations.'

As an anti-foundational pragmatist, Richards believed that all understanding involves guesswork and inference, that interpretation is potentially infinite, that meaning is plural, unstable and contextual, that metaphor in language goes all the way down, and that the mind and its operations are fictions. He rejected a linguistic atomism from the outset with his notion of the 'interanimation' of signs—the way in which they prop each other up. Perhaps it is no wonder that he escaped from Quiller-Couch's Cambridge to China, where he would find what appeared to be a language at home with ambiguity, gratifyingly oblivious of such metaphysical categories as cause, essence, substance, attribute, accident and the like. The Chinese language, as he describes it in *Mencius on Mind*, makes no sharp Western-type distinction between knowing what a thing is and registering its moral significance, thus reminding us that the assumption that knowledge of things is a value in itself is a peculiar, historically contingent one. What supposedly matters to the Chinese philosopher Mencius is the force or 'gesture' of an utterance, the purposive thrust of discourse rather than its bare propositional structure. Verbal forms and structures should be grasped in terms of discursive intentions and effects, not the other way round. Bakhtin was developing just such a view at roughly the same time as Richards, while Brecht, who like Richards was fascinated by Chinese culture, speaks of the *Gestus* ('gist', 'gesture') of an action or statement. The classical name for this view of language, as well as for language of this kind, is 'rhetoric'; and Richards was a rhetorician in the deep, broad sense of the word as well as in the narrower, manipulative one.

Ambiguity, for Richards as later for Empson, is among other things a coded sort of anti-chauvinism. To be hospitable to different meanings is to be open to a diversity of cultures. Empson shared his teacher's bumptious, idiosyncratic spirit, his sceptical, cross-grained, briskly rationalist mind, though his criticism could live with muddle and contradiction, indeed could find them moving and vitalising, as Richards's never could. In some respects, Empson is a Richards shorn of the system, though quite as much of an oddball. Both men, rather like the great émigré artists whom early 20th-century England attracted, were cosmopolitan enough to cast a quizzical eye on Western assumptions. Ambiguity, that is, went hand in hand with anthropology: Malinowski contributed an appendix to *The Meaning of Meaning*, and Richards writes in his *Principles of Literary Criticism* of the extreme cultural relativity of value. He was quick to spot the Eurocentrism of academic psychology, and speculates in his Mencius monograph that there may be a whole range of different but valid mindsets.

For Richards, then, theory was the enemy of reductionism and dogmatic rigidity, not its incarnation. It is common sense which believes in sticking to your own kind, not disciplined speculation. If Richards called for rigour, it was in the name of the non-rigorous, of a finer appreciation of complexity, flexibility and what he called 'multiple definition', whereas the common sense of the common room doggedly trusted that each word had one fixed meaning. Richards dismissed out of hand any simple application of a priori principles to a literary work, and thought in the end that it was all about feeling and judgment. He was far less dogmatic than, say, C.S. Lewis, who once handed Richards a copy of his own *Principles* to read in bed with the tart comment: 'Here's something that should put you to sleep.' He was a lot more abstract than Lewis, to be sure, but it was precisely that power to abstract from his own social situation which made him more adaptive and adventurous.

The quarrel between Richards and Leavis was really about whether to beat science or join it. The American New Critics won themselves the best of both worlds in this respect, yoking hard-nosed analysis to a sense of the numinous. The poem was an examinable object, a taut structure of tensions and polarities, but this lent it an indeterminacy of meaning which had transcendent, even theological implications. Richards took a grim view of modern civilisation, but considered, ironically enough, that a scientifically based criticism and psychology could insulate us from the most degrading effects of a scientific-technological society; or, as he quaintly put it, from 'the more sinister potentialities of the cinema and the loudspeaker'. He was also something of a Benthamite utilitarian in his theory of value. Leavis, for his part, denounced a 'technologico-Benthamite' civilisation which seemed to encompass everything from hairdryers to oxygen tents, and preached instead a pseudo-transcendent humanism. Yet Richards's remark about loudspeakers is pure Leavis, and the two men were at one in holding that art was not only the deepest repository of human value in a mechanised world of declining standards, but that its influence could be socially redemptive. Poetry, Richards observes in vatic Arnoldian vein in *Science and Poetry*, 'is capable of saving us; it is a perfectly possible means of overcoming chaos'.

Both critics clung for different reasons to a continuity between art and common experience, scorning the idea of a specialised aesthetic domain. For Richards, however, science and technology are here to stay, and art can do little more than supplement their emotional deficiencies. Its function is thus emotive rather than cognitive: indeed, this aesthetic emotivism is simply the flip-side of his positivism. A positivism which expels value from the material world can always smuggle it in again by the aesthetic back door as a form of spiritual solace, but only at the cost of refusing art cognitive status and so, ironically, closing ranks with the aesthete. Leavis, by contrast, refused the positivist monopoly of knowledge; for him, art was as much a mode of knowledge as geology, not just a device for refining or adapting our sensibilities. The two men also differed over the status of criticism. Richards despised English as an academic subject and moved off into the philosophy of language. To this extent, he resembled Wittgenstein, who was later to make a number of bungled attempts to give up a lethally addictive philosophy. Since the criticism and philosophy of the time could yield Richards almost nothing, he turned instead to psychology or anthropology or ancient China, as well as to Coleridge, who wrote at a time when art and philosophy could still fruitfully interbreed before the former soared off into idealism and the latter lapsed into positivism. For Leavis, by contrast, English was the vital nub of the whole academic enterprise.

Richards's scientific psychology might be less charitably described as psychologism. He held the view that meaning is a mental process rather than a way of doing things with signs, a doctrine in some ways at odds with his pragmatism. Perhaps he was partly bounced into this opinion by a reaction against Behaviourism (he was a colleague at Harvard of B.F. Skinner), and wrongly supposed that such mentalism was the only alternative to it. When it comes to utterances, he urges us to attend not to what is said, but to the mental operations of the speaker. But it's hard to know how to describe the mental operations behind 'He's gone and smeared mango chutney on it' or 'Thou still unravished bride of quietness' beyond merely repeating the words. Thought, he considers, is a kind of 'mental pointing', a view demolished by the later Wittgenstein. In Kantian vein, he holds that statements about poems are secretly statements about their readers, which makes him a precursor of reception theory as well as a proto-semiotician and post-structuralist.

For all his hostility to empiricism, Richards remains caught in the classic empiricist belief that a successful act of communication—'understanding' a poem, say—consists in transporting a mental experience whole and entire from one mind to another. To make sense of my statement 'Just put it down on the table' is to re-create in your own mind the intricate sensuous experience I have as I pronounce the words, with every bit of its unique flavour and complex density preserved intact. Meaning, according to this view, is a state of mind, not a social practice. It will not do to claim that I can speak or understand these words without having any experience at all, or that even if I do have a few weird flashes behind my eyeballs as they are spoken, they can logically be no part of the meaning of the utterance. If meaning is inherently public and rule-governed, then the fact that I can't read *Treasure Island* without visualising Long John Silver as a one-legged version of my grandmother is of interest only to my psychotherapist and myself. Richards's thought here is bedevilled by the word 'experience', which tempts us to model non-sensory activities on sensory ones, as though reading a poem were akin to deliriously sniffing boot polish every three seconds. He would have been bemused by Wittgenstein's point that intending is not an experience, or by a writer's insistence that he or she was 'experiencing' nothing in particular at the time of writing, or perhaps was feeling a lot of quite disparate, inconsequential things, or was aware of little but the act of writing itself.

Richards's flawed theory of communication is superficially more plausible in the case of poetry, whose language is often (though by no means always) intricately sensuous and densely textured; but it is still a mistake to imagine that the meaning of 'And miles to go before I sleep' is a set of mental images I have, or mental processes I perform, when I read the words. It is a mistake which post-Romantic literary types, with their penchant for the vividly particular, are especially liable to make. One good reason for not holding this theory is that it is hard to know what Milton's 'original experience' was in writing *Paradise Lost*, and therefore hard to know whether you are recreating it correctly in your own head. All you have is a host of readerly 'experiences' of the poem, in which case you are in danger of being landed with as many *Paradise Lost*s as there are readers of it. Richards concedes that the 'original experience' of the poet is now inaccessible to us, and is prepared instead to characterise the poem as the sum total of all its various readers' experiences of it. But a critic as obsessional about order as he is clearly needs to side-step a tidal wave of epistemological anarchy here; so he adds the proviso that the only readerly versions that count are those that do not diverge too widely from the author's experience, which he has just informed us is inaccessible.

For Richards, then, a quality like beauty lies not in the words on the page, but in our response to them. But if you want to claim with the likes of Stanley Fish that the words on the page have no say at all in the matter, then you cannot logically speak of response—you cannot answer the question 'What is it that you are finding beautiful?' Your experience is no more an experience of *this* work of art than is the stomach ache you happen to feel while contemplating it. Richards himself prudently avoids allowing the text to evaporate entirely into the reader, claiming in his psychologistic jargon that the poem is the cause of the experience of beauty in us. But this is just what we mean by saying that the poem is beautiful. Not many critics imagine that beauty is in the poem in the sense that Jeffrey Archer is in jail. That there can be no beauty or envy or agony without an interpreter doesn't mean that to describe a poem is to describe the interpreter. There can be no bank robberies without interpreters either, but it would be a poor sort of legal defence for a robber to claim that his felony was all in their minds. Since Richards holds to a continuity between literary and real-life psychology, what he asserts of literary situations is likely to be true of non-literary ones too, in which case propositions about hostile aircraft only two hundred metres away are also secretly propositions about us rather than the aircraft. In a peculiar epistemological narcissism, all accounts of the world are oblique accounts of ourselves. What might seem to work with poetic beauty, however, sounds less plausible when it comes to things being oblong or poisonous, even though both qualities clearly involve interpretation.

Richards's Kantian view of art is tied up with his controversial opinions about the role of beliefs in literature, and Volume Ten of this edition, *I.A. Richards and His Critics*, valuably documents this and other critical debates about his work. Beliefs in literature are really what Richards calls 'pseudo-statements', to be evaluated not for their truth or falsehood but for their pragmatic role in organising our feelings. It doesn't matter whether Dante actually believed in God, or whether the reader does. What matters is whether such beliefs get something done emotionally. Once again, what seems to concern the object turns out to concern the subject. This is a questionable theory of the relation between poetry and doctrine: it is true that we don't need to be Tories to relish *The Dunciad* or Anglo-Catholics to appreciate *Four Quartets*, but it is also the case that silly, vicious or palpably wrong-headed beliefs in literature, whether sincerely held or merely strategic, can diminish our enjoyment of it. In a similar way, Richards sees that literary utterances are not at root factual propositions even when they happen to be empirically true; but he does not acknowledge that factual inaccuracy or flagrantly nonsensical beliefs can undercut an aesthetic effect. Our faith in the solidity of a realist character is bound to be shaken if he gets from Paris to Berlin in three minutes flat.

Where the notion of pseudo-statement may work rather better is in the theory of ideology. Propositions like 'Prince Charles is a hard-working fellow, not hideously ugly' may be empirically true, but this is not the point. The force of such statements is generally to act as sup-ports for a set of emotive attitudes, such as 'Royalty is an excellent thing.' If the statement in question is falsified, it can be replaced by another without too much disruption to the web of attitudes as a whole. This is one reason why ideology is so resistant to rational refutation: like the statement 'This is sublime' for Kant, it involves the kind of utter-ance which is propositional only in its surface grammar. This is not to say that ideology is simply subjective, any more than aesthetic judg-ments are for Kant; but neither are they quite the descriptions of the world they appear to be.

Richards produced a full-bloodedly naturalistic theory of value, an audacious move at a time when the air was heavy with intuitionism, crypto-religious symbolism and the like. The value of art lies in its power to balance and order our otherwise unruly psychological impulses, organising our desires or 'appetencies' into the fullest, richest, most coherent regime. He thus apparently derives a value from a fact, since to claim that a poem can do this is both a description of it and an evaluation. Once we have solved the communication problem, he announces with strange insouciance, the value question can more or less take care of itself.

This theory of value is utilitarian in origin. Each human subject is a kind of miniature liberal state, which to get the best out of itself must create an equilibrium between its conflicting tendencies, rather as the liberal state holds the ring between competing notions of individual wellbeing. Anything is valuable, in art or life, which satisfies an appe-tency without frustrating a more important one. Richards is aware that unless he is to go transcendent or intuitionist, 'important' has to be defined within the system he has set up; so he characterises an important impulse as one whose thwarting involves a widespread dis-ruption of other impulses. It is hard to see on this hypothesis how murdering one's landlady is objectionable if suppressing the desire to do so throws one into psychic disarray. What Richards would need to appeal to here, as with the model of the liberal state, is how far the fulfilment of one's own desires may involve the frustration of other people's, such as the landlady's right to realise her own appetencies by staying alive. But though Richards occasionally gestures in this direction, his model is too individualist to accommodate this social dimension. It is also vulnerable to the deontological argument that some desires are just bad whether or not they involve thwarting other desires, one's own or other people's. Killing a small child might enhance appetencies all round, but many would find it objectionable even so.

Value, then, becomes 'a problem of organisation', and 'states of mind in general are valuable in the degree to which they tend to reduce waste and frustration'. Richards is a kind of bureaucrat of the soul, a writer who sometimes sounds more like a refuse disposal officer than a critic. In a curious crossing of Bentham and Pater, value is economy, a matter of realising as many impulses as possible with the least sacrifice or curtailment. Like almost all criticism from Aristotle to Northrop Frye, Richards makes the formalist assumption that unity and coherence are goods in themselves, a value-judgment which his system presupposes rather than demonstrates. It is just that he replaces a traditional Romantic organicism with a more up-to-date neurological version of it. Had the England in which he was writing not been so insulated from radical modernism, an art which can celebrate contradiction, dissonance and unfinishedness, he might have paused to re-examine this stock notion. Like many liberals, he assumes that conflict is destructive in itself.

If poetry is important, it is because it represents the subtlest, most economical organisation of human impulses there is. Richards can thus practise his 'scientific' naturalism with no detriment to a Romantic élitism: it is just that the poet is no longer the most visionary of souls but the most neurologically sound. He is to be admired for his normativity, not his eccentricity. The doctrine of art as a disinterested equilibrium of the soul, tempering disruptively partisan interests by balancing them with their opposites, runs back through Arnold to Schiller. But it must now be put on a scientific basis, given the way that modern life, with its brittleness of response, noisy disruptions and drastic impoverishment of experience, has thrown us out of kilter. Richards was thus one of the many critics—Walter Benjamin is perhaps the most celebrated—who recorded the death of experience or decline of bourgeois interiority in the late capitalist epoch. Like Leavis, he imagined that the effects of industry, technology and mass culture could be fended off by sensitive readings of Donne and Hopkins; Benjamin was a little less sanguine in his expectations. The idea that poetry would save us was part of the problem, not the solution.

Culture, however, is not at all as serenely disinterested as it appears. For Arnold, a contemplative aesthetic wholeness had now to translate itself urgently into social action, not least if it was itself to survive; yet the inevitable partisanship of social action would seem to betray the harmony of being which it was meant to realise. Like his Victorian predecessor, Richards is a moralist, educationalist and social reformer as well as a philosopher-critic, for whom poetry must teach the populace psychical disinterestedness for deeply self-interested reasons. The less well-educated, he remarks, 'inhabit chaos', thereby posing a threat to social stability in an age of political upheaval. If he is interested in rhetoric, in suasive rather than cognitive discourse, it is partly because he is tempted by the idea of an enlightened manipulation of popular psychology in the service of social control.

This was not a novel theme in the European culture of his day. There are some dim parallels between Richards's conservative ideological programme and the leftist avant-gardes in Germany and the Soviet Union, which saw in art a similar opportunity to re-educate human feelings in the cause of a new dispensation. Socialism demands a cultural as well as political revolution, the construction of a New Man whose perceptions and responses are geared to action, solidarity and the flux of urban experience. The human mind of the future, Richards warns us, will be far more shifting, provisional and diffuse, which makes that psychic therapy or spiritual hygiene we know as poetry all the more pressing.

Equilibrium, then, is finally in the service of political propaganda; and Richards's emotive theory of art as a reorientating of our responses lent itself to this purpose from the outset. It is not of course that, like Proletkult or the Left Front in Art, he embraces an explicitly didactic view of art. On the contrary, the beauty of his case is that the didacticism lies in the disinterestedness, so that he can avoid aestheticism and instrumentalism at the same time. By being, like the ideal poem, ends in ourselves, we will be all the more instrumental in serving the ideal political state. Richards was perhaps not himself entirely unattracted by 'the more sinister potentialities of the cinema and the loudspeaker'; but he was a critic of remarkable ambition and originality, and this handsome, meticulously prepared edition of his writings represents an intellectual event of some magnitude.

The Frankfurt School

There was once a king who was troubled by all the misery he observed about him. So he summoned his wise men and commanded them to inquire into its causes. The wise men duly looked into the matter, and reported back to the king that the cause of all the misery was him. So runs Bertolt Brecht's parable of the founding in 1923 of the Frankfurt Institute of Social Research, a centre for Marxist studies endowed by a wealthy German capitalist. The English are on the whole rather hostile to schools of thought, which they feel can be left to the over-conceptual Continentals. It is one of the wearier clichés of English cultural commentary that any particular school represents more a mood than a coherent doctrine, an assortment of diverse individuals rather than a unified belief system. The Frankfurt School, as it would come to be called, was certainly diverse in its interests, ranging from Schoenberg to surplus value, psychosis to the laws of capitalism, Baudelaire to bourgeois rationality. But it was united by a revisionist brand of Marxism known as Critical Theory; and from its birth in the Weimar Republic to its later flight to New York and post-war return to Frankfurt, it sustained a tenacious if turbulent institutional existence through the advent of Fascism, the defeat of socialism, the Second World War and the ideological freeze-over which followed on its heels.

Established in the heady aftermath of the Bolshevik Revolution and European insurrection, in the year of Georg Lukács's pioneering *History and Class Consciousness*, the Frankfurt Institute began life with a mission to promote a hard-nosed brand of Marxist science dedicated to the revolutionary overthrow of capitalism. This is a fact worth recalling,

First published as 'In the Twilight Zone' (a review of *The Frankfurt School* by Rolf Wiggershaus) in the *London Review of Books*, 12 May 1994.

given that Critical Theory would later come to signify a soft-focus strain of Marxism which pressed the claims of culture and consciousness against a brutal economic reductionism. Carl Grünberg, the Institute's first director, viewed the transition from capitalism to socialism as a scientific certainty, and worked closely with the Marx-Engels Institute in Moscow on the *Marx-Engels Gesamtausgabe*. Under his aegis, the Institute amassed a unique archive of labour and socialist history, and produced two classics of Marxist economic analysis: Henryk Grossmann's *The Law of Accumulation and Collapse of the Capitalist System* and Friedrich Pollock's *Experiments in Economic Planning in the Soviet Union*. The emphasis, so far, was thoroughly in line with the Marxism of the Second International period: economic, deterministic, full-bloodedly scientistic in working method.

The turning-point came with the appointment in 1930 of Max Horkheimer as Grünberg's successor. Horkheimer was a philosopher rather than a political scientist, more preoccupied by questions of method than with problems of class struggle. The object of the Institute, modestly enough, was now declared to be 'the entire material and spiritual culture of mankind as a whole'; and the school was to steer a resolute course between positivism and idealism, integrating empirical social inquiry into a holistic political theory indebted as much to Hegel as to Marx. In the brief period before Hitler came to power, Horkheimer assembled around him a brilliant coterie of younger intellectuals, of whom Herbert Marcuse and Theodor Adorno were to become the most eminent. In 1934, the Institute, many of whose members were Jews, transplanted itself to the United States and, still under Horkheimer's mandarin rule, set up home as an adjunct of Columbia University. In a darkening situation in Germany, it had already betrayed signs of a retreat from class struggle to critique; now, marooned in a virulently anti-socialist society, it trimmed its materialist sails to the prevailing conservative winds, conducting the kinds of sociological survey it might earlier have denounced as positivist.

Not that its leading luminaries remained any less hostile to capitalism. In *Dialectic of Enlightenment*, published in the wake of the Second World War, Horkheimer and Adorno paint a bleak portrait of a world almost wholly in the grip of instrumental reason, of a paranoid rationality which either ruthlessly gobbles up whatever is other to it, or expels it beyond the limits of the thinkable. Dominion over Nature was necessary for the achievement of human autonomy, freeing the species from the sway of mythologised forces, but Enlightenment reason had now become a form of mythology all of its own. In seeking to emancipate itself by dominating Nature, humanity has repressed its own inner nature, and the repressed has returned with a vengeance as the barbarous irrationalism of Fascism. It would return in another guise, after the war, as the culture industry's manipulation of desire in the name of false sensuality and phony happiness. What allows the human subject to become autonomous is its internalising of the law, but this, in the shape of the punitive super-ego, now simply oppresses the subject from within, so that any chance of resisting authority involves submitting to a more insidious censor. And if the wresting of autonomy from Nature entails self-repression, then the liberated individuals who emerge from this process are, in a woeful paradox, faceless, interchangeable figures drained of all inner richness.

From what vantage-point, however, could Horkheimer and Adorno launch these Olympian judgments? For the critique of Enlightenment must be couched in the language of Enlightenment, and is thus self-subverting. The problem to which Adorno will henceforth address himself, in his philosophy of 'negative dialectics', is how to think against the concept, undoing the prevailing rationality from inside without lapsing into the savage unreason which is its ghostly other. Ideology, in his view, is a matter of 'identity thinking'—the belief that the concept can be equal to the object, exhausting its sensuous being. It is thus a spiritual version of commodity exchange, which for Marx involved a similar denial of the use value of the thing. Negative dialectics, by contrast, seeks to grasp the sensuous residue that the concept leaves over, pressing the claims of specificity, non-identity, contradiction against the hubris of abstract reason.

The result is a transformed view of the social whole, which Adorno developed with his friend Walter Benjamin. Benjamin, with his astonishing blend of Marxism, surrealism, Kabbala, Messianic theology and avant-garde aesthetics, belonged to the fertile Judeo-Marxist current which produced Horkheimer and Adorno. But he was a maverick member of the Frankfurt School, which disastrously turned down for publication part of his great work on Baudelaire's Paris at a time when Benjamin, in exile, could well have used the money. With his collaboration, Adorno hatched the idea of a 'constellation'—a method of examining art works or societies which dismantled their elements into particulars, then reassembled them in fresh configurations, rather like a montage. A surrealist sociology had been brought to birth; a sense of the whole was preserved, but one which refused to reduce it, à la Hegel, to a single determining principle. So it is that in his work on the Parisian Arcades, Benjamin juxtaposes scraps of architectural knowledge with fragments of Freud, images from Baudelaire with stray historical statistics; and so it is that Adorno's very prose style is pitched into a chronic state of crisis, struggling to avoid both a mere 'immediacy' of the individual object, and the tyranny of the universal concept. If Adorno produced a theory of modernism, he also wrote a modernist theory, whose elusive indirectness would challenge the procedures of instrumental reason.

For Adorno, it is above all the modernist work of art which can achieve this. The triumph and the anguish of such art is that it can never be quite identical with itself—that while it may strive to reconcile its various elements, it also knows that any such utopian resolution, in a history which includes Auschwitz, must be an insulting illusion. Modern art turns its back on society, and this refusal to have any truck with a degraded human condition is at once the source of its guilt and its supreme political achievement. The art of Kafka or Beckett is the 'negative knowledge' of social reality, embodying contradictions in its innermost structure, and by its very denial of unity reminding us of what would be necessary for such harmony to be historically achieved. By violently carving up its substance, the modern work exposes the present unity of social life as a lie. Modern art—a commodity like any other—is parasitic on the very society it spurns; and its tortured, self-divided being is the way it internalises this impossible condition. Its aloof autonomy makes of it a kind of fetish; but it also offers us a frail utopian image of a world in which sensuous particularity would have finally come into its own. It thus represents a last-ditch resistance to an almost wholly abstract, administered world. Capitalism, it would seem, was to be countered less by socialism than by Schoenberg; the Frankfurt School had travelled a long way from *The Law of Accumulation and Collapse of the Capitalist System.*

Capitalism had travelled a fair distance too, however. It was no longer just an economic system, but one which had penetrated the innermost reaches of the human psyche. Only this, perhaps, could explain its extraordinary staying power through an era of wars and revolutions. What kept it afloat were libidinal as well as financial investments, its ability to manipulate human fantasy and desire. The first great system of capitalist fantasy was born at a stroke with the high modernism which so fascinated Adorno. Modernist art, among other things, was a strategic response to the emergence of mass culture; and the two, as Adorno remarked in a celebrated phrase, were the torn halves of an integral freedom, to which, however, they did not add up. The more mass culture spawned its spurious harmonies, the more modernism retreated into deviance and dissonance; the more the culture of the people was invaded by the commodity form, the more disdainfully the modernist work turned its back on anything as sordid as sociality. The classical work of art shared a secret compact with its audience, drawing on a set of codes they could be assumed to share; in a world of movies and pop music the modernist text found itself talking in the dark, bereft of an addressee, and thus forced into an endless narcissistic dialogue with itself. The more the 'mass' work slipped painlessly into eye or ear, the more high art fought off a too-easy consumption, thickening its textures and deranging its syntax, fragmenting vision and pulverising meaning. For it to *refer*, in a reasonably intelligible way, was for it to become instantly complicit with the degraded discourses which surrounded it. And since what tied it to such discourses was its content, this had to be purged and dwindled until nothing was left behind but an anorexic purity of form.

It was the Frankfurt School which first turned serious attention to mass culture, and so lies at the origin of what is known today as Cultural Studies. Mass culture, for Adorno, was no more than relief from labour; but it carried into the sphere of entertainment the very processes of exchange and mechanisation which dominated capitalist production. For the first time, cultural production was now an integral part of the capitalist economy as a whole, and so was incapable of performing its traditional role of critique. Instead, it breeds a fake sensuousness and illusory universality which persuade us that utopia has already arrived. But for Adorno's colleague Herbert Marcuse, much the same can be said of high culture too. The art works of a class-based society, by transcending an oppressive present, allow us to imagine alternatives to it; but in playing this utopian role they also sublimate current conflicts into a specious harmony, and so repress the history of unfreedom in which they have their roots. In a grisly paradox, culture, which offers us a taste of freedom and happiness, is only made possible by their absence. And if such freedom and happiness were to be historically realised, culture as we know it would cease to exist.

The Frankfurt School was born only a decade before Germany was gripped by the mass psychosis of Fascism; and it is therefore not surprising that much of its work moves in the twilight zone between Marxism and psychoanalysis. In its exile, the Institute conducted a number of psychological studies on anti-semitism and the authoritarian family, seeking to map the ways in which political power imprinted itself on the human psyche. In an audacious move, Theodor Adorno had brought Freudian categories to bear on mass culture; but the school's leading psychoanalytic theorists were Erich Fromm and Herbert Marcuse, the former practising a socialised form of Freudianism which elevated culture above biology, the latter more concerned to harness the Freudian theory of the instincts to revolutionary ends. In *Eros and Civilisation*, Marcuse accepts Freud's thesis that all civilisation has so far involved repression; but capitalism, he considers, involves a 'surplus repression' which, by depleting the erotic instincts, leaves humanity dangerously vulnerable to Eros's old antagonist, Thanatos or the death drive. Socialism, by abolishing artificial scarcity and thus the compulsion to labour, will lift repression and liberate a joyous instinctual life, freeing erotic energies from their genital confinement and diffusing them throughout social activity as a whole.

It was, for the later Frankfurt School, a most untypical flight of utopian fancy. A more authentically Frankfurtian note is struck in Marcuse's *One-Dimensional Man*. Post-war capitalism has managed, he argued, to contain its contradictions in an anodyne social order from which all vestiges of critical thought have finally been expunged. In a world of 'repressive desublimation', human energies are no longer (as in a more puritanical capitalism) deflected towards 'higher' ends: instead, they may be safely released in trivial, politically innocuous ways. Like some of his Frankfurt colleagues, Marcuse came to see Western capitalism as an essentially totalitarian regime. Having lived through the nightmare of Fascism, they now projected that order onto the liberal capitalism of the USA, finding in the culture industry the most glaring instance of its supposedly all-powerful capacity to process and massage social conflict.

The classical Marxist belief in historical progress was decisively abandoned: there is, so Adorno gloomily remarked, no universal history
stretching from savagery to humanitarianism, but there is certainly one
leading from the slingshot to the megaton bomb. Harassed by Nazism,
overwhelmed by the Holocaust, revolted by the conformism of the post-
war United States, the members of the School sank steadily into dis-
illusion. The Institute returned to Frankfurt in 1950, under the bene-
volent patronage of the Adenauer regime, but it was now a mere spectre
of its former self. Horkheimer became an unashamed apologist for
capitalism; Marcuse stayed on in the USA to savour the sensuous particularity of Southern California, and though a revolutionary to the
finish found increasing consolation in the transcendence of great art.
Theodor Adorno endured a humiliating confrontation with the German student movement, who denounced him as an armchair radical.
The mantle of the school passed to Jürgen Habermas, the Bishop of
Durham of Marxism, proud to be counted among the believers but
critical of just about every major item of the creed.

The most detailed survey of the Frankfurt School to date has been
Martin Jay's *The Dialectical Imagination*, a masterly account which like
most of its author's work suffers from not arguing a case. Much the
same can be said of Rolf Wiggershaus's *The Frankfurt School*, which is
more biography than critique. But this monumental work of scholarship, in which the notes and bibliography alone occupy over a hundred
pages, now provides the definitive history of the Institute, and one it is
hard to imagine being ousted. Jay takes the narrative only as far as 1950;
Wiggershaus, himself a Frankfurt academic, extends it to the present
day, benefits from discussions with former and current associates of the
Institute, and adds a mass of new archival material. The result is an
admirably exhaustive study, which rescues the school from being cate-
gorised purely as an episode in the history of ideas, and returns it firmly
to its political and historical context. Wiggershaus's technique is to
interweave historical information with the explication of ideas; if his
book has a fault, it is that it is considerably stronger on description than
on analysis, and stronger on analysis than on evaluation. It treats the
Institute, quite properly, as a collective phenomenon, but the upshot of
this is that we rarely get a synoptic view of any one of its theorists, much
less an extended assessment of them. It is hard to know what Wiggershaus finally thinks of his topic—how far, for example, the Institute's

patrician aloofness from political struggle was built into its structure at the outset, or how far history was to blame. For the Frankfurt School is the tale of several theorists in search of a practice; and in this sense it offers an allegory of the fortunes of 20th-century Marxism as a whole. It was the key moment in a shift from classical to 'Western' Marxism which Perry Anderson has charted; from politics to culture, revolutionary optimism to a gathering melancholia, materialist science to a reliance on traditional philosophy. Wiggershaus's scholarly nose is too close to his materials to allow for much speculation of this kind, but his Teutonic thoroughness, rendered into lucid English by Michael Robertson, does marvellous justice to his materials. He has even dug out Erich Fromm's great-grandfather, who would sit in his shop all day deep in the Talmud, and when a customer entered ask him whether he couldn't find another shop to go to. If one wanted an image of the Frankfurt School, one might well find it here.

T.S. Eliot

The *Criterion*, T.S. Eliot's periodical, ran from shortly after the First World War to the very eve of World War Two. Or, if one prefers, from one of Eliot's major bouts of depression to another. The two time-schemes are, in fact, related. In 1921, the business negotiations to finance the proposed journal had to be suspended when Eliot suffered a nervous breakdown; it was during his convalescence from this illness that he wrote *The Waste Land*. Though the breakdown had much to do with marital misery, it also reflects something of the post-war cultural crisis of which *The Waste Land* is itself symptomatic. It was as though the old 19th-century doctrines—Romantic humanism, liberal individual-ism, dreams of social progress—had all failed to survive the Somme; and Eliot, like his European modernist colleagues, was dismayed by this spiritual devastation. Among other things, it raised the question of how they themselves were to write, bereft of a nurturing inheritance.

Yet as one who had never believed in liberalism, Romanticism or humanism in the first place, he was energised as well as alarmed by the cataclysm. It may have helped to put him into a sanatorium, but it also turned his thoughts towards a constructive solution. If civilisation lay in ruins, then there was a momentous opportunity to sweep away this heap of broken images and start afresh. Or rather, start once more with the good old things, moving forward to a classical, orderly, tradition-bound past in the face of that squalid cult of anarchic subjectivism, self-expressive personality, economic laissez-faire, Protestant 'inner light' and Bolshevik subversion which Eliot lumped together with cavalier

First published as 'Nudge-Winking' (a review of *The 'Criterion': Cultural Politics and Periodical Networks in Interwar Britain* by Jason Harding) in the *London Review of Books*, 19 September 2002.

indiscriminateness under the name of 'Whiggery'.

This Janus-faced temporality, in which one turns to the resources of the pre-modern in order to move backwards into a future that has transcended modernity altogether, is at the heart of modernism. The pre-modern in Eliot's poetry is a matter of Fisher Kings and fertility cults; in his prose it is a question of classical order, Tory traditionalism and the Christian church. In both cases, however, a discredited individualism must yield to a more corporate form of being, roughly at the time when laissez-faire capitalism was giving way to its international monopoly version. Whether as slain god or submissive Christian, the point of having a self is to give it away. It is the Romantic-humanist heresy which holds that we should nurture our egos rather than abnegate them. 'Tradition' is the order to which the poet must perpetually surrender his selfhood, and writing a poem involves an extinction of personality rather than an affirmation of it. It is no accident that Eliot wrote his doctoral thesis on the philosopher F.H. Bradley, late Victorian deconstructor of the autonomous self. As a rootless, sexually ambiguous American émigré turned pinstriped London banker, his own personal version of that entity had been in question for some time.

Eliot derived his poetics from the French Symbolists, so that it was impossible for him to follow Matthew Arnold in finding a solution to spiritual turbulence in poetry as such. The language of poetry cannot deliver a solution of this kind, indeed cannot even comment authoritatively on such a condition, since to be persuasive—which is to say, for Eliot, to resonate in the reader's nervous system, visceral regions and collective unconscious, not just in the shallow reaches of the mind— such language must be rammed up so closely against sensuous experience as to be well-high indissociable from it. There is, as a result, no space for poetic language to turn round on the experience it records so as to reflect on it critically. The most one can do is gesture through archetype and allusion to some ghostly alternative to the present, or find that alternative in the *sanitas* inherent in such a richly concretised use of language itself.

The task of cultural criticism must therefore be consigned to prose, which is one reason for the incongruity between Eliot's poetic and prose styles. While the poetry is cryptic, allusive and ambiguous, the prose is lucid, oracular, loftily self-assured. The *Criterion* would be Eliot's chief organ of such *Kulturkritik*, dedicated to a revival of classical European Christian civilisation. Nothing less than a kind of EU of the Spirit would now suffice to repel the barbarism of modernity. It was not clear how a little magazine whose circulation probably never topped eight hundred was to put the organic society back on its feet, but Eliot seemed to regard the *Criterion*'s minority status as more conducive to this end than an obstacle to it. Few phrases in his prose seem to yield him a keener, well-nigh erotic frisson than 'only a very few', and he would no doubt have been deeply rattled had his readership shot up by ten thousand overnight.

The second depression of spirits gripped Eliot in October 1938, in the wake of the Munich pact between Hitler and Chamberlain. Three months later, the *Criterion* folded—partly because of the material complications of the advent of war, but no doubt because of its spiritual implications, too. For the war meant that the *Criterion*'s project to rebuild a cultural equivalent of the Holy Roman Empire had collapsed, giving way to an altogether more sinister sort of European empire; and Eliot observed glumly in the final edition of the journal that 'the "European Mind", which one had mistakenly thought might be renewed and fortified, disappeared from view.'

It was Fascism, in short, which helped to close down the *Criterion*, a point overlooked by those for whom Eliot and his magazine were themselves of this persuasion. In fact, Eliot was not a Fascist but a reactionary, a distinction lost on those of his critics who, in the words of Edmund Burke, know nothing of politics but the passions they incite. Ideologically speaking, Fascism is as double-visaged as the modernism with which it was sometimes involved, casting a backward glance to the primitive and primordial while steaming dynamically ahead into the gleaming technological future. Like modernism, it is both archaic and avant-garde, sifting pre-modern mythologies for precious seeds of the post-modern future. Politically speaking, however, Fascism, like all nationalism, is a thoroughly modern invention. Its aim is to crush beneath its boot the traditions of high civility that Eliot revered, placing an outsized granite model of a spade and sten gun in the spaces where Virgil and Milton once stood.

Fascism is statist rather than royalist, revolutionary rather than traditionalist, petty-bourgeois rather than patrician, pagan rather than Christian (though Iberian Fascism proved an exception). In its brutal

cult of power and contempt for pedigree and civility, it has little in
common with Eliot's benignly landowning, regionalist, Morris-dancing,
church-centred social ideal. Even so, there are affinities as well as
contrasts between Fascism and conservative reaction. If the former touts
a demonic version of blood and soil, the latter promotes an angelic one.
Both are elitist, authoritarian creeds that sacrifice freedom to organic
order; both are hostile to liberal democracy and unbridled marketplace economics; both invoke myth and symbol, elevating intuition over
analytical reason. The Idea of Europe, as Eliot dubbed it, is in its own
civilised way quite as exclusivist as the Nazi state which in Eliot's eyes
helped to spell its ruin. It represented, as Thomas Mann understood, a
disabling sublimation of the spirit that left actual human life perilously
open to the assaults of barbarism. Moreover, though racism and anti-
semitism are not essential components of right-wing Tory belief, as they
are of most Fascist doctrine, they flourish robustly in that soil.

It is not surprising, then, that Eliot, like W.B. Yeats, should at times be
found looking on Fascism with qualified approval, or that he should
have made some deplorably anti-semitic comments. The problem with
all such political strictures, however, is that conservatives do not regard
their beliefs as political. Politics is the sphere of utility, and therefore
inimical to conservative values. It is what other people rattle on about,
whereas one's own commitments are a matter of custom, instinct,
practicality, common sense. The *Criterion* was thus embarrassed from
the outset by having to address an urgent political crisis while apparently not believing in politics. Eliot writes that a literary review must be
perpetually changing with the contemporary world; but how can the
idea of a Tory periodical not have a smack of the oxymoronic about it,
given that the principles it embraces are timeless and immutable?
'Times change, values don't', as an advertisement for the *Daily Telegraph*
used to proclaim, written perhaps by a hack who enjoyed burning wit-
ches. Nor can it be a question of 'applying' these unchanging principles
to altering conditions, since the application of universal precepts to the
particular, with its resonance of left-rationalism, is part of what conservatism rejects.

This split between principle and practice is a version of the generic
division in Eliot's writing between prose and poetry—the former being
too aloof from the concrete, and the latter unable to rise above it.
The classical work, in which universal and individual are supposedly

blended, is thus denied in the very form of Eliot's writing, even as it is championed in its content. By the time of *Four Quartets*, this will have become a theological problem too, as transcendent truths seek to clothe themselves in flesh and time. Eliot's theology commits him to a belief in the incarnation of the universal in the particular, the Word in the word, even as his disdain for the material world continues unabated.

One might, to be sure, see modernism as a belated reinvention of this classical unity. The modern artist, so Baudelaire declares, trades in both the eternal and the ephemeral, and this is true of Eliot's own poetic practice. While the fractured surface of the poem is nervously responsive to fleeting sensations, its mythological subtext is stealthily at work converting all this supposedly random stuff into archetypal truths. In this sense, Eliot the poetic avant-gardist and Eliot the Tory traditionalist are secretly at one: if the illusions of suburban consciousness are to be shattered, and the reading subject put in touch with his or her permanent, imperishable selfhood, a good many guerrilla raids on ordinary language will prove necessary. But modernism proves unable to stabilise the relation between the changeless and the contingent—a relation which usually turns out to be frustratingly oblique, or, as the ironic form of Joyce's *Ulysses* would suggest, flagrantly artificial.

The *Criterion*, like all such mandarin *Kulturkritik*, strikes a pose of serene disinterestedness where politics are concerned, committed only to an Arnoldian free play of critical intelligence. A literary review, Eliot insists, must avoid all social, political or theological prejudices. Yet since this, short of drawing one's reviewers from the ranks of the Seraphim, is clearly neither possible nor desirable (what use is a journal without some sort of line?), he also maintains with bland inconsistency that any review worth its salt has a political interest. It is the contradiction of non-political politics. Jason Harding's assiduously researched study of the magazine is excellent at nipping behind its tone of Olympian hauteur to reveal the sectarian, manipulative, suavely malicious politics of the literary marketplace that lie behind it. Framed against a world of literary bruisers and racketeers, the book shows Eliot kneeing a groin here or nudge-winking a reviewer into line there, all the time with his eyes fixed piously on the eternal verities. Harding's book is thus revisionist in spirit, sceptical of grand pronouncements, attentive to ad hoc forces and pressures, aware that what tends to survice of history is the general statement rather than its all-revealing local context.

The *Criterion* was rather more disinterested on some occasions than on others. It was, for example, extravagantly Olympian about the Spanish Civil War, urging that any partisanship should be held 'with reservations, humility and misgiving', and commending in this respect the admirable equipoise of Arjuna, hero of the *Bhagavad Gita* and Matthew Arnold's Asian lookalike. Curiously, however, Eliot makes no such judicious invocation of Arjuna when it comes to combating Communism. He also betrays remarkably little reservation, humility or misgiving in his hostility to 'free-thinking Jews', or in his solemn proposal, speaking as an expatriate from St Louis, that 'it would appear to be for the best that the great majority of human beings should go on living in the place in which they were born.'

The battle against Bolshevism, in fact, was part of the magazine's raison d'être, and perhaps also part of the reason for its decline. The most important event of the First World War, Eliot writes, was the Russian Revolution; and he clearly views the conflict between it and 'Latin' civilisation as a spiritual war between Europe and Asia. Yeats thought much the same: if the Spirit of Europe needed reviving, it was largely because Bolshevism broke out first in the East. The *Criterion* was among other things a response to the creeping power of Marxism, a creed which Eliot admired rather as one can imagine Pope Pius XII having a sneaking respect for Stalin. He praises Communism more than once in the magazine for its orthodoxy, moral conviction and deep-seated principles, and evidently regards it as one of the few ideological adversaries worthy of his attention. As a Tory reactionary, he himself objects to the 'dictatorship of finance' and the fetishism of the economic quite as fervently as the political Left. Indeed, his view of most Conservatives of his day is more or less Roger Scruton's view of Thatcherites: they are liberals in traditional Tory clothing, elevating liberty over order. But Communism may also have played its part in the journal's demise, since by the close of the Marxising 1930s and with the looming of global war, its brand of aristocratic, Anglo-Catholic classicism was bound to appear less than burningly relevant. As the Eliot of *The Idea of a Christian Society* was advocating a largely rural society living by the rhythms of the seasons, Hitler's troops were marching into Poland.

Harding does not seek to deny Eliot's 'élitist and imperialist cultural politics', though he perhaps underestimates how nasty they could actually be. He does, however, highlight the relative open-mindedness of the *Criterion*, which actively courted the Communist Hugh Mac-Diarmid, was mutedly enthusiastic about Maynard Keynes, and by its final phase was publishing Auden, Spender and the Surrealists. He organises his study partly by investigating the journal's intricate relations to surrounding periodicals (the *Adelphi*, the *Calendar of Modern Letters*, *Scrutiny* and *New Verse*); partly by an overview of its cultural politics; and partly by examining the work of five of its key reviewers. This approach risks burying the *Criterion* itself beneath accounts of other journals, sectarian squabbles and reviewers' biographies; but it has the advantage of illustrating just how politically and aesthetically diverse its contributors often were. Herbert Read, its most frequent book reviewer, was a Surrealist and anarcho-syndicalist educated in a Halifax orphanage, whereas the debonair dilettante Bonamy Dobrée, an odd compound of Strachey and Kipling, bellettrist frivolity and public school backbone, was educated at Haileybury and Cambridge. As the critic John Peter has put it, 'parts of the *Criterion* resembled a supplement to the *Tablet*—while, incomprehensibly, other parts were crowded with Marxists and moderns.'

Read was an anarchist who accepted a knighthood, a champion of avant-garde art who also edited the fashionable *Burlington Magazine*; such contradictions are typical of the *Criterion* in general. The money for the journal came from Viscountess Lilian Rothermere, the estranged wife of the newspaper magnate, who was keen to promote the sort of radical-chic production that might make a stir in London drawing-rooms. She played the kind of supervisory role in the conduct of the *Criterion* that the imperious Annie Horniman did in the running of Yeats's Abbey Theatre. Eliot, himself an unstable compound of bourgeois stuffiness and literary saboteur, thus found his journal caught between High modernism and High Society, too dull for some and too daring for others. He himself moved between bohemian Soho and genteel Mayfair, a polarity that conceals an affinity. For modernism was among other things a reaction against middle-class modernity, which therefore attracted both patricians and poetic drop-outs, the socially outmoded and the socially passed-over.

The *Criterion* pulled in writers such as Woolf, Lawrence, Yeats, Aldous

Huxley, E.M. Forster and Wyndham Lewis, but also gave Proust, Valéry, Cocteau and other European writers their first airing in English. Conservative reaction, like socialist internationalism, was distinctly un-English in its lack of provincialism. If the journal espoused an unpleasant brand of right-wing Christianity, it was at least an intellectually taxing discourse centred on Dante, Aquinas and Parisian neo-Thomism, rather than the parochial pseudo-religiosity of a Philip Larkin. In the epoch of high modernism, it was for the most part the radical Right, rather than the liberal or social democratic centre ground, that opened up cosmopolitan perspectives in a stiflingly claustrophobic England, as exiles and émigrés such as Conrad, Wilde, James, Shaw, Yeats, Joyce, Lawrence, Eliot and Pound shuttled between cultures and languages in order to reap those symbolic resources for their art that England alone could not furnish.

Not all of these authors were right-wing; but the predominance of that outlook among them is nonetheless striking. In an epoch of cultural crisis, it was the displaced and deracinated who could respond to their historical moment in answerably ambitious terms; and it was these, therefore, who in raising the most searching questions about modern civilisation, were able to produce the finest literary art. But nobody is more in love with autocracy than the anxious and insecure. The fact that so many of these writers responded to the historical crisis with apocalyptic pleas for absolute authority and the violent exclusion of subversive elements is the price we have to pay for such art, if we should choose to do so.

Georg Lukács

Changing the world involves a curious kind of doublethink. For us to act effectively, the mind must buckle itself austerely to the actual, in the belief that knowing the situation for what it is is the source of all moral and political wisdom. The only trouble is that such knowledge is also desperately hard to come by, and perhaps in any complete sense unattainable. What is difficult is not so much solutions, but grasping the way it is with a particular bit of the world. If you get this right, it will intimate the kind of solutions you should look to. Answers are not the hardest thing.

The problem is not only that there are many competing versions of how it is with the world, including the postmodern belief that it is no way in particular; it is also that to bow our minds submissively to the actual requires a humility and self-effacement which the clamorous ego finds hard to stomach. It is an unglamorous business, distasteful to the fantasising, chronically self-deceiving human mind. Seeing things for what they are is in the end possible only for the virtuous.

There is no point in demanding an end to capitalism if the system was wound up several decades ago and one has simply failed to notice. In this broad sense, all prescriptions about what to do imply descriptions of what is the case. Values must be in some sense linked to facts. But at the very moment the mind is required to be chaste, rigorous and self-forgetful, it is also asked to spurn the actual in the name of the possible.

It must combine the indicative mood with the subjunctive one,

First published as 'Kettles Boil, Classes Struggle' (a review of *A Defence of History and Class Consciousness* by Georg Lukács) in the *London Review of Books*, 20 February 2003.

yoking a coldly demystified sense of the present to a warmly imaginative leap beyond it. It must respect and refuse the world in the same act. The mind is called upon to be both mirror and lamp, faithfully reflecting its surroundings while shedding a transformative light upon them. The flights of fantasy which get in the way of trying to see the situation straight are vital to imagining an alternative to it. We must be moved by visions of a future in which men and women would be made physically sick by the act of dominating others, while remaining stony-faced and churlishly suspicious before the blandishments of the present. If the Romantic conforms the world to his or her desire, and the realist conforms the mind to the world, the revolutionary is called upon to do both at once.

In this sense, radical politics demand a strangely hybrid kind of human being, one who is both more sceptical and more trustful than the average run of folk. Such characters are more gloomy in their view of the past and present than most conservatives, but also more open to a transformed future than most liberal reformists. Because what is awry with the present is a structural affair, it runs far deeper than individual folly or knavery, which is the bad news; but for the same reason it can in principle be changed, which is the good news. It is when radicals are decried as Jeremiahs by the liberals and as starry-eyed utopians by the conservatives that they know they have got it more or less right.

This duality crops up in Marxist theory as a contention over how much power one should assign to the subject and how much to the object. But since 'subject' here means the revolutionary masses, and 'object' something like history or class society, the epistemological is also the political. How far is change up to us, and how far is it constrained by objective conditions? Pushed too far, the former keels over into voluntarism, and the latter into determinism. The combination of these two heresies is known as middle-class society, which believes politically speaking in self-determination, and economically speaking that the individual is merely a pawn in the marketplace. The voluntaristic doctrines of capitalism—the sky's the limit, never say never, you can crack it if you try—are a convenient screen for the 'truth' of its determinism—for the fact that the human subject is shunted around by random economic forces which are within nobody's control. But they also reflect a genuine belief in democracy, hard though that is to reconcile with economic anarchy.

What, then, of the Marxist version of this problem? Marx himself tended to speak of practical human subjects in his youth and of objective, law-like processes in his middle age. Some of his disciples claimed that these were just different ways of talking about the same thing, whereas others of them, not least humanist or Hegelian Marxists like Jean-Paul Sartre, regarded talk of law-like processes as itself a form of alienation. For the early Antonio Gramsci, Marx had immatured with age, and *Capital* was to be discarded. The 'Back to the young Marx!' slogan of the humanists was shouted down by the 'Forward to the middle-aged Marx!' rallying-cry of Louis Althusser and his acolytes, for whom Marx's youthful talk about living human subjects was simply a regrettable Hegelian hangover, and the 'mature' Marx was the genuine scientific article.

For some bourgeois apologists of Marx's own day, the essence of human subjects was their freedom, whereas the objective historical process was governed by inexorable laws. Some Marxists had problems with the first bit of this, since it smacked of laissez faire; but it was hard to reject freedom out of hand and still clamour for social change. Marx himself sometimes sounds as though he is a determinist, and sometimes not. The Marxism of the Second International was robustly determi-nistic, which left the subject rather at a loose end. If socialism was predestined by the laws of history, what exactly was the point of men and women trying to bring it about? Why struggle for what will happen anyway? And why should one suppose that the inevitable is also desir-able? The reverse is usually the case. Marxist philosophers like Kautsky and Plekhanov had no very cogent answer to this latter question; though some of their colleagues, aware that a positivist form of Marxism could yield no ethical criteria to establish why socialism was worth embracing in the first place, laced this sterile historicism with a dash of Kantian ethics.

The apparent superfluity of the human subject, however, could be dealt with after a fashion. Socialism was indeed inevitable—but this included the inevitability of working-class insurrection. The proletariat was bound to rise up and overturn the system once it found its condi-tion sufficiently intolerable, and once it had attained consciousness of its allotted historical role. In its wily way, historical determinism had already factored in the free behaviour of human agents, just as divine providence does not dispense with our free decisions but works in and through them. My freedom is not an embarrassing oversight in God's plan for the world, since it is God who lies at the very source of that freedom, and who has calculated in my freely chosen actions from all eternity. God did not force me to dress up as a parlour maid and call myself Milly last Friday; but being omniscient, he knew that I would, and could thus shape his cosmic schemes with last Friday's Milly business well in mind. There is no stopping the kingdom of God from coming, but only because the fact that Christians work to bring it about is equally preordained. The notion of divine providence thus deconstructs the opposition between subject and object, liberty and necessity. In the modern era, it takes the form of the Hegelian Absolute.

Even so, all this scarcely left the subject centre-stage. What changed everything in this respect was the Bolshevik revolution. If that cataclysm was the ruin of the Tsar, it also threatened the ruin of the mechanistic materialism for which the human subject was a mere symptom of the historical process. The establishment of the first workers' state reminded the Marxist theory which helped to give it birth of what it had almost forgotten: that it is men and women, not History, who write the human narrative. In eras of revolution, Marxist theory tends to turn with fresh vigour to questions of consciousness; but it also does so in periods of reaction, when, as with much Western Marxism, political questions which have grown intractable can be displaced by matters of culture and philosophy. The problem is how to give voice to the importance of the subject without giving comfort to the bourgeois idealists, who are fond of hearing that injustices can be put right by a bit more will power, and that a change of heart is always more deep-seated than a mere change of property relations.

What the Bolshevik revolution revealed was that Marxist theory had lagged behind socialist practice—not exactly the most pressing of problems for left politics today. Today's left, bereft of the political opportunities of a Lenin or Lukács, is accustomed to practise limping behind theory, or even being replaced by it. Once radical protest was flushed off the streets of Paris in 1968, 'discourse' or the floating signifier could keep it warm. It is not unknown for followers of Michel Foucault to celebrate the anarchic force of madness while voting Liberal Democrat. You can back Tony Blair and Pierre Bourdieu with equal enthusiasm. In the era of Bolshevism, by contrast, theory had at times to hobble hard to keep abreast with what was happening on the streets.

The Petersburg Soviet tore up and rewrote Marxist theories of political power, while the Bolshevik uprising struck hard at the kind of Marxism for which human agency was a kind of agreeable bonus.

Philosophically speaking, Lenin championed the kind of quaint epistemology for which ideas are copies or reflections of real objects. Politically speaking, however, this largely passive model of the mind hardly answered to what had broken out in the farms and factories of Russia. Leninist practice outstripped the theory. To account for what had happened, you had to swap one bourgeois philosopher for another, reach back to Hegel rather than Kant, and retrieve an idea of consciousness as active intervention rather than accurate picturing. There was need for an Hegelian recasting of Marxism, which would rewrite history in retrospect and supply Bolshevism, after the event, with its missing epistemology. The World Spirit accordingly summoned the Hungarian philosopher Georg Lukács to accomplish this task.

Lukács did so most resourcefully in *History and Class Consciousness* (1923), the chief intellectual monument of Western Marxism. No other work of Marxist philosophy has proved so richly influential. Among other things, the book reinvents the young Marx's theory of alienation, at a time when his writings on the subject were still unknown. It is alienation which leads us to forget that the object has its source in the labour of the subject. The history of modern Western epistemology begins to look different once you see that its innocent 'object' is in fact a reified commodity. It is only then, in Lukács's view, that we can see why Immanuel Kant is forced to posit a mysterious individual freedom on the one hand and an impenetrable, law-bound object on the other.

What will bridge the gap between them is the dialectic. History and subjectivity, Lukács insisted, were simply different poles of a single dialectical process. In the shape of working-class consciousness, the mind was a transformative force within reality, not an obedient reflection of it. Objectivity was not to be achieved by the disinterested contemplation typical of 'bourgeois' natural science: rather, truth is a product of the interaction of mind and world, not of the banishment of the subject from the object so that it may view it more accurately. On this perverse notion, the subject can know the object best by disappearing altogether from the scene of inquiry.

For Lukács, by contrast, truth is achieved by the working class becoming aware of itself as the universal subject of history. A universal subjectivity is effectively identical with objectivity. You can thus hope to historicise truth while avoiding relativism. For Hegel, the truth of history is the World Spirit becoming conscious of itself; for Lukács, it is the self-knowledge of the working class. The *Zeitgeist* has become incarnate in the wretched of the earth.

Lukács recognised, in short, that there is a category which mediates between subject and object, namely self-knowledge. In the act of knowing myself, I become subject and object simultaneously. This peculiar sort of knowledge also dismantles the dichotomy between thought and action, or fact and value—for to know myself is to alter myself in that very act, and to grasp the truth of my condition is to know what I would need in order to be free. Is this to claim, then, that Marxist theory is no more than the historical self-understanding of the working class, as Hegel's Absolute is no more than history brooding upon itself? If so, what has become of Lenin's insistence that such theory must be brought to the working class from outside, or of the role of revolutionary leadership?

Well received at first, Lukács's great work soon ran into trouble with the custodians of Marxist orthodoxy. 'If we get a few more of these professors spinning their theories', screamed Zinoviev at a Communist Party congress, 'we shall be lost'. A photograph of Lukács appears on the front of A *Defence of 'History and Class Consciousness'*, looking like a cross between a mad professor and a punk. He himself was later to disown the book. Indeed, recantation came as easily to this accomplished groveller as optimism did to Trotsky. What nobody knew, however, is that Lukács had penned a response to the virulent criticisms of his work, which turned up recently in the Soviet Communist Party archives and is published here for the first time.

Lukács's main aim in this passionate polemic (he accuses one critic of 'fatalistic tailism', a grave, potentially infectious disorder) is to establish his credentials as a sound Bolshevik. Indeed, he had excellent reasons for doing so, given that the Hungarian Workers' Republic of 1919, in which he himself had been active as a political commissar, was routed partly because of its disastrously feeble leadership. Like *Paradise Lost, Ulysses* and a good many other distinguished pieces of writing, *History and Class Consciousness* is the fruit of a botched revolution. Lukács does not regard his historicist theory of knowledge as incompatible with a notion of theory as implanted by an avant-garde. The workers may come to see that they are exploited, but they will hardly come to grasp the finer details of surplus value or the Asiatic mode of production simply by feeling hard done by. Mechanical materialism must be resisted: insurrection is an art, a semi-intuitive seizing of the moment, not a stage in some drearily predictable development. Here, at least, the subjective moment has decisive predominance.

The kind of determinist Marxism which Lukács is out to worst is particularly keen on the so-called dialectics of Nature, a piece of metaphysical materialism hatched by Engels out of 19th-century positivism. The doctrine was crudely (though non-satirically) summarised in the words of a Marxist worker of my acquaintance: 'Kettles boil, dogs' tails wag, and classes struggle'. Lukács tips his hat to this piece of reductionism, but is much more enthused by the idea that our knowledge of Nature is always socially mediated.

This is one of several issues which divides John Rees, who writes an erudite, illuminating introduction to this book, and Slavoj Žižek, who provides a characteristically provocative 'Postface' for it. Roughly speaking, Rees seeks rather stiffly to reclaim Lukács for a certain Marxist orthodoxy, whereas the more imaginative Žižek ends up by making him sound more like an existentialist than a materialist. His Lukács is really an exotic mixture of Jacques Lacan and Alain Badiou, a thinker who breaks with evolutionism for the 'radical contingency' of the revolutionary act. If Rees risks taking the novelty out of Lukács, Žižek makes him sound more like an avant-garde Parisian than a Hungarian Communist.

Rees is anxious to co-opt Lukács for 'diamat' or the dialectics of Nature, and claims him as an orthodox Leninist without probing too deeply into the tension between historicist and vanguardist theories of consciousness. He seems to approve of the fact that Lukács brutally consigned his own valuable pre-Marxist writings to the ashcan of history, whereas the truth is that Western Marxism would have been woefully impoverished without its non-Marxist philosophical resources.

Rees is also a zealous advocate of Lukács's belief that false consciousness is ultimately rooted in the reified, fetishistic nature of capitalist society. This, the conceptual keystone of *History and Class Consciousness*, is indeed a powerful case; but Rees fails to see that it is a reductionist one, too. There are all kinds of ideological forms which have precious little to do with reification, not least those unconcerned with social class. Rees himself falls prey to reification when he speaks of 'the dialectic', but not particularly because he is a victim of the fetishism of commodities.

The tragic irony of Lukács's career is that he himself moved from being a revolutionary subject to becoming, as a stalwart of Stalinism, the symptom of a determined historical process. His personal trajectory was in this sense true to Marx's intellectual one. Born in Budapest in 1885, the son of a leading Hungarian financier and of a mother who sprang from one of the oldest and wealthiest Jewish families of Eastern Europe, Lukács hardly seemed cut out for a Communist career. His early philosophical preocccupations, cast in a sombrely tragic mould, were ethical and idealist, and his politics a form of Romantic anti-capitalism. Works like *Soul and Form* (1910) and *Theory of the Novel* (1916) reflect an abstract, utopian rejection of bourgeois civilisation, influenced by a curious blend of Hegel, Kierkegaard, Dostoevsky, Tolstoy, Georg Simmel and Max Weber.

It was the Bolshevik revolution which turned Lukács gradually from tragic metaphysics to historical materialism; and it was the collapse of the Hungarian *ancien régime* in 1918 which was to thrust him into the arms of the Hungarian Communist party of Bela Kun. The young Kierkegaardian philosopher was now political commissar for education and culture in Hungary's ill-fated Soviet Republic of 1919, throwing open theatres to the workers and launching a controversial sex education campaign which introduced children to the idea of free love and denounced their monogamous parents. Communism would resolve the tragic antitheses of essence and existence, fact and value, subjective and objective, individual and totality, which had haunted his earlier speculations.

A harmonious totality of social powers which the young Lukács had discovered in the world of classical antiquity was now given a change of tense and shifted to the socialist future. Marxism was the consummation of the great bourgeois humanist heritage. The later Lukács was accordingly in favour with the Comintern whenever it was bent on a political alliance with the bourgeois West, as in the Popular Front period, and out of favour whenever it lurched away from such *détente* (the pre-Second World War era in which social democracy was denounced as 'social fascism', the Nazi–Soviet pact, the height of the Cold War). It was less a matter of Lukács zig-zagging to adapt to Soviet policy, than of Soviet policy zig-zagging around him.

In one sense, the Lukács of the Hungarian revolution had simply translated into material terms a metaphysical conflict between authentic spiritual value and the corruptions of temporal existence. The former now staged an appearance as the revolutionary proletariat, while the latter took on the guise of bourgeois society. Still absolutist in his habits of thought, the neophytic Marxist Lukács preached that no compromise between the two was tolerable, and had accordingly to be rebuked by Lenin for infantile ultra-leftism. He was to change his political tune not long after Lenin's death, championing the Stalinist doctrine of 'socialism in one country' and launching some high-minded assaults on the revolutionary cultural avant-garde in the name of a more classical Marxist aesthetics. Having failed to bend reality to his desire, either in philosophical speculation or revolutionary practice, he settled stoically for trimming his desire to a harsh Soviet reality.

Yet Lukács's loyalty to classical culture, not least to the great bourgeois humanist heritage, was also a silent critique of Stalinist philistinism. Totality, having shifted from the ancient past to the socialist future, now took up home in the realist novel, banished there by the failure of revolutionary hopes. Utopia, glimpsed fitfully in Dostoevsky, had flared briefly in insurrectionary Hungary only to be snuffed out in the tragic decline of socialism into state oppression. It was now to be rediscovered in the mighty lineage of European literary realism from Balzac and Scott to Tolstoy and Thomas Mann. It was in *Waverley* and *Le Rouge et le Noir*, not in the World Spirit or the workers' republic, that individual particular and organic whole, sense and reason, the actual and the ideal, could be reconciled. Indeed, realism was simply a name for authentic art, a standard against which the whole decadent modernist enterprise from Flaubert to Brecht was to be measured and found lacking. If it could serve to imply a patrician contempt for images of brawny Soviet ploughmen, it was also a way of rubbishing almost everything from Zola to Joyce.

It was thus as a literary critic that Lukács became a name to conjure with in the West—one of a venerable lineage of Western Marxist thinkers whose preoccupation with culture and philosophy seemed to soften the edges of a historical materialism which was otherwise rather raw and angular for Western intellectual taste. It is ironic, then, that as this book reminds us, Lukács's 'turn to the subject' was not one away from bloody revolution, but represented a decisive move towards it.

Northrop Frye

If someone were to ask why art and culture have proved so vital to the modern age, one might do worse than reply: to compensate for the decline of religion. It is certainly a more convincing response than claiming that modern society finds art particularly valuable, as opposed to richly profitable. What modernity finds precious is less works of art, which are just one more commodity in its marketplace, than the idea of the aesthetic. And this reverence for the aesthetic reflects the way in which art, or at least a certain exalted notion of it, is forced in the modern age to stand in for a religious transcendence which has fallen on hard times.

T.E. Hulme caustically described Romanticism as 'spilt religion'; but much the same could be claimed of art in the post-Romantic epoch, an epoch which is forever on the prowl for plausible secular versions of good old-fashioned metaphysical values. The dilemma of modern societies is that they need such strongly foundational values to legitimate their authority, but find themselves constantly discrediting them by their own rationalist behaviour. Art or literature, then, can restore an aura of mystery to a bleakly disenchanted world. And though this is a hope full of tremulous pathos, it is by no means entirely fatuous. Art, after all, has a good deal in common with religious belief, even in the most agnostic of environments. Both are symbolic forms; both distil some of the fundamental meanings of a community; both work by sign, ritual and sensuous evocation. Both aim to edify, inspire and console, as well as to confront a depth of human despair or depravity which they

First published as 'Having one's Kant and eating it' (a review of *Northrop Frye's Late Notebooks 1982–90* edited by Robert Denham) in the *London Review of Books*, 19 April 2001.

can nonetheless redeem by form or grace. Each requires a certain suspension of disbelief, and each links the most intense inwardness to the most unabashedly cosmic of questions.

From Matthew Arnold's portentous idiom of sweetness and light to George Steiner's reverent talk of artefacts as real presences, art is a domain of displaced transcendence. It is the one remaining intimation of immortality for those who mourn the spiritual barbarisms of modernity, but are modern enough themselves to feel thoroughly out of place in a pew. For Matthew Arnold and his progeny, literature is religion without theology—the edifying, poetic spirit of Christianity emptied of its increasingly rebarbative doctrines. To this extent, literature becomes a sort of aesthetic analogy of liberal Anglicanism, full of the atmosphere of belief without an embarrassing amount of doctrinal lumber. Just as it sometimes appears that you can be a zealous member of the Anglican Church while rejecting the existence of both God and Jesus, so literature as transcendence commits you to little beyond a sense of the numinous which makes a virtue out of not knowing what it means. But as Arnold recognised, such degutted religion is a way to preserve discipline and social order among a populace who are less and less inclined to enthuse over the Virgin Birth.

The affinities between art and religion can be multiplied. Literary interpretation takes its cue from hermeneutics, originally a theological discipline. The decoding of the word was always at some level a deciphering of the Word. Sacraments, which are traditionally thought to bring about what they signify, are instances of so-called performative discourse, just like the language of poetry. In both cases, the sign is incarnational rather than merely denotational. The metaphor of artistic 'creation' has always been latently theological, a reenactment of God's fashioning of the world ex nihilo. And just as the world is autonomous of its creator (which is part of what is meant by calling him 'transcendent'), so the work of art is mysteriously self-generating and self-dependent, conjuring itself up miraculously out of sheer nothingness, obedient to no law but that of its own unique being. As a concrete universal, it is as much a coupling of sense and spirit, time and eternity, as the Incarnation itself, a microcosmic model of Christ. Art is all about inspiration, the wayward impulses of the Holy Spirit of the imagination; but like the Church it is a corporate, hierarchical, code-governed affair as well, conscious of being the bearer of tradition and convention, preserving canons of esoteric texts and grooming acolytes in their initiation into them.

Like the Church, too, art has had its popes and heretics, its martyrs and apostates. F.R. Leavis pulled off the improbable trick of being all four, as an outcast rebel against orthodoxy who nevertheless did a fair bit of canonising and excommunicating himself. The critical élitism he practised was a version of what Coleridge had dubbed the 'clerisy', a sort of secular priesthood. The artist as secular priest crops up as late as Joyce's *Portrait of the Artist as a Young Man*, as Stephen Dedalus exchanges consecrating the eucharist for that transformation of the bread of daily experience into the host of sacred nourishment which he calls art. Flaubert and James, Proust and Joyce are adepts who immolate themselves on the altar of their own art, gathering profane experience into the artifice of eternity.

For Leavis, the most precious novel is one which reflects a 'reverent openness before Life', and the religious idiom here is wholly calculated. It is inherited from D.H. Lawrence, for whom the novel was the 'Book of Life', the sacred scripture of a post-metaphysical social order. 'Life' for both Lawrence and Leavis is a transcendent rather than empirical affair, a matter of laying oneself trustingly open to a profoundly impersonal force which flows in its own sweet way through the spiritual elect. Like God, it is a force which is at once utterly inhuman and unfathomable and yet which lies at the very core of the self. One or two later commentators, in a profane equivalent of so-called negative theology, have given this elusive, quicksilver force names like 'power', 'difference' or 'desire'. Leavis's colleague I.A. Richards announced with stunning self-assurance that poetry 'was perfectly capable of saving us', while an English lineage from Henry James to Iris Murdoch discovered in the novel the quintessentially ethical form which would transfigure the whole concept of morality, shifting it from Kant to Kafka, from obedience to a code to the texture and quality of lived experience. It is art which will now answer the ultimate moral question: what, finally, do we live by? And though the answer may come only in sporadic flashes known as epiphanies, heard between two waves, in the ominous echo of an Indian cave, in the moment in the rose garden or in a sudden shout in the street, it can scarcely be claimed by the more conventionally religious that the Almighty's own utterances are either less infrequent or less enigmatic.

Literature as religion, however, is a project doomed to failure. For one thing, the cultivation of the former involves too few people to be a plausible substitute for the latter. Religion is a symbolic form or ritual practice, sometimes of a highly arcane kind, which nevertheless engages countless millions of men and women in the course of their sublunary lives, and which connects their beliefs about when the universe was created with their beliefs about when it is permissible to fib or fornicate. If the champions of cultural studies were not so theologically illiterate, they would long since have identified it as history's most astonishingly successful solution to the division between high and low culture. Within a single ecclesiastical institution, an intelligentsia of clerics is organically linked by both theory and practice to the mass of the faithful. No secular cultural project has come even remotely close to matching this extraordinary achievement, bought often enough at the cost of blood, bigotry and oppression. If culture in the artistic sense is too minority a phenomenon for such purposes, culture in the anthropological sense is a good deal too contentious.

For another thing, art is too delicate, and too impalpable, to be bent to such ambitious ideological ends. If you try, as has been tried so regularly since the Romantics, to atone for the death of God by fashioning art into a political programme, an ersatz theology, a body of mythology or a philosophical anthropology, you will impose on it a social pressure which it isn't really robust enough to take, and end up producing in it what Jürgen Habermas has called 'pathological symptoms'. The result will be an absurd inflation of this modest, marginal phenomenon, evident enough in the Leavisian faith that by analysing Hopkins's syntax or Austen's narrative form you were somehow contributing to the overthrow of commercial society.

It was perhaps inevitable, even so, that this steady convergence between theology and literature should finally assume literal, flesh-and-blood form in the shape of a major critic who was also a committed Christian. The Canadian Northrop Frye, previously known chiefly as a critic of Blake, burst on the literary world in a big way in 1957, with the publication of his remarkably original and ambitious study, *Anatomy of Criticism*. With previous North American criticism, we had moved within a modest discourse of tensions, ironies and ambiguities, of the poem as urn or icon; now, suddenly, we were plunged into a murky world of archetypes and fertility cults, male and female principles, humours and elements, emasculated kings and resurrected gods—as though the fin-de-siècle Cambridge School of Anthropology had suddenly been reborn according to its own rhythms of death and renewal in post-war Toronto. Such criticism represented everything that the briskly rationalist William Empson, who detested religiose aesthetics like those of Eliot, found most nauseating. It was enamoured of charts and diagrams, polarities and sub-divisions, with that odd combination of rigorous categories and occult contents which one associates with magic. Magic, as Yeats knew, is one of the most meticulously precise systems of fantasy, and in that sense resembles nothing quite so much as paranoia.

Indeed, it was just this combination of mystery and methodology that the age demanded. In the era of post-war reconstruction, the humanities had a choice between opposing technology and imitating it. If Leavis and the Christian Right took the former path, I.A. Richards, behaviourist psychology, positivist sociology and the early structuralists plumped for the latter. Literary studies had to decide between toughening up their methods to qualify as a kosher science and asserting the superiority of the creative imagination to any merely rationalist mode of cognition. The New Criticism which prevailed in North America when *Anatomy of Criticism* first appeared aimed in this respect for the best of both worlds, blending a belief in the poem as quasi-sacramental with a hard-nosed analytical criticism. Frye followed suit, cross-breeding the sacred and scientific to remarkable effect. Criticism, he considered, was in a sorry, unscientific mess, full of subjective value-judgments and idle gossip, and badly needed transforming into an objective system. At around the same time, Claude Lévi-Strauss was hatching much the same ambitions for anthropology. In Frye's view, criticism's task was to seek out the objective laws by which an apparently random assemblage of literary texts secretly operated, and these laws were to be found in the modes, myths, genres and archetypes according to which all literary works functioned. The phrase 'a science of literature' need no longer be regarded as an oxymoron. A science of the unique particular, to be sure, would be a contradiction in terms, and literary works might well be seen as exactly that; but there was also the question of literary form, which was general rather than particular and which could thus constitute a valid object of scientific investigation.

Here, then, was a literary discipline appropriate to a technological age; but its beauty lay in the way that it united this brisk technocracy of the spirit with a pastoral, pre-urban insistence on literature as myth. Myth, that is to say, in the post-Nietzschean sense of a source of primordial wisdom incomparably deeper than any drably discursive knowledge. A scrupulously categorising, religious-humanist criticism could thus have its Kant and eat it. Even more, it could outflank the New Critics while remaining just as formalist and unhistorical. For Frye, literature is an 'autonomous verbal structure' quite without reference to reality, powered by its own internal processes. If his own critical system is internally consistent, it is because it is equally remote at all points from empirical reality. Yet literature also represents an insatiable hankering for utopia, a collective dreaming which reflects the latent dynamic of all human history. It can thus figure as a substitute history for the one we actually have, uniting a rejection of actual historical life with a totalising sweep which would be the envy of any Hegelian. As with Eliot's Tradition, there is an ideal order behind secular time which is more real than reality. The author of literature, which represents the true narrative of humanity, is the human species itself, which finds in myth the one place where it can be free from the bondage of empirical history. The only mistake, so Frye informs us, is that of the revolutionary, who naively imagines that such freedom might be historically realised. Here at least, is one sloppily subjectivist value-judgment which he is unafraid to pronounce. A literature severed from all sordid connection to social reality ends up more or less capable of telling us which way to vote.

Northrop Frye, who died in 1991, ended up as a Glastonbury-type guru who might well stage a comeback as a cult figure for the New Age. Certainly these latest, meticulously annotated volumes in the handsome Collected Works now being published from the University of Toronto pull out all the coolest spiritual stops. Frye kept notebooks for over fifty years, and these two collections of them, the fruit of the last eight years of his life, are crammed with allusions to apocalypse, Atlantis, Plato, Eros, God, Anti-Christ, Prometheus, Doppelgängers, the Book of Revelation and the like. Yet if some of the contents are dippy enough, the tone is brisk, racy, occasionally pugnacious. In language somewhat less than Papal, he tells us that 'the Spirit is the successor or Son of the Word. Anyone who calls this a lot of crap can stick it up his ass with the rest of his own crap.' The tension between the spiritual content and the brusquely self-assertive form, here as elsewhere in Frye's work, is telling.

Since I myself stage a brief appearance as 'that Marxist goof from Linacre College', it is more than usually munificent of me to note just how formidably erudite these jottings are, for all their hothouse hermeticism. Even by the time of *Anatomy of Criticism*, Frye seemed to have read just about everything; and though he puts his learning to some eccentric uses, inquiring into the distinction between the cosmos and the universe or between white-goddess and black-bride imagery, it is the mark of one of the last great humanists of our time. That his schemes, like Casaubon's, are as free from obstruction as a plan for threading together the stars, is simply the price he has to pay for this visionary idealism.

Another such price is bathos. Frye moves in a heady sphere of angels and demons, Moses and mandala symbols, and thinks that such workaday pursuits as marking students' essays should be done by machines. All structure and no texture, he has little of the literary artist's sense of the contingent detail, the eloquent nuance, the ambiguous gesture. It is no wonder that he assigns realist fiction such lowly status in his critical hierarchy. Rarely has the creative imagination been lauded in such sterilely abstract a style. As a Christian, Frye is interested in Jesus as Hermes figure, androgyne or (can he be joking?) ballet dancer, not in the Jesus who spoke up for the common life and the dispossessed.

Yet all of this high-toned, heroic stuff comes down in the end to the most tritely conventional of wisdoms. Here, as in his book *The Critical Path*, Frye informs us that he is all for counterbalancing freedom with order. The mighty march of the human spirit from Adam to Auerbach culminates in such incontrovertible banalities, finding its niche somewhere between left-wing Tories and right-wing Labourites. It also seems to find its natural focus in one Northrop Frye, who receives by far the longest entry in the index, a good few pages longer than the one for Jesus. These two renowned figures are at one point closely paralleled: the difference he feels between his true self and his public image, so Frye tells us, is rather like the difference between the resurrected Jesus and the Jesus of the Gospels.

Not that he is lacking in Christian humility. In a coda to these notebooks, he observes that many scholars and critics have been more intelligent, better trained and more accurate or competent than himself. It is a pity that he then rather tarnishes this winning modesty by adding that he, unlike anyone else in the humanities known to him, had genius. This pronouncement is headed 'Statement for the Day of My Death', and as such seems deliberately intended as his last word. It would have been far preferable for him to have left a note reminding his nearest and dearest to feed the goldfish. It is rather as if Christ had asked for a notice to be pinned to his cross proclaiming: 'I may not be a hotshot scholar but at least I'm the Son of God.' Frye's breathtaking arrogance in the face of death is not an uncommon trait of his unpleasantly vaunting brand of humanism. A man whose last notebooks include a good deal on Adonis but only one passing reference to Auschwitz seems not to have learnt Yeats's lesson that no humanism can be authentic which has not passed through its own negation—that nothing can be whole without being rent. But that would be a question of tragedy; and though Frye can find ample room for such tragedy in his literary typologies, he can find damagingly little space for it in his sense of life—if there is any for him—outside the text.

Isaiah Berlin and Richard Hoggart

The First and the Last brings together Isaiah Berlin's earliest surviving piece of writing, a short story that he penned at the age of twelve entitled 'The Purpose Justifies the Ways', and his last essay, 'My Intellectual Path', a summary of his thought for a Chinese publication. To pad out these two slender projects, a handful of brief memorials of Berlin by various philosophical colleagues are thrown in at the end. Since the childhood story is precocious but scrappy, and the résumé of Berlin's thought lucid but unremarkable, the upshot is a few rather scrawny bits and pieces masquerading as a book. 'My Intellectual Path' is evidently to be published anyway in a forthcoming English translation of the Chinese volume; one of the concluding encomia has already appeared in a journal, and another, by Noel Annan, has a familiar ring to anyone who has read his chapter on Berlin in his recently published work on Oxbridge dons. This is rather a lot of non-exclusive material for 141 pages.

Berlin, Henry Hardy observes in an introduction, had a 'lifelong horror of violence'. This is strange, since the schoolboy short story that follows on the next page is nothing if not bloodthirsty. In revenge for the murder of his patrician father at the hands of the Bolsheviks, young Peter shoots the officer responsible and then exultantly kills himself. It might be more accurate to claim that Berlin had a lifelong horror of totalitarian violence; liberal-capitalist brutality, such as the US war in Vietnam, seems not to have disturbed him quite so deeply. He is not on public record as objecting to the invasion of Guatemala or the bombing

First published as 'All Souls can't speak to all souls' (a review of *The First and the Last* by Isaiah Berlin and *First and Last Things* by Richard Hoggart) in the *Times Higher Education Supplement*, 25 February 2000.

of Iraq. Anyway, it is not as though most individuals have a lifelong relish for violence, and Berlin stands out among this shabby crew as some sort of saint. Most people find violence abhorrent while endorsing its use in extreme circumstances, as Berlin seems to have done himself.

Hardy also notes Berlin's aversion to 'justifying present suffering as a route to some future imaginary state of bliss'. He was indeed an eloquent witness against such tyrannical teleology; but he seemed not to have noticed that the social system he supported goes in for it all the time. Assuring the poor that they are en route to becoming rich, and so should put up with their deprivation for a bit longer, is as familiar (if not as terroristic) a tactic in Westminster and the White House as ever it was in Stalin's Kremlin. Similarly, Berlin quite properly rejects the idea that scientific élites should tell the rest of us how to behave; but he seems to have in mind only party theoreticians rather than capitalist technocrats, an odd exclusion for a liberal.

The first and the last in Berlin are more closely linked than this volume brings out. It was a childhood encounter with Bolshevik violence, registered in his short story, that more or less determined the philosophical career recorded in 'My Intellectual Path'. Berlin's abiding intellectual motifs—monism, freedom, pluralism, determinism and the like—were to some extent pre-set for him by an early political trauma. It is on these 'anti-totalitarian' themes, rather than on, say, justice, compassion or solidarity, that his writing for the most part muses.

Philosophy is no doubt all the better for being driven by passionate personal conviction; but there is also a sense in which Berlin's intensely personal agenda, the unusually direct relation between his opinions and his life history, pulls against the disinterested liberal pluralism that he so tirelessly promotes. If his liberalism has the authority of bitter experience, it is also all too obviously partisan, in a way that liberals are not usually expected to be. He would be more convincing on these matters if he devoted as much time to expounding philosophical topics that could not be suspected of being, among other things, coded bits of anti-communism. And his anti-communism itself would be more persuasive if he seemed less loftily sequestered from the indignities that sometimes inspire ordinary men and women to revolt. Berlin the schoolboy writes that the Russian people 'enjoyed their life thoroughly' until the Bolsheviks came along; and though this is of course a piece of childish naivety, not every twelve-year-old in Russia would have been so naive.

A genuinely open-minded thinker would not write, as Berlin does so carelessly here, of the 'iron laws' of Marxist historical theory, of Marx's championing of the 'Party', or of his single-minded pursuit of 'perfection'. Nor would he so grossly caricature the concept of equality. It may well be the case, as Berlin so persuasively urged, that the pursuit of social perfection is potentially lethal; but it is sheer All Souls ignorance to imagine that Marx himself was in the least enthralled by the notion. On the contrary, he spent his career ferociously satirising all forms of idealism and utopianism. 'Perfection' was an idea that appealed to him about as much as feudalism.

In any case, Berlin writes as the spokesman of a social order that can afford its dystopian scepticism. Utopian ideas belong, by and large, to social classes that are still aspirant; once comfortably ensconced in power, they are more likely to talk about how damnably difficult it is to change things. Such dreams of perfection were the invention not of Marxists, but of an earlier stage of the middle-class civilisation with which the émigré Berlin threw in his lot. Without its early progressivism, that social order might never have won out, and Berlin would thus have had nothing to join. Moreover, if you choose to join a particular club, it is natural to want it to stay pretty much as it is. You do not set about briskly reconstructing the life raft onto which you have just scrambled. In any case, there is no particular reason why a don who enjoyed the company of the rich and powerful should have backed radical change. Unlike his less fortunate fellow citizens, he had little need of it. Seeing such change as idle perfectibilism is thus a convenient enough gambit, even if one also believes it.

'My Intellectual Path' records Berlin's laudable attempt to retrieve the more liberal, universalist aspects of the Enlightenment from its dogmatic objectivism, while rescuing the pluralism of the Romantics from their holism and relativism. He is, however, a mite too anti-pluralist on some counts. He seems to believe, for example, that variety is always a good thing, whereas a true liberal would surely want to be a little less dogmatic on the question. Some forms of variety are commendable, while others—a diversity of fascist parties, for example—are surely not. Similarly, he appears to hold that having many different opinions around the place is always better than having only one, a case that fares rather better with Racine than with racism. The academicist remoteness of such views is very telling. For Berlin, one is either a dreary monist or a reveller in the free play of the mind. This leaves scant room for those who, while rejecting monism, think that there are some issues that it is rather important to get right, and on which some opinions are a great deal more valuable than others. Berlin the fervent Zionist presumably believed this too, whereas Berlin the High Table wit was rather more doubtful.

Berlin's distaste for monism takes the predictable form of an aversion to 'isms'. A list of such 'isms' in this book (socialism, nationalism, fascism and the like) unaccountably omits liberalism. Perhaps 'isms', like halitosis, are what the other fellow has. Marxism or fascism are fully fledged creeds, whereas a Berlin-like belief in private property, market forces, social élitism and the occasional imperialist war is apparently not. The disingenuousness of this omission, for such a slavishly adulated thinker, is remarkable. But then Berlin was on the whole a more intellectually distinguished figure for those who knew him than for those who did not. There is an ontological gulf between those of the coterie who could hear his voice while reading him, and those consigned to the outer darkness who could not. And if you are going to judge him great, then it helps—as it does not so much with, say, Hume or Spinoza—to agree with him.

To turn from Isaiah Berlin's clipped, patrician tones to the unbuttoned colloquialisms of Richard Hoggart is to cross more than a linguistic boundary. Hoggart has nothing like the intellectual acuity of Berlin; but there is a power of ordinariness in his work that Berlin's cult of genius shuts him uncomprehendingly out from. It is hard to imagine the high-toned Sir Isaiah referring to his 'Aunt Lil', or drawing moral conclusions from his trips around a Farnham supermarket. Hoggart's rather rambling reflections on religion, social mores, the English, social class and the like would probably have struck Berlin as intolerably folksy; but Hoggart, though certainly no revolutionary, is alert to how common lives are being blighted and damaged by the social order for which Berlin was so loquacious an apologist. If the trauma at the source of Berlin's intellectual trajectory was Bolshevik terror, the 'first things' for Hoggart are resonant with a less melodramatic sort of violence. His own 'true moment of beginning' was a visit to his mother's pauper's grave in Leeds.

In fact, Berlin and Hoggart have a surprising amount in common. Both are secular, empiricist humanists, resolute anti-metaphysicians who trust to the evidence of their senses, relish the sensuous textures of things, reveal a strong moral sense and admire what they see as the tolerance and decency of their English countryfolk. But their respective Englands are different worlds; and this is not simply a matter of delectable difference but of debilitating inequality. Isaiah Berlin wrote finely against political tyranny; but no such critique will be fully convincing unless it acknowledges the truth that the alternative to social change involves, in one shape or another, a pauper's grave.

Ludwig Wittgenstein

How do you photograph philosophy? What shape and colour are ideas? To make a film about Ludwig Wittgenstein, perhaps the greatest philosopher of the 20th century, is to try to span the abyss between thought and image, what can be said and what can be shown. It was a gap, incidentally, which interested the younger Wittgenstein a good deal. As he argues in his early masterpiece the *Tractatus*, our language can show us what the world is like, but cannot articulate it, and since the *Tractatus* itself tries to do exactly this, the reader must recognise it as nonsense in order to understand it.

Putting Wittgenstein in the movies thus involves Wittgensteinian problems. (He was an avid consumer of bad Westerns himself, partly because he didn't reckon much to reading.) In the end, it is as impossible to film philosophy as it is to write about the smell of garlic, but Wittgenstein lends himself to art more than many. For one thing, unlike most of his fellow philosophers, he led a dramatically enthralling life. Born into one of the wealthiest families in the Austro-Hungarian empire, a schoolmate of Adolf Hitler, he was brought up in the Vienna of Freud and Schoenberg in a home with more grand pianos than they could count. Three of his brothers committed suicide, and Ludwig himself gave away all his money and turned up in Manchester as an aeronautical engineer. He then wandered off to Cambridge to pester Bertrand Russell, and produced the beautiful, unintelligible *Tractatus*, a kind of philosophical equivalent to Schoenberg's music.

First published as 'A suitable case for treatment' in the *Guardian*, 18 March 1993.

Much of this work was written in the trenches of the First World War—a war in which Wittgenstein threw military headquarters into constant confusion by demanding to be transferred to ever more dangerous postings. Death, he thought, might shed some meaning on his useless life, but the Allies didn't oblige, and he passed the rest of his life in a state of chronic spiritual torment. He was austere, imperious, autocratic, an old-world aristocrat who thought philosophy pointless and urged his disciples to give it up. He detested Cambridge, and was continually running off to work as a monastery gardener, live by a Norwegian fjord or in a solitary cottage on the Galway coast. He turned up at one point in Moscow, demanding to train as a humble doctor in Stalinist Russia. He was a cross between monk, mystic and garage mechanic, preferring detective fiction to Aristotle and adept at manual labour, for which he had an almost religious reverence. On the few occasions he was invited out to dinner in Cambridge, he would cart all the dirty dishes upstairs to the bath and swish around with gusto, scrubbing them with all the obsessional attention to detail with which he had designed a starkly unadorned house for his sister in Vienna.

It is not surprising, then, that this profound, self-torturing eccentric has proved so fascinating to artists. Kant is a philosopher's philosopher, and Russell or Sartre every layperson's image of the sage, but Wittgenstein is the philosopher of poets and novelists, playwrights and composers, and the archive of creative works on him continues to accumulate. Bits of the tantalisingly opaque *Tractatus* have even been set to music, its sentences croaked out in a stage-German accent in a hilariously poker-faced spoof.

If Wittgenstein lends himself so well to art, it is ultimately because he was a great artist himself. Philosophy, he considered, could say something—but nothing that was really important. For that you had to go to Tolstoy or Dostoevsky, Mendelssohn or Saint Augustine. Philosophical problems look deep, but they are really just puzzles which arise from mistaking one 'language game' for another, talking in inappropriate ways. The philosopher's job, then, isn't to deliver us the secret of the universe—that is for the poets—but to act as a kind of therapist, disenchanting our minds of the pseudo-problems which beset them, and so packing us off poorer but more honest. It was a style of philosophising which was to fit well the suavely debunking ethos of Oxbridge, but behind it lies a passionate intensity which Oxbridge could only find amusingly foreign. Wittgenstein is one of the last great Judaic moralists, a man who had to fight hard just to keep his spiritual feet, a disinherited son of European humanism adrift in an alien 20th century.

So should a film about him go for the man or the ideas? Both ideally, but this raises a thorny problem, for what is most striking about the mature Wittgenstein is the contrast, rather than continuity, between the life and the thought. The man himself is a suitable case for treatment: rigidly repressed, obsessively perfectionist, demanding more devotion from his friends than the Virgin Mary, and ready to abandon any of them if they stood in the way of his quest for holiness. But the *Philosophical Investigations*, the great work of the later period, is humorous, laid-back, open-ended, much more like a tissue of jokes, images and anecdotes than a piece of high-toned philosophising. You want to grasp the public nature of criteria? Think of a man who says 'But I know how tall I am!' and places his hand on top of his own head. You want to fathom the mysteries of truth and identity? Imagine someone who buys himself a second copy of the morning newspaper to confirm that what the first copy said was true. This is the style of a man affably at home in the world, which is the very last thing that Wittgenstein was.

As the scriptwriter for *Wittgenstein*, I have an interest in ideas but little visual imagination. The director, Derek Jarman, is just the opposite. The two of us together, then, might be thought to add up to a reasonably competent person, and when the film is really buzzing, this is what happens. But because film has to present ideas in terms of characters, there's always the danger of reducing them to it—of catering to the prurient English interest in biography, and so reinforcing a very English anti-intellectualism. Jarman, for all his admirable radicalism, has a very English middle-class sensibility, which is light years removed from the austerity and intellectual passion of his subject. The film, then, is not uniformly brilliant. Hunky young men for whom Spinoza is probably a kind of pasta shamble around ineptly disguised as philosophers. A camp Martian crops up for no particular reason, uttering wads of embarrassing whimsy. (None of this, I swear, was in the original script.) But Karl Johnson, a veritable Ludwig lookalike, is splendidly intense and intelligent, and much of the movie scintillates with Jarman's bizarrely creative imagination. Does it manage to photograph ideas? I doubt it. Nobody will emerge with a grasp of the finer points of the *Tractatus*. If you are filming the story of a philosopher, you need a director with some respect for the mind. But *Wittgenstein* gives you a reasonable general idea of what Ludwig was on about, along with some memorable images of the life.

Norberto Bobbio

The political left has always had trouble with ethics, in theory as well as in practice. The practical problems hardly need recounting. It was one of the great tragedies of the 20th century that socialism proved least possible where it was most necessary. A vision of human emancipation which presupposed for its success all the precious fruits of modernity—material wealth, liberal traditions, a flourishing civic society, an educated populace—became instead the guiding light by which wretchedly impoverished nations bereft of such benefits sought to throw off their chains. Shunned by those well-heeled nations who might have smoothed their path to freedom, they marched their people into modernity at gunpoint, with criminal consequences. One would not describe Fascism as tragic, whatever the tragic destruction to which it gave birth. But Stalinism was tragedy of a classical kind, as the noble intentions of socialism were deflected into their opposites in that fatal inversion which Aristotle calls *peripeteia*.

The theoretical problems were less catastrophic, though just as severe. Marx, for example, could never decide whether ethics was what he was up to in his own work, or a bourgeois mystification implacably opposed to it. If he sometimes appeals to notions of justice, denouncing the wage-relation as 'robbery', he more often dismisses moral ideas as ideological baggage, superstructural fictions by which our rulers aim to sweeten their sovereignty. There would be no need for justice in a Communist society, since the very concept implies a scarcity which would have been surpassed. Morality, rather as for Nietzsche, belongs to

First published as 'For the hell of it' (a review of *In Praise of Meekness: Essays on Ethics and Politics* by Norberto Bobbio) in the *London Review of Books*, 22 February 2001.

pre-history; it is a child of the realm of necessity, and there will be no place for it in the kingdom of freedom.

Marx's contempt for morality is especially ironic, since he himself was a moralist in the most classical sense of the term. As Norman Geras has remarked, Marx believed in moral notions, but he did not know that he did. He did not know it because he wrongly identified morality with bourgeois moralism, which he quite rightly rejected. He was, in short, too respectful of his opponents' formulations, rather as some unwary leftists today disown 'tradition' because they are thinking of the Changing of the Guard rather than the Chartists. Moralism is the belief that there exists a realm of specifically moral questions, but as Aristotle understood, there is no autonomously 'moral' issue which can be abstracted from the complex institutional life of the polis. It is only the modern age which has come up with this alienated view, just as it holds that there is something called the aesthetic which is not only independent of the social, but more or less its antithesis. Aristotle observes at the beginning of his *Ethics* that there is a science which deals with the supreme good, and then tells us—surprisingly, given the title of his book—that its name is politics.

Marx was a closet Aristotelian, and a traditional moralist just because he set questions of justice, equality and the like in their social and historical contexts. If this made it fatally easy for him to relativise them away, it also saved him from the modernist error of those for whom adultery is a moral affair but public ownership a political one, for whom ethics is what you do in bed, and politics or economics what you do when you get out of bed. But Marx is an Aristotelian also because he sees ethics in terms of virtues rather than obligations. Like Aristotle, he recognises that the good life is all about enjoying yourself, that the end of human life is happiness or wellbeing, and that this involves a many-sided flourishing, realising your historically-bred powers and capacities to the full. It is this which class society forestalls, and what it forestalls it with, among other weapons, is morality. Freud would later identify moral ideology, or the super-ego, as a kind of sickness, a frenzied sadistic idealism which drives us to self-destruction in the name of righteousness.

What Marx has done here, without appearing to be aware of it, is to shift the whole question of ethics from the 'superstructure' to the 'base'. It is not, as he seems to think, that he has got rid of ethics, simply relocated them without noticing the fact. For the material 'base' of society includes not just the forces and relations of production, but human productive powers; and the good life for Marx lies in their perpetual self-realising and unfolding. This, for him, would include such activities as tasting a peach or listening to a concerto; his idea of production, far from being too crabbedly economistic, is actually rather too capacious for comfort. The ethical life then consists in allowing these creative powers to break through whatever 'superstructure' is currently suppressing them, which includes moral ideology. In this, too, Marx is at one with his compatriot Friedrich Nietzsche, and indeed with William Blake.

Such an ethics is not, needless to say, without its difficulties. As a curious cross-breed of Aristotle and Romantic humanism, it tends to assume that human powers become morbid only by virtue of being repressed. It is not clear that this is the case with the urge to boil infants alive. If Marx believes with an off-the-wall libertarian like D.H. Lawrence that all our powers should be realised just because they are ours, then he is guilty of a naive naturalism; but if he does not hold such a disreputable view, then he has to name some criteria by which we select suitable candidates for self-realisation from among our various capacities, and this is hard to do once you have thrown out transcendent norms.

In his early *Economic and Philosophical Manuscripts*, he tries to circumvent the so-called naturalistic fallacy with such concepts as 'species being', which hover indeterminately between fact and value. He wants to work his way up from our condition as a material species to questions of quality and value. This, once more, is a thoroughly traditional moral project, which Thomas Aquinas would have had no trouble in recognising. Moralism and idealism must be refuted, and the question of what we ought to do must somehow be anchored in the way it is with us. But the spectre of reductionism is not simple to exorcise, and it is easier to derive moral norms from the facts of human nature if you have already smuggled a few of them into your description of that nature in the first place.

Some later 19th-century Marxism turned from this ambitious moral anthropology, looking instead to Kant for moral guidance. Positivist forms of historical materialism might proclaim that socialism was inevitable, but they could not guarantee that it was desirable. Indeed, the historically inevitable might always turn out to be thoroughly unpleasant. Such Marxism could make no room for questions of value, and so, in the worst of all worlds, tacked an idealist morality onto its mechanical materialism. It was not until the Marxist rediscovery of Hegel, most notably with the writings of Georg Lukács, that this sterile coupling could be set aside. It has cropped up again in our own time in the incongruous Kantian turn of some post-structuralist thought, which is just as incapable as mechanistic Marxism of plucking moral norms from its view of the world. But whereas the problem for mechanistic Marxism was that its view of the world excluded value from the outset, the problem for post-structuralism is that it has no view of the world. For this vein of thought, you cannot get from the way the world is to what we ought to do, since the world is no particular way at all. For the pragmatist, determining the world as being a certain way is the result of what you want or ought to do, not the reason for it.

Kantian morality, with its universal obligations and imperatives, might seem quite incompatible with the 'virtue' morality of an Aristotle or Marx. Alasdair MacIntyre and Bernard Williams have both famously contrasted the two lineages, and for rather different reasons shown Kantian morality the door. The Italian political philosopher Norberto Bobbio is somewhat more prudent. In these essays on ethics and politics, he regards the two doctrines as different rather than opposed. This is the case with Marx, though Bobbio does not go on to spell out how. Marx is right to hold, *pace* the Kantians, that morality is about happiness, not primarily about duty or prescription; but he is also right *contra* the virtue moralists and Romantic humanists to insist that the creation of the good life for all is bound to involve such otherwise unpalatable phenomena. You cannot build socialism without them, just as you cannot build it without self-sacrifice.

MacIntyre has bluntly dismissed such self-sacrifice as a 'vice', and in one sense it is; it is certainly not an exemplary way to live, as feminists do not need to be reminded. For Marx, however, this 'vice' is tragically necessary if the good life is to be secured all round. This would not be the case were history not as direly oppressive as it is. Unhappy the land in need of martyrs, or indeed in need of radicals. Given that history has been so atrocious, however, its transforming will inevitably mean some people having to abnegate at least part of their own fulfilment for the sake of others. Marx himself was one such example; and this is why he has his Kantian as well as his Aristotelian side.

The self-disciplined, self-sacrificial revolutionary is thus the last person to furnish us with an image of an emancipated future. He or she is not a sign of that future, but of how much it takes to achieve it. As a poem by Bertolt Brecht comments: 'Oh we who tried to lay the ground for friendship, / Could not ourselves be friendly.' Similarly, the monk or religious celibate is no image of heaven, just a dramatic signifier of how much, in an unjust world, will have to be jettisoned to achieve it. All such renunciation is a kind of negative utopia. Bobbio, who comes from the land of Machiavelli, has much of interest to say in this slim volume of the doctrine that the end justifies the means; but the creative disjunction between them in Bobbio's account is rather different from how it is set out in *The Prince*. Ascesis, prohibition, prescription, self-repression can be 'bad' means to a good end—'bad' in the sense that unless they contribute to that end, they cannot be commended as ways of life in themselves. But history, alas, has seen to it that they are in fact essential to that goal, and it is this that the laid-back pragmatists and postmodernists fail to see. For the less sophisticated among them, all prohibitions are instances of a malevolent Law, as though being forbidden to set fire to a cat was a wanton restriction of one's self-fulfilment.

Bobbio, whom Perry Anderson has called 'the moral conscience of the Italian political order', has been a remarkably influential figure in practical politics. A leading luminary of the political wing of the Italian Resistance, twice imprisoned by Mussolini, he became after the war a sympathetic yet stringent critic of the Italian Communist Party. His critique of the Party laid the ground for the Eurocommunism to which it was to turn in the early 1970s, while a few years later he collaborated in drafting the constitution of the Italian Socialist Party. Today, still active at the age of 91, he is an Italian life senator, an emeritus professor, and a figure of sage-like, oracular status.

The Resistance had impelled Bobbio from liberalism to socialism, twinned forces in the struggle against Fascism, and the relation between the two creeds was to form a major theme of his philosophy. Convinced that socialism is liberalism's natural completion, he has nevertheless spoken up for what he calls 'the value of enquiry, the ferment of doubt, a willingness to dialogue, a spirit of criticism, moderation of judgment, philological scruple, a sense of the complexity of things'. To adapt the slogan of his most celebrated Marxist compatriot, it is a case of socialism of the intellect, liberalism of the heart. These sometimes rather slight pieces on democracy, prejudice, racism, truth, tolerance and allied topics betray the marks of old age, despite their absurdly inflated hardback price. But they also have some sharp insights to offer into the distinction between tolerance and scepticism, the sources of human prejudice and the relations between ethics and politics. Since they also sing the praises of meekness as a political virtue, they are unlikely to prove Peter Mandelson's favourite reading.

Bobbio distinguishes four kinds of relation between ethics and politics. There are two brands of monism which respectively reduce ethics to politics (Hobbes) and politics to ethics (Erasmus, Kant); a more flexible form of monism which holds that politics should be ethical but with certain exemptions; and a full-blooded dualism for which the political constitutes its own autonomous domain distinct from the ethical (Machiavelli). For the latter current of thought, ethical actions have an intrinsic value, whereas political actions have an instrumental one. What dismantles this opposition, though Bobbio does not argue the case here, is the very phenomenon which has absorbed his attention over a lifetime: democracy. What divides Left and Right on this score is the question of whether democracy has an intrinsic or a purely instrumental value. For much conservative thought, democracy may have its uses, but it is hardly a good in itself. Better for a single sovereign to reach the right decision than for a sovereign people to botch the business. And though democracy may thrive in English soil, it may well not suit the Portuguese. For the Left, democracy has both intrinsic and instrumental merit: it is a way of arriving at sound judgments by involving as many arbiters as possible, but the self-determination it involves is also a moral good. Indeed, it remains so even when the decisions in question are disastrous. For the Left, human beings may abuse their freedom, but they are not wholly human without it; for the Right, what matters by and large is not that we decide but what we decide.

One essay in this volume, 'The Gods that Failed', is devoted to the problem of evil. Unlike some rather more coy radicals, Bobbio is properly unafraid to pronounce the word, demanded as it is by the monstrosities of the century through which he lived almost from one end to the other. One needs some such language to distinguish the Final Solution from the Great Train Robbery, and it need carry no metaphysical implications. But Bobbio misses an opportunity here to relate the question of evil to his opposition between the intrinsic and the instrumental. The purges of Stalin and Mao, however monstrous, were done with a purpose; the Holocaust, by contrast, represents that more puzzling, elusive form of evil which seems fundamentally without motive. It had, to be sure, pragmatic aspects; but it is hard not to agree with Geoffrey Wheatcroft's claim that the most difficult truth of all about it is its meaninglessness. Primo Levi points out that there was simply no point in subjecting one's victims to cruelty and humiliation, dragging them on a senseless journey across Europe, when you were going to exterminate them anyway. Why not just kill them in their beds? If you say that the reason for the slaughter was the Nazi desire for racial purity, this simply pushes the question back a stage: why did they desire that? There is no rational motive for such a wish, as there may be for desiring political freedom or a more buoyant economy.

In traditional mythology, the devil is portrayed as delighting in destruction for its own sake. Indeed, it is the only way that he can ease his intolerable pain. The damned are in torment, yet exult in their wickedness. This kind of motiveless, Iago-like malignancy seems to be an end in itself, and so joins a rather select class of objects which includes God and art. It has the baffling quality of things which are brutely themselves. It comes as no surprise that the devil was once an angel, since goodness is similarly non-functional. In a world as shabby as this, goodness doesn't get you anywhere, which is why, as Henry James knew, it is as gloriously pointless as the aesthetic. In the end, one has to be virtuous just for the hell of it. The demonic are those who sense some frightful non-being at the root of their identity, and who find this sublime chaos embodied in a particular figure, whether Jew, woman, homosexual or foreigner. Exterminating this otherness then becomes the only way of convincing yourself that you exist. Only in the obscene enjoyment of dismembering others can you plug the gap in your own being, warding off the threat of non-being by creating even more of the stuff around you.

So the destruction does, after all, have a purpose: it is done to lend you an identity. But since there is no particular reason for wanting that, and since the pleasure one reaps from annihilating others is an end in itself, it can also be seen as purely self-sustaining. The damned cannot relinquish their torment because it is bound up with their *jouissance*, cannot escape the brutal sadism of the Law because this is just what they desire. And this is why they are in despair. But since we all desire the cruelty of the Law, at least if Freud is to be credited, evil of this kind is at once gratifyingly rare and exceedingly commonplace. It has, however, some formidable opponents, and they are listed in Bobbio's title essay as humility, modesty, meekness and other such virtues—the alternative ethics, so he argues, of those 'who die without leaving any other trace of their presence on this earth than a cross in a cemetery bearing their name and a date'.

Jonathan Dollimore

Literary theory is in love with failure. It looks with distaste on whatever is integral, self-identical, smugly replete, and is fascinated by lack, belatedness, deadlock, self-undoing. Works of literature catch its attention once they begin to come unstuck or contradict themselves, when they unravel at the edges or betray an eloquent silence at their heart. Like some remorseless therapist, the theorist is bent on exposing just how spiritually dishevelled such texts really are, despite their pathetic attempts to appear plausible and coherent. Literary theory is an aesthetics of the underdog, championing the humble particular which plays havoc with the structure of an epic or the intentions of a novelist.

This labour of the negative, as Hegel called it, seems appropriate to a politically sceptical age, in which no one is much impressed any more by robust vitality or unqualified commitment, and when irony or ambiguity seem the closest we can come to what a more confident past knew as the truth. In all of this, the concept of desire has a key role to play. Since, according to psychoanalysis, desire is a nameless hankering, unfulfilable by any of its particular objects, it fits supremely well with this negative standpoint. It is less a craving for literary stardom or a square meal than an empty, intransitive yearning whose various targets all turn out to be arbitrary substitutes for one another. Like a turbulent child, desire shatters whatever is hastily produced to keep it quiet and moves restlessly on to the next breakable bauble. It has its source in lack, and is intent simply on keeping itself in business, hijacking bits of

First published as 'Good dinners pass away, so do tyrants and toothache' (a review of *Death, Desire and Loss in Western Culture* by Jonathan Dollimore) in the *London Review of Books*, 16 April 1998.

rubber, dreams of omnipotence or the desires of others for this obtusely obsessive end. But because none of its objects can really satisfy it, desire figures also as a furious excess, a perpetual refusal with something of the uncompromising drive of revolutionary politics.

Politically speaking, then, this latest metaphysical hero of cultural theory is able to have it both ways. If it is a pure negation which can't be pinned down, it also has all the positive force of an insurrection. In this it resembles death, which is also beyond representation—death is the last thing we experience, in more senses than one—while being at the same time brute reality. It is no wonder, then, that 'desire' crops up so often in the titles of books by disillusioned radicals whose zeal for overthrowing everything in particular is matched only by their doubt that this could ever come about. A rather less high-minded motive for such book titles is that they promise to win you a double readership, hovering as they do between scholarship and sensationalism, cultural studies and bodice-poppers. The authors of these books usually insist on the need to historicise, but rarely glance sideways at the historical context of their own attraction to desire.

Jonathan Dollimore's *Death, Desire and Loss in Western Culture* manages to pack no less than three resonant negations into its title, an emphasis on depletion at odds with the ambitiousness of his project. In remarkably wide-ranging survey from Anaximander to Aids, Dollimore presses his case that the drive to relinquish the self has always lurked within Western notions of identity and can be found above all, 'perversely, lethally, ecstatically' in sexuality. This, among other things, is a coded rebuke to those postmodern theorists for whom the affirmative 'humanist' subject has now given way to the 'decentred' one. (Such theorists, oddly, also regard thinking in terms of historical stages as part of an oppressive rationality.) On the contrary, as Dollimore shrewdly shows, the Western subject was never more affirmative than when it was falling apart.

The book centres, as all current theoretical studies should, on an unthinkable deadlock. Mutability is at once the enemy of desire and its very medium, so that 'the very nature of desire is what prevents its fulfilment, what makes it "impossible".' From the ancient Greeks to the author of Ecclesiastes, from Buddha and St Augustine to the Renaissance poets, death is not simply an ending but an internal undoing which, like the subversive motions of desire, undermines us from within. If mortality, like prohibition, is what makes our pleasures sweeter, it is also what punctures them; if desire deliriously unbinds the unity of the self, it does so only to prefigure a more absolute dissolution. For the Romantic libertarians, desire is baulked by forces external to it, which in theory it can always resist; the rather less sanguine truth is that desire digs its own grave, defaces whatever it embraces.

The book skilfully traces these motifs through Shakespeare, Montaigne, Raleigh, Donne and an array of Early Modern others, before turning to consider the denial of death implicit in Enlightenment thought. As Jean Baudrillard remarks, there is a sense that for modernity 'it is not normal to be dead'—that the dead are committing some kind of unspeakable solecism simply by no longer being around. Not to exist at all is a disturbing form of extremism. Dollimore himself doubts this thesis, as Michel Foucault doubts that the Victorians were coy about sexuality. In Dollimore's view, death has been not so much repressed by modernity as resignified, in ways which permit a never-ending analysis of it. His own book is presumably an example. But this passes too lightly over the fact that death is bound to appear scandalous to a hubristic culture which believes that nothing can escape its mastery. The true Platonism of our time, the idealist fantasy which seeks to disown material limits altogether, is surely to be found in the postmodern body, that infinitely pliable non-entity which can be pierced, plumped up, scooped out, remoulded, regendered, but cannot finally be prevented from turning into garbage. The sacred rituals which used to promise eternal life—burning incense, drinking the blood of the god, slaying a fatted calf—have now become the liturgy of burning off fat, drinking fruit juice and not eating calves at all.

Dollimore pursues his theme through modern philosophy. Hegel's dialectic seeks to incorporate death into life, and his Spirit finds its truth only in the process of dismemberment. For Heidegger, the only authentic life is one which embraces death as an inner structure of *Dasein* or human existence, while for Sartre humanity is simply the 'desire to be', a tragically unfinishable project driven on by its own lack or *néant*. In Schopenhauer's gloomy writings, desire, now retitled Will, is a striving bound to thwart itself, one which can be assuaged only in death or in the disinterested contemplativeness of the aesthetic. Freud, for whom life is just an elaborate detour en route to death, is forced to conclude that 'something in the nature of the sexual instinct itself is unfavourable to the realisation of complete satisfaction'. Rather than lose itself in fulfilment, desire prefers to be crushed out of existence altogether by the death drive.

There is a distinctly potted feel to this whirlwind trip around European thought, with seven and a half pages on Hegel, one and a bit on David Hume and so on. The *Monty Python* 'Summarise Proust' contest, in which competitors had thirty seconds to deliver a précis, springs irresistibly to mind. Like the motion of desire itself, the book drives remorselessly from one author to another, raiding them for what it needs but careless of their specific textures. Literary works are plundered for their abstractable content, with scant sensitivity to questions of artistic form. The structure of the book parodies its own thesis: the subject of desire is what keeps this narrative in motion, but also what forms a kind of internal blockage to its full realisation. As with desire, too, the various objects examined, from Parmenides to Cavafy, turn out to look oddly alike.

Even so, this is an impressively versatile survey, although it passes over an important moral dimension of its subject, unsurprisingly in an age when the erotic is more in vogue than the ethical. In a few comments on Christianity, Dollimore rightly resists the usual left-humanist caricature of the creed as morbidly life-denying. He sees that asceticism has an emancipatory aspect to it, concerned with future transformation rather than present self-loathing. He might have added that for the supposedly anti-fleshly St Paul, it is the sexual coupling of bodies which symbolises the relationship between Christ and his people, and that in Christian tradition celibacy is meant to be a sacrifice. Since it is no sacrifice to surrender what you regard as worthless, Christian asceticism is a rather more complex affair than the scoffings of a Nietzsche might suggest. But for Christian theology the supreme model of such sacrifice is not celibacy but martyrdom. In a discussion of Marx and Feuerbach, Dollimore speaks of Marxism as 'socialising' death, shifting attention from the perishable individual to the rather more durable species. But martyrdom is a socialising of one's own death, too, converting it into a means of life for others. Since the martyr willingly abandons his life, he looks at first sight much like the suicide. The difference is that the suicide relinquishes what has become unbearable to him, whereas the martyr gives up his most precious possession in the hope that good may flow from it.

In Christian theology, what determines whether or not you can embrace death in this way is how you have lived. If you have failed in life to divest yourself for the sake of others, you will be trapped like William Golding's Pincher Martin in a hell which is the inability to die. By the end of Golding's novel, Martin has dwindled to a pair of huge, lobster-like claws tenaciously protecting his dark centre of selfhood from the 'black lightning' of God's ruthless mercy. Martin refuses to be picked apart: he is one of the damned who regard themselves as too important to undergo anything as squalid as personal extinction. W.B. Yeats may not have landed among that select company, but the hair-raisingly blasphemous epitaph he wrote for himself—

> Cast a cold eye
> On life, on death.
> Horseman, pass by!

—disdains death as a vulgarity fit only for clerks and shopkeepers.

It is the martyr's meaning of death-in-life which St Paul has in mind when he comments that we die every moment. To live selflessly is not to exist in a state of self-dissolution but to behave in a certain style, one which requires keeping your wits about you and having a reasonably resilient ego. True self-abnegation is not a matter of political submissiveness or the heady *jouissance* of sexual pleasure, but of anticipating one's death by living in the service of others. It is this which Heidegger lamentably misses, in his failure to link what he calls *Mitsein*—living with others—with the authenticity of being resolute for death. The latter is then debased to a kind of solitary heroism, with unsavoury fascistic overtones. If death is what gives shape to life, it is because it signifies a self-abandonment which is the pattern of the good life. It is not just because the worm lurks in the bud, or because our achievements turn to ashes in our mouths, or an awareness of our finitude restrains us from hubris, or the brevity of life renders our sensations more intense.

'To know how to live,' Dollimore wisely comments, 'one must first know how to die.' As the most dramatic event ever to befall most of us, death is to be performed rather than endured, something we have to get good at, like playing the trombone or tolerating bores. Whether we can pull it off with any degree of élan depends, like any dramatic performance, on practice. For a venerable moral tradition, the name of that ceaseless rehearsal is living. But this is not to see life as a mere antechamber to death, since to know how to live in the knowledge of death is to know how to flourish.

Dollimore's study is as much about mutability as it is about death or desire, a theme which is at once profound and banal. (Something similar could be said of the author's literary style, which deals with momentous issues in a depthless, drably functional prose.) Few things are more mind-shaking than the truth that everything perishes, and few more corny either. Rather late in the book, Dollimore seems to recall that mutability isn't always such a bad thing after all. If good dinners pass away, so do tyrants and toothache. Samuel Johnson regarded all change as a great evil, whereas Brecht seemed to see the sheer fact of change, as opposed to particular unpleasant instances of it, as inherently comic. In one of his fables, Herr Keuner returns to his native village after a lengthy absence to be cheerily told that he hasn't changed a bit. 'Herr Keuner,' Brecht writes, 'turned pale.'

If Dollimore leans rather too heavily on the miseries of transience, he also exaggerates its centrality. Much that is oppressive in human existence springs from inertia and recalcitrance, not from the fall of the leaf. Postmodern and historicist thought, as Francis Mulhern has pointed out, tends to reduce history to change; but 'history is also— decisively, for its greater part—*continuity*.' Nothing is more persistent than the idea of ephemerality, as this book demonstrates without being quite aware of the irony. In Dollimore's speculative striding from the ancient *polis* to the gay bar, the history of ideas would indeed seem at times no more than a footnote to Plato. Mutability may provide the book's subject-matter, but it is treated in a remarkably invariant way. For political radicals, it is precisely the fact that things don't change all that much—Marx's paralytic 'nightmare of history', to snap out of which demands such a struggle—that is the problem.

Death, Desire and Loss in Western Culture is a boldly transhistorical book from one who would lay claim to the title of cultural materialist. Once or twice, it pauses to historicise its otherwise rather repetitive storyline. From Heraclitus to Schopenhauer, Dollimore observes, meditations on death tend to crop up in conditions of historical crisis, when failures of political praxis lead to high-minded renunciations of human society. Freud's great work on the death drive, after all, has its root in the First World War. The Schopenhauer who held that we would all have been far better off not existing at all was also the man who reputedly helped out a soldier taking aim at a revolutionary mob by handing him his opera glasses. It is an instructive allegory of the relations between culture and politics.

In *Modern Tragedy*, Raymond Williams deals with what one might call the politics of death, insisting on how culturally variable it can be so as to counter what he sees as a reactionary metaphysics: 'To say that man dies alone is not to state a fact but to offer an interpretation. For indeed men die in so many ways: in the arms and presence of family and neighbours; in the blindness of pain, or the blankness of sedation; in the violent disintegration of machines and in the calm of sleep.' For a humanist like Williams, the statement 'we all die alone' is no more informative than the claim that we all eat or sleep alone. It is just a way of saying that it is I who am doing this particular piece of dying, even if you are pegging out alongside me. But there are two opposed ways of refusing the view that death is inherently tragic, an intolerable self-estrangement which strikes meaning from human life and so plays into the hands of conservative absurdists. There is Williams's way, which is to argue that the idea of death is simply an abstraction from culturally different ways of expiring, just as you might claim that the imposingly singular 'desire' of psychoanalysis is an abstraction from diverse sorts of want. Or you can take the opposite path and view death as a value-free biological fact, as intrinsically indifferent to significance as a rumble in the gut. From this viewpoint, death is no more tragic or affirmative, absurd or emancipatory, than the cawing of a rook.

Dollimore's study refuses both of these strategies. It insists, rightly in my view, that there is indeed a transhistorical fact to be examined here, which no historicism can dissolve conveniently away. In this sense, the repetitiveness of the book's narrative is part of the point. But it is also wary of the naturalistic alternative to the culturalist account, finding in death, like Hamlet *contra* Claudius, something scandalously in excess of all natural occurrence. The book has its emotional source in a profound sense of sorrow—that of a gay intellectual for whom the latest tragic conspiracy of death and desire lies in the catastrophe of Aids. The final section of the study, which turns directly to this topic, contains its most moving, intricate explorations. Yet the naturalistic and culturalist viewpoints need not be at odds. Death is indeed natural; but it belongs to our nature to be able to make something of the biologically given, just as it belongs to desire to be in excess of biological need. To perform one's death is to convert fact into value, conjuring something out of nothing; and whether we can do this depends not just on the conditions in which we die, but on how we have lived. Robert Maxwell probably departed this world in circumstances which, in any literal sense, made the whole notion of such performance quite irrelevant. But even if he had passed away in bed with all his faculties intact, it is doubtful that he would have been able to do much more than die in something like the way that he digested or perspired.

Peter Brooks on Bodies

There will soon be more bodies in contemporary criticism than on the fields of Waterloo. Mangled members, tormented torsos, bodies emblazoned or incarcerated, disciplined or desirous: it is becoming harder, given this fashionable turn to the somatic, to distinguish the literary theory section of the local bookshop from the soft porn shelves, sort out the latest Jackie Collins from the later Roland Barthes. Many an eager masturbator must have borne away some sexy-looking tome only to find himself reading up on the floating signifier.

Sexuality began in the late Sixties, as an extension of radical politics into regions it had lamentably neglected. But as revolutionary energies were gradually rolled back, an increased concern with the body came to take their place. In the Seventies we had class struggle and sexuality; in the Eighties we had sexuality. Erstwhile Leninists were now card-carrying Lacanians, and everyone shifted over from production to perversion. The socialism of Guevara gave way to the somatics of Foucault and Fonda. As usual, this happened on the most spectacular scale in the United States, which had never had much grasp of socialism to begin with, and where the Left could find in the high Gallic pessimism of Foucault a sophisticated rationale for their own political paralysis. The fetish, for Freud, is that which plugs an intolerable gap; and sexuality itself has now become the greatest fetish of all. In classrooms from Berkeley to the Bronx, there's nothing more sexy than sex; and a concern with physical health has now escalated into an American national sickness.

First published as 'It is not quite true that I have a body, and not quite true that I am one either' (a review of *Body Work* by Peter Brooks) in the *London Review of Books*, 27 May 1993.

The body, then, has been at once the focus for a vital deepening of radical politics, and a desperate displacement of them. There is a glamorous kind of materialism about body talk, which compensates for certain more classical strains of materialism now in dire trouble. As a stubbornly local phenomenon, the body fits well enough with the postmodernist nervousness of grand narratives, as well as with American pragmatism's love-affair with the concrete. Since I know where my left foot is at any particular moment without needing to use a compass, the body offers a mode of cognition more intimate and internal than a now much scorned Enlightenment rationality. In this sense, a theory of the body runs the risk of self-contradiction, recovering for the mind just what was meant to deflate it; but if the body provides us with a little sensuous certitude in a progressively abstract world, it is also an elaborately coded affair, and so caters to the intellectual's passion for complexity. It is the hinge between Nature and Culture, offering surety and subtlety in equal measure. Indeed what else is psychoanalysis but the thinking person's horror fiction, a discourse which wonderfully combines the cerebral and the sensational?

For the philosophers and psychologists, 'mind' is still a sexy notion; but literary critics have always been wary of the unhoused intellect, preferring their concepts to come fleshed and incarnate. To this extent, the new somatics is simply the return in a more sophisticated register of the old organicism. Instead of poems as plump as an apple, we have texts as material as an armpit. The turn to the body sprang first from a structuralist hostility to consciousness, and represents the final expulsion of the ghost from the machine. Bodies are ways of talking about human subjects without going all sloppily humanist, avoiding that messy interiority which drove Michel Foucault up the wall. For all its carnivalesque cavortings, body talk is thus our latest brand of repression; and the postmodern cult of pleasure, not least in its Parisian variants, is a very solemn, high-toned affair. Either, like Peter Brooks in *Body Work*, you write about this bizarre stuff in an impeccably academic idiom, thus risking an incongruous clash of form and content; or, like some of his American colleagues, you let the body take over your script and risk disappearing up your own pretentious wordplay and idle anecdotalism.

For the new somatics, not any old body will do. If the libidinal body is in, the labouring body is out. There are mutilated bodies galore, but few malnourished ones, belonging as they do to bits of the globe beyond the purview of Yale. The finest body book of our era is Maurice Merleau-Ponty's *Phenomenology of Perception*; but this, with its humanist sense of the body as practice and project, is now distinctly *passé*. The shift from Merleau-Ponty to Foucault is one from the body as relation to the body as object. For Merleau-Ponty, the body is 'where there is something to be done'; for the new somatics, the body is where something—gazing, imprinting, regimenting—is being done to you. It used to be called alienation, but that implies the existence of an interiority to be alienated—a proposition of which somatic criticism is deeply sceptical.

It is part of the damage done by a Cartesian tradition that one of the first images the word 'body' brings to mind is that of a corpse. To announce the presence of a body in the library is by no means to allude to an industrious reader. Thomas Aquinas thought that there was no such thing as a dead body, only the remains of a living one. Christianity pins its faith to the resurrection of the body, not to the immortality of the soul; and this is just a way of saying that if the afterlife doesn't somehow involve my body, it doesn't involve me. The Christian faith has, of course, much to say of the soul too; but for Aquinas the soul is the 'form' of the body, as wedded to it as a meaning to a word. It was a point taken up by the later Wittgenstein, who once remarked that the body was the best image we had of the human soul. Soul talk was necessary for those confronted with a mechanical materialism which saw no real distinction between the human body and a banana. Both, after all, were material objects. In this context, you needed a language which sought to capture what differentiates the human body from the things around it. Soul talk at its best was a way of doing this. It easily backfired, though, since it is well-nigh impossible not to picture the soul as a ghostly sort of body, and so find yourself simply slipping a fuzzy object inside a grosser one as a way of accounting for the latter's uniqueness. But the human body does not differ from jam jars and elastic bands because it secretes a spectral entity they lack; it differs from them because it is a point from which they can be organised into significant projects. Unlike them, it is creative; and if we had had a language which adequately captured the human body's creativity we would perhaps never have needed soul talk in the first place.

What is special about the human body, then, is just its capacity to transform itself in the process of transforming the material bodies which surround it. It is in this sense that it is anterior to those bodies, a kind of 'surplus' over and above them, rather than an object to be reckoned up alongside them. But if the body is a self-transformative practice, then it is not identical with itself in the manner of corpses and dustbins; and this is a claim that soul language is also trying to make. It is just that it locates that non-self-identity in the body's having some invisible extra which is really me, rather than seeing the real me as a creative interaction with my world—a creative interaction made possible and necessary by the peculiar sort of body I have. Badgers and squirrels can't be said to have souls, however winsome they may be, because their bodies are not the kind that can work on the world and so necessarily enter into linguistic communion with those of their kind. Soulless bodies are those which do not speak. The human body is that which is able to make something of what makes it; and in this sense its paradigm is language, a given which continually generates the unpredictable.

One can see the point, then, of dropping talk of having a body and substituting talk of being one. If my body is something I use or possess, then it might be thought that I would need another body inside this one to do the possessing, and so on *ad infinitum*. But this resolute anti-dualism, though salutary enough in its way, is untrue to a lot of our intuitions about the lump of flesh we lug around. It makes perfect sense to speak of using my body, as when I suspend it courageously across a crevice so that my companions can scramble to safety across my spine. Nothing is more fashionable in modern cultural theory than talk of objectifying the body, feeling somehow that it is not my own; but though plenty of objectionable objectification goes on, not least in sexual conduct, the fact remains that the human body is indeed a material object, and that this is an essential component of anything more creative we get up to. Unless you can objectify me, there can be no question of relationship between us. The body which lays me open to exploitation is also the ground of all possible communication. It was Marx who ticked off Hegel for equating objectification with alienation, and the rampant culturalism which marks today's avant-garde theory needs to learn the lesson anew.

Merleau-Ponty recalls us to the fleshly self, to the situated, somatic, incarnate nature of being. His colleague Sartre has a somewhat less upbeat narrative to tell of the body as that 'outside' of ourselves we can never quite get a fix on, that otherness which threatens to deliver us to the petrifying gaze of the observer. Sartre is anti-Cartesian enough in his notion of consciousness as mere hankering vacancy, but sufficiently Cartesian in his sense of the nameless gap which separates mind from members. The truth does not, as the liberals say, lie somewhere in between, but in the impossible tension between these two versions of bodiliness, both of which are phenomenologically just. It is not quite true that I have a body, and not quite true that I am one either. This deadlock runs all the way through psychoanalysis, which recognises that the body is constructed in language, and knows too that it will never entirely be at home there. For Jacques Lacan, the body articulates itself in signs only to find itself betrayed by them. The transcendental sig-nifier which would say it all, wrap up my demand and deliver it whole and entire to you, is that imposture known as the phallus; and since the phallus does not exist, my bodily desire is condemned to grope its laborious way from partial sign to partial sign, diffusing and frag-menting as it goes. It is no doubt for this reason that Romanticism has dreamt of the word of words, of a discourse as firm as flesh, or of a body which has all the universal availability of a language while sacrificing none of its sensuous substance. And there is a sense in which con-temporary literary theory, with its excited talk of the materiality of the text, its constant interchanges of the somatic and semiotic, is the latest version of this dream, in suitably sceptical postmodernist style. 'Mate-rial' is one of the great buzz-words of such thinking, a sound at which all progressive heads reverently bow; but it has been stretched beyond all feasible sense. For if even meaning is material, then there is probably nothing which is not, and the term simply cancels all the way through. The new somatics restores us to the creaturely in an abstract world; but in banishing the ghost from the machine, it risks dispelling subjectivity itself as no more than a humanist myth.

Body Work is one of the more distinguished products of a rather suspect genre. Peter Brooks ranges with admirable acuity from Sophocles to scopophilia, the novel to the visual arts. The book is lav-ishly furnished with plates of the naked female form, so that male readers can gaze upon the way they gaze upon them. Brooks is one of our best Freudian critics, and here brings a wealth of psychoanalytic insight to bear on the body in Balzac and Rousseau, James and Zola,

Gauguin and Mary Shelley. If there is a unifying theme in this impressively diverse exploration, it is the way the body must be somehow marked or signed in order to enter narrative, pass from brute fact to active meaning. 'Signing the body', Brooks writes, 'indicates its recovery for the realm of the semiotic'; and from Oedipus to Hans Castrop he maps this recurrent conversion of flesh into text.

This is a fertile notion; but it has to be said that it is one of the few genuinely original bits of conceptualisation in an oddly predictable book. There is the sense of a rather conventional mind at work on unconventional materials; and few of its manoeuvres are as arresting as Brooks's earlier reflections on the unconscious dynamics of narrative in *Reading for the Plot*. The orthodox heterodoxy of the new somatics remains firmly in place, determining each critical move; and though this results in some brilliant local readings, the book never offers to press beyond a now familiar set of motifs. Thus, Brooks has some excellent comments on the relations between privacy, the novel and an increasing attention to the body. The rise of the novel, he points out, is closely tied to the emergence of a private sphere of domestic relations, and the theme of the private body rudely invaded is central to writers like Richardson and Madame de Lafayette. It is also a vital concern in Rousseau, with his tiresome compulsion to bare his behind, and Brooks has a good deal to say of the *Confessions* and *La Nouvelle Héloïse*. But what he has to tell us, in effect, is that the body in Rousseau is a place 'where scenarios of desire, fulfilment, censorship, and repression are played out'; and this is hardly world-shaking news.

There are some genuinely original insights about the staging of the body in the French Revolution, which Brooks, who in a previous work pulled off the improbable trick of making the topic of melodrama theoretically exciting, sees as a melodramatising of it. But he then turns to Balzac and spends a good deal of time meticulously hunting down semiotic markings of the body in his work. This is a fresh way of reading the texts, but it does little to elaborate the 'marking' theory itself, beyond offering yet more exotic instances of it. There is an equally scrupulous account of the fetishisation of Emma Bovary's body, which, so Brooks deftly demonstrates, is always perceived in bits and pieces; but while this illuminates Flaubert interestingly enough, it fails to push forward a reach-me-down psychoanalytic discourse of metonymies and objectifying gazes, desiring subjects and recalcitrant objects, exhibitionism and epistemophilia. Zola's *Nana* is seen as engaged in a fruitless pursuit of the truly naked body, the real material thing, as it strips its heroine bare; but we are still caught here within a constricted language of concealing and revealing, nudity as culture and nakedness as nature. A chapter on Gauguin deals with the primitivist, exoticised body—a way of seeing which Brooks considers is not just stereotypically objectionable but actually turned by the artist to some productive uses. This is an unpredictable move to make; but it is made within a still rather predictable set of critical strategies.

It has been apparent for some time that literary theory is in something of a cul-de-sac. Derrida has written little of substance for years; de Man produced his most stunning effects by dying and leaving an unsavoury past to be unearthed; Marxism is licking its wounds after the collapse of the post-capitalist bureaucracies. The pathbreaking epoch of Greimas and the early Kristeva, the Althusserians and avant-garde film theorists, radical Barthes and reader-response theory, now lies a couple of decades behind us. Few truly innovative theoretical moves have been made since; the new historicism, for all its occasional brilliance, is theoretically speaking a set of footnotes to Foucault. It is as though the theory is all in place, and all that remains to be done is run yet more texts through it. This, in effect, is what *Body Work* does; but Peter Brooks has proved himself capable in the past of generating genuinely new ideas, and it is an ominous sign of the critical times that this latest book never offers to transfigure the concepts on which it relies. Caught in its modish conceptual universe, *Body Work* is quite incapable of rounding upon itself to inquire into its own historical conditions of existence. Why produce three hundred pages on the body in the first place? Well, it's all the rage at the Modern Language Association. But to produce a less banal response to that question would require a rather grander narrative than American criticism, for entirely understandable reasons, is at present prepared to deliver.

Peter Brooks on Confession

In the wake of the Second Vatican Council, some progressively minded Catholics began to reintroduce into the Mass the ancient practice of public confession. Individuals would rise from their pews and accuse themselves in comfortably imprecise terms of various moral lapses, begging forgiveness of their brethren. At one such Mass, a young woman rose and proclaimed to the piously suppressed excitement of the congregation that she had committed adultery. 'With that man over there,' she added, pointing a finger at a young man with a baby on his lap who was turning a slow crimson. Then she added, 'In thought,' and sat down again.

'In thought' is a nice Papistical touch. It betrays the Cartesian bias of much modern Catholicism, the belief that what matters is what goes on in your head. It is all right to possess nuclear weapons as long as you don't intend to use them. The practice of confession raises all sorts of slippery issues about truth, self-deception, intentionality and the like, most of them subtly dissected in Peter Brooks's rich, stodgily written new study. The fact that Brooks is an American is not accidental in this respect, since after Stalinist Russia the United States is surely the most neurotically confessional culture in modern history. When Brooks speaks of the modern demand for a 'generalised transparency', he has a point; but he is also mistaking his own neck of the woods for some grander entity called Western culture. It was not the inhabitants of Franche Comté who invented TV shows in which people fess up to having sex with an alligator. The belief that whatever is not instantly

First published as 'Qui s'accuse, s'excuse' (a review of *Troubling Confessions: Speaking Guilt in Law and Literature* by Peter Brooks) in the *London Review of Books*, 1 June 2000.

externalised is inauthentic belongs more to California than Calabria. And though this blend of puritanism and consumerism now increasingly permeates Europe, too, it is still hard for some Europeans to get by in a United States which seems not to value reticence or obliquity. The country is awash with witness, therapy, victimage, public self-exculpations, lowlier-than-thou protestations.

One of several troubled passages between the private and the public, the act of confession links the most private—sin, sexuality and the like—to the most dauntingly public (law courts, police stations). And this is bound to be of interest in a society like the United States, whose citizens, like people elsewhere only more so, are at once cloistered in their own private space and remorselessly on public show. The connection between these spheres was once known as republicanism or civic humanism: it is now known as selling your sex life to the papers.

Both puritanism and consumerism make a fetish of transparency; but a little more transparency in Western culture, even so, might not come amiss. For the other side of the phoney immediacy of the chat show is the deception and skulduggery by which some people reap a profit from such spectacles, not to speak of the lying politics which prop up that acquisitive system. While some chatter artlessly away about incest and aliens, others huddle conspiratorially together in smoke-free rooms. The more private lives are conducted in a glasshouse, the more sinisterly inscrutable grows the public realm. Capitalist culture's hunger for transparency is, among other things, an excessive reaction to excessive opacity, just as the mandarin jargon of academia is in part a resistance to the over-consumable speech of the marketplace. For every post-structuralist fastidiously sceptical of truth, there are millions of ordinary folk out there for whom seeing is believing.

This, no doubt, is one reason for the success of post-structuralist theory in the United States, well past its sell-by date though it now is. Another reason is the American fetish of personal responsibility. With the possible exception of 'Blessed are the losers', few statements are less permissible in the United States than 'It wasn't my fault.' It is a fanatically voluntaristic society, in which appeals to the social determinants of selfhood are seen as a moral cop-out almost everywhere except in literary theory seminars. The legal notion of confession depends, as Peter Brooks points out, on the assumption of a free, rational will, so that to cast doubt on the concept is more ideologically subversive in the

States than it is in stoical, deterministic, history-ridden Europe. Hence the US origins of postmodernism, which overreacts to a hubristic American affirmation of the self by undoing or dissolving it.

In a society obsessed with discourse, the subject of confession is bound to prove alluring. There is the question—deftly examined by this book—of whether a 'free confession' can ever be more than an oxymoron; and this is especially relevant in a culture much preoccupied with issues of free versus oppressive or coercive speech. And if the act of confession seems to blur the line between the free and the involuntary, so it obscures the distinction between the natural and the artful. It is thus of particular relevance to that running battle between puritanism and postmodernism, the spontaneous and the constructed self, which we know as the United States. *Qui s'accuse, s'excuse:* there is usually an element of crafty self-exculpation about coughing up, which for Brooks is one reason why it is an inherently duplicitous, unreliable speech act. The force of this case is somewhat diminished by the fact that, for some of the theories from which it springs, every speech act from promising to shouting 'Fire!' is unstable and unreliable. Even so, he shows with admirable resourcefulness how confession can involve power, propitiation, dependency, self-humiliation; how it can pleasurably generate the very guilt it seeks to assuage; how it may be a way of provoking as well as avoiding punishment, or of vaunting the self in the act of abnegating it. There is also, if one recalls the young woman at Mass, confession as come-on.

All this is alarming stuff for a society which believes that what you see is what you get. The idea that our selfhood spontaneously seeks its naked self-disclosure can withstand the news that there are forces around to stop this happening, but not that being oneself is a form of play-acting. That sincerity involves artifice, just as the immediacy of the TV image involves fabrication, is not what either puritan or avid consumer wants to hear. Even so, Brooks's view of confession reflects the very liberal values he wants in some ways to challenge. The book revolves on some intricate parallels between confessions to priest, psychoanalyst and police interrogator, while acknowledging vital distinctions between them. Unlike priests, for example, psychoanalysts are more interested in their confessees' involuntary rather than voluntary disclosures, in their resistances rather than their confidences; and unlike lawyers or police interrogators, psychoanalysts make no direct use of the material they elicit. Brooks might have added that religious confessors don't either: the point of the 'seal of confession' and the closed, private nature of the confessional, which the book views at times as mildly sinister, is to protect the confessee. What Brooks reads as obscurantist mystery is in part enlightened policy.

The most obvious difference between religious and legal acts of confession is that the former is about forgiveness while the latter is about punishment. Penance is not the point of confession, even if it is still its official theological name; and this is something that *Troubling Confessions*, which scarcely uses the word 'forgiveness', fails almost entirely to see. In off-the-peg Foucauldian style, Brooks views the Catholic confessional as little more than a blend of consolation, moral cleansing, self-discipline and spiritual policing, in which the authoritarian role of the confessor is to pluck the truth of a suitably 'abjected' confessing subject from the depths of his tormented inwardness. In fact, this is hardly true to the empirical experience of the Catholic confessional, which is usually as perfunctory an affair as buying a pound of carrots. It is clear from his work that Michel Foucault was never in the box himself, though some might think he needed it. 'Confessional', in the Oprah Winfrey sense of the word, is the last thing that confession is. Indeed Brooks himself perceptively notes the parallel between the impersonality of the confessional, where the priest sits behind a screen or with face averted, and the impersonality of the scene of analysis, where the analyst usually sits out of sight of the recumbent analysand. Had Brooks a little more theological expertise, he might have added that the impersonality of the confessional has much to do with the fact that the priest is present as a representative of the Christian community rather than as an individual in his own right. This is why it doesn't matter if he is even more sinful than you.

Through this normalising apparatus, in Brooks's view, the hapless confessee is reintegrated into the community and 'subjected to a regimen of orthodoxy in behaviour and belief'. As a good liberal, Brooks is fashionably suspicious of orthodoxies, just as he seems not to relish the law overmuch. It does not seem to occur to him that being 'subjected' to an orthodoxy of humane belief and behaviour is rather preferable to being a heterodox thug. Feminism is not an orthodoxy in Nepal, and more's the pity. Nor does he seem to appreciate in his piously liberal way that the law can be emancipatory as well as oppressive, nurturing

and protective as well as injurious; or that to be accepted back into a
community one has offended may be more than some darkly incor-
porative device. To complete his liberal orthodoxy, Brooks uses words
like 'guilt' and 'shame' somewhat distastefully, as though there were
not a great deal for us to feel guilty and ashamed about. The fact that
guilt has become a thriving cottage industry in the United States should
not blind us to this fact.

It is true that the Catholic confessional has probably served as much
to oppress as to emancipate, and Brooks shrewdly points out that it
emerges in the Middle Ages at about the same time as Inquisitorial
hunts for heresy. But this legalistic model of religious confession, for
which confessing one's sins to a priest is like coughing to a cop, will
hardly stand up against, say, the theology of William Blake. The name
'Satan' in the Old Testament means something like 'accuser', and
represents the demonic image of God of those who insist on regarding
him as an avenging judge. Part of the point in seeing God in this
hostile, Nobodaddy fashion is to make one's own acts of trying to
appease him seem meaningful. If God is a judge, then there would
seem to be some point in trying to keep in his good books, bargaining
our way to salvation by being remarkably well-behaved. This is the kind
of behaviour commonly known as 'pharisaical', though the term is
something of an insult to the historical Pharisees, a much more interesting and creditable bunch than the gospel-writers saw fit for their own
political reasons to make out.

What the devotees of this Satanic, patriarchal image of God find
scandalous is the idea that he does not need to be appeased because he
has always already forgiven us. To add insult to injury, he accepts us just
as we are, in all of our squalor and disagreeableness, and there is no
point in trying to impress him by embarking on some twelve-step self-
improvement programme. For Christian faith, as Blake understood, this
alternative way of imaging God is known as Jesus. Jesus is God in the
shape of human frailty, no longer the judge on the bench but the
political criminal who becomes an advocate alongside us in the dock.
To be open to one's own weakness in this way is known as repentance,
and involves *metanoia* or 'radical transformation'. It is of this that
confession is a signifier or, as the theological jargon has it, sacrament. It
is properly part of the communal Mass, not a privatised, hole-in-the-
corner affair, as it has been since the 16th century witnessed the inven-

tion of the confessional. It takes its cue from the scriptural injunction that if you arrive at the altar with your offering to find that you have a quarrel with your brother, you should first be reconciled to him before going ahead. Human righteousness is more important than religious ritual, as the Old Testament Yahweh keeps irritably reminding his tiresomely cultic people.

Nobody is being asked to believe all this; but to write about confession untheologically, as Peter Brooks does, is rather like writing about the electoral booth as though it were merely a device for manipulating the public, ignoring the fact that it is also a key part of democratic philosophy. Secular liberals may dislike the idea of confession because it smacks of secrecy and autocracy, but they may also dislike it because quaintly old-fashioned words like repentance are no part of their lexicon. They smack instead of some bone-headed Evangelicalism. But when Brooks speaks sceptically of the notion that redemption may depend on confession, one might ask him what else he thinks it might depend on. An acceptance of one's frailty and failure is the only sure basis for any more enduring achievement, as the South African Truth and Reconciliation Commission (passed over rather too casually by this book) might suggest. They are not busy simply consoling, therapising and disciplining themselves down there in Pretoria.

Brooks sometimes writes as though humility were merely some sort of unpleasant grovelling offensive to human dignity, rather than a necessary acknowledgment that, despite all one's fancy attainments, one remains something of a worm. One of the founding narratives of the United States is George Washington's confession to having committed an offence, but its point is to show that he is man enough to acknowledge his trespass. The self is thus amplified in the very act of being abnegated, rather as in the wrong kinds of martyrdom. In a more minor key, you can now get by in US literary academia as a professional confessant, winning promotion by writing critical essays which mention your impending divorce or how you visited the lavatory after finishing the preceding paragraph. This is confession as therapy rather than repentance, quite different from what is afoot in Chile or Northern Ireland. This book's conception of confession, like that of any study, is limited by its social context.

Not that forgiveness is without its problems, as *Measure for Measure* would suggest. It must not, for example, be allowed to make a mockery of justice. Mercy or forgiveness breaks the vicious circle of vengeance, overriding its tit-for-tat or exchange value in an act of creative superfluity. As Portia remarks in *The Merchant of Venice*, its quality is not 'strained' (constrained). But this gratuitousness also risks devaluing its object, just like the commodity form. Mercy must not become a form of blithe indifference; it must pay for its lavishness by reckoning the cost and feeling the pain of the injury it has endured. And there are always those like the psychopathic Barnadine in Shakespeare's play who cannot be redeemed not because they are too wicked, but because they cannot see any meaning in moral language at all, any more than a squirrel could make sense of algebraic topology. In this sense, oddly, they resemble the innocent, who, as William Golding observes in *Free Fall*, cannot forgive because they do not understand that they have been offended.

Troubling Confessions is a radical book with a liberal one struggling to get out. What the wilder, more Foucauldian Brooks gives with one hand, the tamer liberal humanist takes back with the other. Sometimes he seems hostile to the whole notion of police confessions, while at other times he is content to suggest rather feebly that they should be handled with care. There is a sense of theoretical overkill here, as a lot of big conceptual guns are wheeled up to fire off such a mild conclusion. His prose style is nervously subjunctive, full of self-protective 'mays' and 'mights'. Whereas the liberal in him wants to defend the right to silence, the radical suspects that such privacy is yet another cunning construct of power. At times he flirts with the flamboyant thesis that confession created the modern private self in the first place (capitalism might be a more plausible candidate), and displays a modish postmodern aversion to subjective depth and inwardness. At other times the cautious liberal takes over to remind us that legal confessions have their place and that individual responsibility is more than just a fiction.

Troubling Confessions, which dexterously weaves together Rousseau, Dostoevsky, Church history, Freud, US case law and a host of other sources, reflects a growing American interest in the relations between law and literature. This is partly because law can serve as a mediation between literature and society, as politics did in a more hopeful age. The most exact, rigorous language is thus being brought together with the most figurative; and one effect of this, as Brooks remarks, is to show up legal discourse as more fuzzy, more dependent on the vagaries of interpretation, than some have considered. It is a pity that the interchange has not been more two-way, and critical language infused with something of the precision of the juridical. The book is entirely convincing on just how central to Western culture the idea of confession has been—how natural the narrating of the self appears to be. It is not a modern phenomenon: Charles Taylor has fingered St Augustine as the first great apologist for personal inwardness. Nor is it, as Brooks sometimes implies, just a way of fashioning a subjective space within which we can be all the more cravenly subjected to power. If inwardness is a prison, it is also a set of capacities; if the narrative of the self is vital for subjection, it is equally crucial to emancipation. It is perhaps not surprising that, in the world of Oprah Winfrey, this book should so often lose grasp of that doubled truth.

Peter Conrad

Of all historical periods, modernity is the only one to designate itself, vacuously, in terms of its up-to-dateness. Does this imply that the Renaissance lagged behind the times, or that classical antiquity (from where, ironically, we derive the word 'modern') could never quite catch up with itself? The fact is, of course, that in their own eyes the Stuarts were quite as modern as the Spice Girls, but labels like 'modernism' and 'modernity' tend to obscure this fact. Every epoch suffers from the disability of being contemporaneous with itself, and of having no idea where it might lead. In some ways, we know a good deal more about the doctrine of divine right than the Stuarts did, not least that it failed to survive them for very long.

Why should modernity define itself in purely temporal terms, rather than by reference to a cultural style, a mode of production, an intellectual climate, a reversion to the past or the sway of a particular monarch? The answer must surely be that though all ages are bang up-to-date, not all of them are as entranced by the fact as our own epoch. All periods are modern, but not all of them live their experience in this mode. Indeed the classical is a way of living one's current experience as though it were simply a reprise of the past, so that only those bits of it which bear the legitimating seal of tradition can be regarded as authentic. In this view, what is important about the contemporary is precisely what is least new-fangled about it. Modernity, by contrast, sees itself not just as one more phase of time, but as a phase of time which re-evaluates the very notion of temporality, and thus as in and out of time simultaneously. What strikes it as most typical about itself is the

First published as 'Newsreel History' (a review of *Modern Times, Modern Places* by Peter Conrad) in the *London Review of Books*, 12 November 1998.

dazzling, dismaying experience of time, which no longer comes wrapped in history or habit or custom but is now becoming almost their opposite. The modern is that which reduces everything which happened up to half an hour ago to an oppressive traditionalism; it is less a continuation of history than an abolition of it.

This, to be sure, is an ironic enough notion, since nothing is more time-honoured than efforts to break with the past. A great deal of history has followed from attempts to blow history to pieces. Hegel believed that the Zeitgeist had arrived at its final consummation inside his own head, but this simply provided a cue to Marx, Kierkegaard, Nietzsche and a range of others to keep it going by challenging Hegel's assumption. Marx's cavalier declaration that all previous history had been no more than 'pre-history' was as modernist a gesture as Fauvism. Pronouncements of the end of history simply contribute another event to the history they declare over and done with, as Francis Fukuyama has no doubt been discovering from his post-bag. They are self-disconfirming prophecies, Cretan Liar paradoxes which, like all appeals to make it new, add one more item to that venerable lineage known as the avant-garde. Besides, you can only break with history if you are already standing somewhere inside it, and the instruments with which you emancipate yourself from it must be fashioned from its own unpromising stuff. It is also hard to be sure that your power to transcend the past is not itself determined by it—that you are not the plaything of history in the very act of leaping free of it. Modernity is the era in which time speeds up because democracy and technology now allow us to fashion our own destinies instead of waiting on the *longues durées* of Nature or Providence; but the same technology comes to be felt as an implacable, quasi-natural force of which we are the mere passive products.

Even so, the claims of modernity are not entirely bogus. The modern era really is different from what preceded it. The world has probably changed more swiftly and deeply in the last two centuries than ever before, and our own century can lay claim to being easily the bloodiest on record. Until quite recently, most men and women lived their modernity as tradition: truth was a contract between yourself, your ancestors and your progeny, and radical innovation was either wicked or unthinkable. All the most important truths were already known, since God would not be so prejudiced as to reserve them only for future generations. One moved backwards into the future with one's eyes fixed on the past, and in this way was less likely to come a cropper. The present was what had the most history behind it, not what was struggling to awaken from it; and if the present knew more than the past, it was the past that it knew. The modern idea that one lives best as an amnesiac, that history is somehow behind us and that the present is necessarily the new, could find no foothold here.

In any case, the modern is not really about up-to-dateness. To seize the time is to find that nothing is more eternal than nowness. It is also to discover that this apparently self-contained moment is secretly fractured, hollowed out by a future on whose brink it is perpetually trembling. In a curious crossing of tenses, 'futuristic' is sometimes used to mean the latest thing, and *le dernier cri* is nicely ambiguous, meaning the latest but also the last. In the modernist time-scheme, every moment ushers in some fleeting future which will be instantly superseded, rather as for Walter Benjamin even the most perishable of historical moments is the strait gate through which the Messiah might enter. If classicism, which slows time down, undermines the importance of the contemporary, the same might be said of modernism, which speeds time up. The present is now continually undercut by a future which can never quite arrive—partly because in some sense it is already here, partly because it will arrive only under the sign of its own instant negation.

The problem with trying to characterise the modern age in these terms is that it is almost impossible not to lapse into high cliché. Historical textbooks always seem to make three claims about the era they are dealing with: it was a period of change; it was essentially a transitional epoch; and the middle classes went on rising. Since all this is truer of the 20th century than of any other time, the clichés are bound to be compounded. Fragmentation, a sense of space shrunken and time accelerated, giddying technological advance, the crumbling of moral certitudes, the rise of the faceless masses, the human individual as fractured, estranged, disorientated: all this is now as drearily familiar a discourse as the Elizabethan world picture, if somewhat more accurate. Peter Conrad's monumental study of modernism falls foul of such platitudes from time to time, not least in its tendency to a kind of newsreel history. 'The 19th century, powered by the internal combustion engine, was a time of hectic, propulsive dynamism.' Conrad's do-it-yourself sociology contrasts sharply with the subtlety of his analyses of art, in what is surely the most wide-ranging book on the subject yet to appear in English.

Conrad organises his book around topics, not authors or art-forms. There are chapters on primitivism, apocalypse, the body, the image, light, militarism, dehumanisation, space and time, political revolution, technology, language and a good deal else; Charlie Chaplin is the only modernist icon to be granted a section to himself. Each chapter pulls in a formidable array of artists, art-forms, movements, scientists and philosophers, raiding them for examples of its theme. The book's method thus reflects its subject-matter: Conrad has produced a kind of modernist montage of modernism, a curved, centreless space in which any item can be permutated with any other. Each chapter is a mesh of connections but self-contained, so that in a modernist smack at realist notions of narrative order, no chapter can claim priority over another. The form of the book is Einsteinian rather than Newtonian; indeed the Einsteinian world picture is a subject it explores at length. Relativity, like everything else in the book, is treated relativistically: Conrad's prose leaps mercurially from one cultural illustration of the doctrine to another, weaving an intricate web of relations in which they all come to seem indifferently interchangeable. If the book wasn't so nervous of cultural theory, one might even detect in this method a trace of Walter Benjamin and Theodor Adorno's notion of 'constellations', a brand of surrealist sociology which abandons hierarchies and abstractions and lets its general ideas emerge from the interaction of minute particulars. This, anyway, would be a charitable way of avoiding the conclusion that Conrad is just a good old empiricist who happens to enjoy Continental art.

Einstein's continuum of time and space, so Conrad claims, was just what the reckless gang of Italian Futurists thought they could experience when they drove their racing-cars, and there are submerged relations between the theory of relativity and J.M. Barrie's unageing Peter Pan. Modern railways involve a mutual adjustment of disparate places, just like T.S. Eliot's theory of a sensibility which could devour any kind of experience. Proust wanted characters you could walk around, like the Cubists' cones, and his Albertine 'with promiscuous relativity ... distributes herself around the world'. In his great work on dreams, Freud discovered inside the mind something like the continuum which Einstein had revealed in the physical world. Meanwhile, 'the expanding universe of the new physics matched the geopolitical world of the 20th century, with its revised or erased borders and its fleeing populations.' And just as Rutherford's account of atomic structure had shown matter to be volatile and improvised, so modernist architecture had to come to grips with this perturbing lack of solidity. The vacuity which both Rutherford and the X-ray machine had uncovered was imaged in the Eiffel Tower, which seems to repel any definitive way of being looked at or any mandatory standpoint from which to do so. 'Here,' Conrad remarks, 'was the relativity theory built in iron, or the uncertainty principle absorbed in a merry, maddening dance.' Atomic physics would reappear later in the figure of Charlie Chaplin, described by one commentator as 'an atom that must journey alone through the world'. As for vacuity, this crops up later in the book in the guise of the vacuum cleaner, another mode of dematerialisation which 'gobbles mislaid wedding rings as if they were cobwebs'.

Freud, as it happens, had a name for this obsessive perception of affinities (he called it paranoia), but a more literary word for it is allegory. Some of the modernists favoured allegory over symbolism because it forged connections in a fragmentary world while retaining an ironic sense of their arbitrariness. Allegory allowed for a number of possible resemblances between things, and so made it clear that any particular set of relations sprang from a specific standpoint. Conrad writes as though the parallels he perceives between different bits of modernism are somehow objectively there, and indeed some of them are; but he is least impressive when they seem forced and fanciful, the product of his own relative viewpoint. The Russian painter Malevich's steady distancing of the material world is said to be like our view of a plane taking off, while in the Weimar Republic, so Conrad remarks, the same printing presses which manufactured journalistic lies also churned out economic fictions like one thousand billion mark bills. The communal latrines of the First World War were part of a 'renunciation of personality' which crops up in all kinds of modern artistic manifestos. The war itself 'redesigned the human body', and thus has affinities with Cubism.

If anything can mean anything else, as allegory tends to believe, then it is both enriched and impoverished; and this is also true of the procedure of this book. Some of Conrad's parallelisms are perceptive, some of them are slick, and others are clever in both the laudatory and limiting senses of the word. *Modern Times, Modern Places* is an astonishingly well-informed piece of work, which roams from ballet to Berg, Fritz Lang to Jack Nicholson, with the omnivorous energy of the modernist art it addresses. But Conard's pithy style, which hardly stumbles for over seven hundred pages, also sails close to a sort of colour-supplement smartness, hovering somewhere between epigram and sound-bite ('Freud's thought turned reality upside down'). If his writing is pointed it can also be glib, covertly sensationalist beneath its clipped impersonality: early 20th-century Vienna possessed 'a Jewish clerisy, excluded from power, which in revenge exposed the discontents suppressed by civilisation, released the empty air pent up in language, and dismantled the melodic scale'. A lot of the book is more high-class cultural journalism than rigorous inquiry. Social context is conveniently packaged, and though there is much play with scientists and philosophers, one doesn't sense that the author could hold his own in a discussion of primary narcissism or perlocutionary acts.

With commendable impudence, Conrad refuses to disfigure his text with a single footnote, even if some readers may feel that he wears his learning too lightly. Unlike some avant-garde works of art, this book erases all traces of the labour which produced it. What is worrying, however, is less the absence of footnotes than of original thought. Conrad's general ideas about modernism are for the most part standard stuff; what is gripping is the intelligence with which he puts them concretely to work. But this vivid quiltwork of allusions lacks conceptual depth. Analysis gives way to metaphorical resemblances—a flurry of analogies which, as in the Martian school of poetry, are sometimes coruscating and sometimes callow.

In this, *Modern Times, Modern Places* is more postmodern than modern. Modernist art may be allergic to absolute meanings, but it cannot rid itself of a dream of depth, plagued as it is by a nostalgia for the days when truth, reality and redemption were still notions to be reckoned with. If the modernist artwork has shattered into fragments, what this leaves at its centre is not just a blank, but a hole whose shape is still hauntingly reminiscent. Unlike the postmodern work, the modernist artefact cannot give up its hermeneutical hankering, its belief that the world might just be the kind of thing that could be meaningful. For postmodernism, by contrast, this is just a kind of category mistake, a scratching where it doesn't itch, part of a post-metaphysical hangover which deludedly assumes that for a thing to lack a sense is as disabling as for a person to lack a limb. Postmodernism, being too young to remember a time when there was truth and reality, is out to persuade its modernist elders that if only they were to abandon their hunger for truth they would be free.

Modern Times, Modern Places is a brilliantly two-dimensional book, miles wide but only a few feet thick, which has all the virtues of what Eliot called an art of the surface. Its dispassionate, hard-boiled style filters the lurid through the clinical in true postmodern fashion, as in the account of Picasso's *Guernica*, in which Conrad's prose seems to be casting a sideways glance at itself: '*Guernica* picks out the soft, sensitive extremities which are of interest to torturers: the sole of the foot and the palm of a hand, both scored with stigmata, anchor the composition in its bottom corners. Nipples seem to be squeamishly detachable, mouths are megaphones for broadcasting agony.' The scrupulous alliteration of 'scored with stigmata', the suave placing of 'squeamishly', the overpitched final image: all this stylistic self-consciousness creates a postmodern 'lack of affect', which is evident in other ways, too. Most of the time, it is hard to know what Conrad actually feels about his subject, as everything is churned through the mill of his blankly non-judgmental style. Style is the universal medium which translates one thing into another but somehow levels and neutralises them in the process. The point of this oddly positivistic study is not to evaluate but to describe. To judge, for Conrad, would presumably be to court the perils of political radicalism, which fondly imagines that things might have been different and cannot accept that the world is simply whatever is the case. But the sceptical, streetwise, postmodern Conrad is at odds with the patrician modernist who clearly finds much in the modern world thoroughly distasteful; and the problem is how to pass judgment on this world without lapsing into the naiveties of utopian thought. Conrad's answer to this dilemma is style, which in Flaubertian fashion clings to its object while managing to rise imaginatively above it.

It is a cliché of cultural history that England had to import most of its modernist writers from abroad. By the time modernism arrived on the scene, realism was too deeply entrenched a cultural mode in English society for any homegrown artistic experiment to have much chance of flourishing. The only region of these islands to produce a vigorous modernism earlier this century was also the most alien and unstable: Ireland. Since then, English critics addressing the topic of modernism have regularly betrayed a philistine parochialism, from F.R. Leavis onwards. Fortunately, however, Peter Conrad is not English but Tasmanian, and brings to bear on his subject the synoptic view of a genuine cosmopolitan. Like all the best commentators on modernist art, he is something of a hybrid and exile himself, adept at shifting between different cultures and rather more open to their cross-influences than the fans of Philip Larkin. Whatever its limits, his book communicates the exuberance of modernism as few native English critics have managed to do, and does so with an elegance and concision in which each sentence strives to be an aperçu. If his analogies are sometimes strained, they are rarely less than suggestive. *Modern Times, Modern Places* tells the story of modern cultural history with unflagging freshness, and without an ounce of surplus stylistic fat.

Paul de Man

Imagine a current of literary theory notable for its belief that meaning is indeterminate, language ambiguous and unstable, the human subject a mere metaphor, history a frequently 'undecidable' text, an endless self-ironising the nearest we can approach to authenticity. One of its most familiar typographical devices is the use of scare quotes—'How to "speak", "now", the "truth" of this "real" "event"?'—and one of its favoured stylistic figures an archly mannered use of the rhetorical question: 'What am I saying? Can I even pose that question? What would it be to "know"? For "I", precisely, to "know"?' (If this is a parody, it is hardly less so than the opening of Samuel Weber's contribution to *Responses on Paul de Man's Wartime Journalism*: 'What are we talking about? What have we been talking about? Does it make any sense to begin with such questions?' The implication, of course, being that only some flat-footed vulgarian would rush forward with anything as ill-bred as an answer.)

For this intellectual milieu (commonly known as deconstruction, or 'deconstruction'), everything is quite agonisingly *difficult*, and little or nothing can be known for certain. It thus combines a dash of radicalism *vis-à-vis* the complacent dogmatism of our rulers with a hermetic élitism in respect of the gullible plebs. Suddenly, into this radical sphere, drops a grossly palpable 'fact'. One of this theory's most eminent and brilliant

First published as 'The emptying of a former self' (a review of *Wartime Journalism 1939–1943* by Paul de Man and *Responses on Paul de Man's Wartime Journalism*, both volumes edited by Werner Hamacher, Neil Hertz and Thomas Keenan; *Paul de Man* by Christopher Norris; *Critical Writings 1953–1978* by Paul de Man, edited by Lindsay Waters; and *Reading de Man Reading*, edited by Lindsay Waters and Wlad Godzich) in the *Times Literary Supplement*, 26 May–1 June 1989.

exponents, so a busy young researcher has revealed, contributed in his youth a sizeable number of reviews and articles to German-controlled newspapers in Belguim, during the period of that country's occupation by the Nazis. The pieces in question, now published in smudged photocopy format with the appearances of low-grade pornography, included one outrageously anti-Semitic article, and comprised a broad sprinkling of fantastic sentiments. In the most uncontrollable irony of all, history, politics and ethics, none of them exactly the *forte* of the deconstructionists, emerge from the limbo of indeterminancy with a vengence. 'Deconstruct *that* one', the critics of this creed wrathfully or gleefully murmur.

A few of the contributors to *Responses*, it must be said, have a fair old try. Andrzej Warminski goes for the rhetorical question: 'What do you know about the man, his circumstances, the place, the time? Who are you to draw a line between good man and bad man, resistance and collaboration?' It is clear, Warminski writes, that one cannot deal with this matter along the lines of some binary opposition between good and evil, politically correct and incorrect and so on, which we all know Jacques Derrida to have finally spirited away. It is a fact that the young de Man mentions with approval the possibility of establishing an isolated colony for Jews, claims that the war will fuse the 'Hitlerian' and German souls into a single unique force, and enthusiastically praises Fascist authors and cultural events; but is there anything really *determinate* here to be judged? Isn't it all terribly *difficult?* Samuel Weber prefers the evasion of scare quotes, which he drapes around the word 'collaboration' in an essay considerably more irascible about de Man's detractors than about his early politics. Timothy Bahti, in a fit of petulance, concludes his reflections on the affair by suggesting that the offending articles would have had to have been invented did they not exist. It's all an anti-deconstructionist plot. Nobody actually suggests that the stuff was forged by Christopher Ricks, but there are one or two desperate hints that de Man might have been bluffing. Perhaps he was a fifth columnist all along. Rodolfe Gasché is deeply doubtful that de Man, who wrote of 'the impeccable behaviour of a highly civilised invader' only five months after the first anti-Jewish decrees were passed, was anything as vulgar as a collaborator. In a bold gesture, however, he does concede that the youthful de Man, who described the Nazis' attitudes to their subject peoples as worthy, just and humane, reveals in these writings 'a strong traditionalist and conservative bent'.

In a subtle, learned essay, Cynthia Chase displaces attention from the early de Man to the later, more acceptable figure, and insinuates that those who oppose his work may simply not have read him. The booby prize for special pleading, however, must doubtless be awarded to a tortuous, deeply embarrassing contribution from Jacques Derrida, which he should certainly have thought twice about writing. His title, 'Like the Sound of the Sea Deep Within a Shell: Paul de Man's war', alludes not only to the actual war in which Jews were deported from Belgium to the gas chambers, but to the spiritual agony which—purely speculatively, since he never spoke of it—we can impute to the later de Man himself, or indeed to the 'war' supposedly waged against him by his critics. Derrida contrives to make de Man himself, rather than in the first place the victims of the regime he supported, appear a poignant, persecuted figure, and excuses his lifelong public silence about the affair on the grounds that the controversy consequent upon a confession would have distracted him from his work. De Man told hardly anyone about his earlier incarnation; but perhaps, Derrida ruminates in the style of a bad French movie, he was telling us all along. The trusty old rhetorical questions are duly wheeled up—Who can tell? Who has the right to judge?—and the essay concludes by displacing the whole issue to the malice of de Man's critics. It is they who are the true 'totalitarians'. Some good, however, will spring from all this: at least we will now all have to keep reading de Man over and over again. How fortunate, in other words, that the deconstruction industry has been lent a new lease of life, just at the point where it appeared to be flagging. Derrida's essay lends strength to the conviction that the main qualification for writing about de Man is not to have known him personally.

These patches of shabby sophistry are more than compensated for elsewhere in the volume, which contains some impressively cogent pieces both pro and con, and which displays throughout a quite admirable moral seriousness and intellectual force. They are also more than compensated for by the reckless hyperbole and falsification of some of de Man's enemies. A man who is in his very early twenties, in an atmosphere of widespread collaboration among the intelligentsia, published for a relatively brief period a number of sometime equivocal pro-fascist reviews, has been directly compared to Goebbels and Waldheim, pilloried as the Klaus Barbie of New Haven. His later literary theory, so it is slanderously claimed, is merely the continuation of the same sinister business under a different name. Conservative journalists and academics affronted by the genuinely subversive elements of deconstruction have seized on these saddening revelations, with unscrupulous opportunism, to impugn as so much 'nihilism' a fertile, original vein of critical enquiry. A man who can no longer speak up for himself (de Man died in 1983) has been travestied and vilified by commentators whose true target is often any idea which questions the current critical establishment. The guardians of de Man's reputation have every right to be enraged by the intellectual dishonesty and moral irresponsibility of this onslaught. There is a dim analogy, perhaps, with the plight of the Marxist philosopher Louis Althusser, whose critics, on hearing that he had killed his wife in the grip of severe psychosis, muttered that they had suspected all along that there was nothing in his ideas.

Many of the issues involved in the de Man affair are indeed as yet indeterminate. Several of his pro-fascist formulations are devious and double-edged, hedged around the qualifications. In notably non-fascist style, he defends art's autonomy of politics, and can be taken as wishing to preserve Flemish cultural independence against German imperialism. There is evidence to suggest that he was not personally anti-Semitic. But it is not, as Derrida thinks, a matter of weighing an 'on the one hand' against an 'on the other hand'. Such apparent judiciousness, curious for one so wary of binary oppositions, bestows a spurious symmetry on what are in truth quite unequal phenomena: de Man's deplorable collaborationism and whatever implicit reservations he may have signalled about it.

As far as the relation, if any, between earlier and later de Man is concerned, his most implacable opponents tend to be 'continuists' and his supporters 'anti-continuists'. The former, assiduously combing the later work for buried evidence of earlier attitudes, seize upon a number of 'mature' de Manian doctrines as blatantly self-exculpatory devices: the past is a fiction, error is inevitable, forgetting is essential, language is beyond our control. Considerably more convincing is the view taken by Christopher Norris in his excellent new study, *Paul de Man: Deconstruction and the critique of aesthetic ideology*, that the later work can be read as a silent, reparative undoing of the earlier. De Man's horror of totalities and teleologies, of organicist and 'immediatist' doctrines, of the 'aestheticizing' of cognition and brandishing of absolute truth claims, represent a secret deconstruction of his earlier aesthetic nationalism. The extreme bleakness and ascesis of his work, one might reasonably speculate, are signs of a violent, renunciatory emptying out of the self he had once been. There is an interesting parallel between de Man's vertiginous ironies and the post-war work from Theodor Adorno, whose 'negative dialetics' evince an extreme revulsion from all definitive statements and final solutions. Simply to *propose*, in an epoch where provisional language has been used as an instrument of geno- cide, is to be guiltily complicit with one's antagonist. What Norris fails to point out in his study, the brisk lucidity of which may well offend some card-carrying de Manians, is that de Man's discontinuous career thus manifests a remarkable continuity: a resolute opposition to emancipatory politics. The early extreme right-wingism mutates into a jaded liberal scepticism about the efficacy of any form of radical poli- tical action, the effects of which will always proliferate beyond our control.

To turn from this depressing debate to de Man's *Critical Writings 1953–1978* is to be sharply reminded of why his early 'aberrations' matter so desperately to his followers. For though these 'middle period' pieces are by no means the most conceptually intricate, bizarrely dis- turbing of de Man's essays, they display an erudition, philosophical acumen and strenuous originality of thought to which hardly any other Western critic can hold a candle. This is the de Man of the 1950s and 60s, before the 'rhetorical turn', still preoccupied in Heideggerian and phenomenological fashion with selfhood and inwardness. But most of the motifs of the later writings are embryonically present: the pathos of temporality, the perpetual non-coincidence of mind and world, the incapacity of knowledge to name anything but its own failure.

Intellectually speaking, the master has been fortunate in his disciples, as the pieces collected in *Reading de Man Reading* well enough testify. The sheer strangeness and recalcitrance of his thought have attracted, and formed, some of the United States's most brilliant critical minds, many of whom line up here to pay homage to the lost leader. There are some finely perceptive essays from Neil Hertz, J. Hillis Miller, Geoffrey Hartman, Timothy Bahti and others, though only Bill Readings tackles the vexed question of the politics of deconstruction. The volume dives illuminatingly down the labyrinthine byways of its subject's writings, but in doing so curiously overlooks the figure in the carpet which Norris brings out so well: the utter centrality to de Man of what can be called the ideology of the aesthetic, of which he was at first mystified adherent and later a relentless scourge.

In other ways, the master has been rather less well served by his acolytes. Of the fourteen contributions to this book, only a typically searching essay by Gasché manages to voice anything like a systematic critique. It is hard to think of a critic since F.R. Leavis who has inspired a more extraordinarily submissive posture in his devotees, and the fact that both men were rogue steers within the academy has no doubt much to do with this. You do not shoot the general in the back when he is under fire from up front. It is ironic, even so, that the man who so caustically demystified the deceptive authority of writing did so only for his own pronouncements to be accorded, often enough, the status of sacred scripture. From what one hears of de Man, there is no reason to believe that such a reception would have made him feel anything but uneasy. It would certainly be unpardonably reductive for his supporters, one feels, to attempt to place his work historically—to see him, for example, as belonging to a disenchanted, post-war, 'end of ideologies' epoch, in which authenticity becomes identical with stating one's own bad faith, decisive action is always premature and self-blinded, and history lapses into an empty, broken temporality. De Man's self-paralysing ironies and disabling aporias, the doleful insistence on failure and indeterminateness, the authoritative disclaiming of authority: all of these, unwrapped from their philosophical idiom, are embarrassingly close to the liberal commonplaces of a politically baffled, dispirited intelligentsia.

If there is much in de Man to disturb the White House, there is also quite a bit to lend it comfort. The self-ironising insight of deconstruction rests upon a historical self-blindness. The young de Man was entangled in an unsavoury history from which he strove painfully to extricate himself; but he did not thereby cease to reflect a later history, suspect the term though he might. The unearthing of the early writings is a stark illustration of Fredric Jameson's dictum that we may forget about history, but history, for better or worse, will not forget about us.

Gayatri Spivak

There must exist somewhere a secret handbook for post-colonial critics, the first rule of which reads: 'Begin by rejecting the whole notion of post-colonialism.' It is remarkable how hard it is to find an unabashed enthusiast for the concept among those who promote it: as hard as it was in the '60s or '70s to find anyone who owned up to being a structuralist. The idea of the post-colonial has taken such a battering from post-colonial theorists that to use the word unreservedly of oneself would be rather like calling oneself Fatso, or confessing to a furtive interest in coprophilia. Gayatri Spivak remarks with some justification in this book that a good deal of US post-colonial theory is 'bogus', but this gesture is *de rigueur* when it comes to one post-colonial critic writing about the rest. Besides, for a 'Third World' theorist to break this news to her American colleagues is in one sense deeply unwelcome, and in another sense exactly what they want to hear. Nothing is more voguish in guilt-ridden US academia than to point to the inevitable bad faith of one's position. It is the nearest a postmodernist can come to authenticity.

The second rule of this samizdat handbook reads: 'Be as obscurantist as you can decently get away with.' Post-colonial theorists are often to be found agonising about the gap between their own intellectual discourse and the natives of whom they speak; but the gap might look rather less awesome if they did not speak a discourse which most intellectuals, too, find unintelligible. You do not need to hail from a shanty town to find a Spivakian metaphorical muddle like 'many of us are trying to carve out

First published as 'In the Gaudy Supermarket' (a review of *A Critique of Post-Colonial Reason: Toward a History of the Vanishing Present* by Gayatri Chakravorty Spivak) in the *London Review of Books*, 13 May 1999.

positive negotiations with the epistemic graphing of imperialism' pretentiously opaque. It is hard to see how anyone can write like this and admire the luminous writings of, say, Freud. Post-colonial theory makes heavy weather of a respect for the Other, but its most immediate Other, the reader, is apparently dispensed from this sensitivity. Radical academics, one might have naively imagined, have a certain political responsibility to ensure that their ideas win an audience outside senior common rooms. In US academia, however, such popularising or *plumpes Denken* is unlikely to win you much in the way of posh chairs and prestigious awards, so that left-wingers like Spivak, for all their stock-in-trade scorn for academia, can churn out writing far more inaccessible to the public than the literary élitists who so heartily despise them.

It might just be, of course, that the point of a wretched sentence like 'the in-choate in-fans ab-original para-subject cannot be theorised as functionally *completely* frozen in a world where teleology is schematised into geo-graphy' is to subvert the bogus transparency of Western Reason. Or it might be that discussing public matters in this hermetically private idiom is more a symptom of that Reason than a solution to it. Like most questions of style, Spivak's obscurantism is not just a question of style. Its duff ear for tone and rhythm, its careless way with verbal texture, its theoretical sound-bites ('Derrida has staged the homoeroticity of European philosophy in the left-hand column of *Glas*'), spring quite as much from the commodified language of the United States as they do from some devious attempt to undermine it. A sentence which begins 'At 26, graphing himself into the seat of *Aufhebung*, Marx sees the necessity for this critical enterprise' combines the vocabulary of Hegel with the syntax of *Hello!* Spivak's language, lurching as it does from the high-toned to the streetwise, belongs to a culture where there is less and less middle ground between the portentous and the homespun, the rhetorical and the racy. One whiff of irony or humour would prove fatal to its self-regarding solemnity. In the course of this book, Spivak writes with great theoretical brilliance on Charlotte Brontë and Mary Shelley, Jean Rhys and Mahasweta Devi; but she pays almost no attention to their language, form or style. Like the old-fashioned literary scholarship it despises, the most avant-garde literary theory turns out to be a form of good old-fashioned content analysis.

Spivak rightly sets her face against the left philistines for whom any idea which will not instantly topple the bosses is about as politically useful as algebraic topology. But she is far more reluctant to recognise the seed of truth in their point of view: that radical theory tends to grow unpleasantly narcissistic when deprived of a political outlet. As the semioticians might put it, the theory then comes to stand in metaphorically for what it signifies. Political revolution may have many perils, but failing to concentrate the mind wonderfully is not among them. The endless digressions and self-interruptions of this study, as it meanders from Kant to Krishna, Schiller to Sati, belong, among other places, to a politically directionless Left. More charitable readers will see this garrulous hotch-potch as a strike at the linear narratives of Enlightenment, by one whose gender and ethnicity these violently exclude. If colonial societies endure what Spivak calls 'a series of interruptions, a repeated tearing of time that cannot be sutured', much the same is true of her own overstuffed, excessively elliptical prose. She herself, unsurprisingly, reads the book's broken-backed structure in just this way, as an iconoclastic departure from 'accepted scholarly or critical practice'. But the ellipses, the heavy-handed jargon, the cavalier assumption that you know what she means, or that if you don't she doesn't much care, are as much the overcodings of an academic coterie as a smack in the face for conventional scholarship.

If an abrupt leaping from *Jane Eyre* to the Asiatic Mode of Production challenges the staider compositional notions of white male scholars, it also has more than a smack of good old American eclecticism about it. In this gaudy, all-licensed supermarket of the mind, any idea can apparently be permutated with any other. What some might call dialectical thinking is for others a pathological inability to stick to the point. The line between post-colonial hybridity and postmodern anything-goes-ism is embarrassingly thin. As feminist, deconstructionist, post-Marxist and post-colonialist together, Spivak seems reluctant to be left out of any theoretical game in town. Multiplying one's options is an admirable theoretical posture, as well as a familiar bit of US market philosophy. For Spivak to impose a coherent narrative on her materials, even if her title spuriously suggests one, would be the sin of teleology, which banishes certain topics just as imperialism sidelines certain peoples. But if cultural theorists these days can bound briskly from allegory to the Internet, in a kind of intellectual version of Attention Deficit Disorder, it is partly because they are free from the inevitably constricting claims of a major political project. Lateral thinking is thus not altogether easy to distinguish from loss of political purpose. Even the books which Spivak has *not* written cluster like unquiet ghosts within her footnotes, reluctant to be excluded. Indeed, an essay remains to be written on the unpublished writings of Gayatri Spivak, which would take as its subject all those footnotes in which she has announced a work which never actually appeared, or—as here—describes a work that she will not or cannot write.

Spivak's hankering to say everything at once is not perhaps entirely innocent of a desire to impress; but it is a great deal more than that, just as the obscurity of a theorist's style can sometimes signal insecurity quite as much as arrogance. The fact is that Spivak has a quite formidable span of reference, which leaves most other cultural theorists looking dismally parochial. Few of them could remotely match the range and versatility of this book, which stretches from Hegelian philosophy and the historical archives of colonial India to postmodern culture and international trade. Much post-colonial writing behaves as though the relations between the North and South of the globe were primarily a 'cultural' affair, thus allowing literary types to muscle in on rather more weighty matters than insect imagery in the later James. Spivak, by contrast, has a proper scorn for such 'culturalism', even if she shares a good many of its assumptions. She does not make the mistake of imagining that an essay on the figure of the woman in *A Passage to India* is inherently more threatening to the transnational corporations than an inquiry into Thackeray's use of the semicolon. The relations between North and South are not primarily about discourse, language or identity but about armaments, commodities, exploitation, migrant labour, debt and drugs; and this study boldly addresses the economic realities which too many post-colonial critics culturalise away. (For some of them these days, any reference to the economic is ipso facto 'economistic', just as any allusion to the lungs or kidneys is 'biologistic'.) If Spivak knows about graphemics, she also knows about the garment industry. It helps, too, that she is among the most coruscatingly intelligent of all contemporary theorists, whose insights can be idiosyncratic but rarely less than original. She has probably done more long-term political good, in pioneering feminist and post-colonial studies within global academia, than almost any of her theoretical colleagues. And like all such *grandes maîtresses*, she has now to deal with that ultimate source of embarrassment, her devoted acolytes.

She accomplishes this task with rather too much grace. *Somebody* should write a critique of post-colonial reason, assessing both its achievements and its absurdities, but this book is too well-mannered, as well as too episodic, to be that. If its subtitle is only just intelligible, its title is positively misleading. Spivak is at once the best and worst-placed author to carry out such a project, and her failure to do so is both disappointing and understandable. She is the best-placed because as an immigrant in the West she can spot those conceptual limits which are less obvious to insiders. There is a great deal of timely good sense, if Spivak would forgive the phrase, in pointing out to the more idealist employees of the Western post-colonial industry that nativism is not to be romanticised; that ethnic minorities within metropolitan countries are not the same as colonised peoples; that there is nothing 'essentialist' about civic rights; and that for subaltern groups to become institutionalised citizens is an undesirable goal only for card-carrying primitivists. Unlike some of her more starry-eyed colleagues, Spivak does not see the transition from ethnic immigrant to business executive as unequivocal progress, or feel the need to disavow the reality of 'ethnic entrepreneurs ... pimping for the transnationals and selling their women into sweated labour'. She is equally aware that feminists working for 'gender justice' in the West are inevitably helping to shore up a social order whose global operations stifle such rights elsewhere.

Yet this withering criticism of the post-colonial Western liberals never quite comes to a head. If Spivak has an uncannily keen nose for Western cant, patronage and hypocrisy, she is notably reluctant to break ranks. In one sense, this is an admirable refusal to indulge in the gamesmanship of those in the know confronted with those who want to be. There is enough futile self-laceration in American academia without Spivak mauling the victim a little further. It is also a brave acknowledgment of her own compromised condition, as an academic superstar who speaks of caste and clitoridectomy. But there is more to her reticence than that. This book takes a few well-deserved smacks at the wilder breed of post-colonialist critics, whose fascination for the Other is in part a demoralised yearning to be absolutely anyone but themselves. But it is also tinged by the bland, anodyne consensus of US academia, where outright conflict is too often muffled by a common 'professionalism'. Despite its revealing habit of using the word 'aggressive' as complimentary, the United States is a culture deeply fearful of contention, which perhaps explains why wrestling, a game which converts real combat into simulated spectacle, is the most popular of its TV sports.

Spivak is the worst-placed of critics to write the book which her title deceptively promises because she is too much the insider, as one of the major architects of the whole post-colonial enterprise in the West. Her fellow architect Edward Said has become increasingly impatient with what they have jointly succeeded in constructing, and in his attractively caustic manner is not averse to saying so; but Spivak is more eirenic than her occasionally embattled prose-style would suggest. Her comment that much in the area is 'bogus' is largely an aside. If she rightly distinguishes between ethnic minority and colonised nation, she fails to drive home the point that a good deal of post-colonialism has been a kind of 'exported' version of the United States' own grievous ethnic problems, and thus yet another instance of God's Own Country, one of the most insular on earth, defining the rest of the world in terms of itself. For this exportation to get under way, certain imports known as Third World intellectuals are necessary to act as its agents; yet though Spivak has reason to know this better than most, she never pauses long enough in this book to unpack its implications. To do so would require some systematic critique; but systematic critique is for her more part of the problem than the solution, as it is for all those privileged enough not to stand in need of rigorous knowledge. These individuals used to be known as the gentry, and are nowadays known as post-structuralists. If she can be splendidly scathing about 'white boys talking post-coloniality', or the alliance between cultural studies, liberal multiculturalism and transnational capitalism, these wholesome morsels surface only to vanish again into the thick stew of her text.

There is, to be sure, a great deal more to be said for post-colonial studies than that, and Spivak herself says much of it in these pages. Whatever its romantic illusions and secret self-regard, this most rapidly growing sector of literary criticism signals the entry onto the Western cultural stage, for the first time in its history, of those the West has most injured and abused. There can thus be few more important critics of our age than the likes of Spivak, Said and Homi Bhabha, even if two of that trio can be impenetrably opaque. Unlike one of the two Calvary thieves being saved, this is hardly a reasonable percentage. But there are discreditable as well as creditable reasons for the speedy surfacing of post-colonialism, and Spivak remains for the most part silent about them. Its birth, for example, followed in the wake of the defeat, at least for the present, of both class struggle in Western societies and revolutionary nationalism in the previously colonialised world. American students who, through no fault of their own, would not recognise class struggle if it perched on the tip of their skateboards, or who might not be so keen on the Third World if some of its inhabitants were killing their fathers and brothers in large numbers, can vicariously fulfil their generously radical impulses by displacing oppression elsewhere. This move leaves them plunged into fashionably postmodern gloom about the 'monolithic' benightedness of their own social orders. It is as if the depleted, disorientated subject of the consumerist West comes by an extraordinary historical irony to find an image of itself in the wretched of the earth. If 'margins' are now much in vogue, it is partly because those who inhabit them clamour for political justice, and partly because a generation bereft of political memory has cynically abandoned all hope for the 'centre'. Like most US feminism, post-colonialism is a way of being politically radical without necessarily being anti-capitalist, and so is a peculiarly hospitable form of leftism for a 'post-political' world. Gayatri Spivak, by contrast, has kept faith, however ambiguously, with the socialist tradition; but though she has a good many striking perceptions about Marxism in this book, she is too deeply invested in feminism and post-colonialism to launch a full-scale socialist critique of these currents. And just as she straddles two worlds here, so her work's rather tiresome habit of self-theatricalising and self-alluding is the colonial's ironic self-performance, a satirical stab at scholarly impersonality, and a familiar American cult of personality.

There are some kinds of criticism—Orwell's would do as an example —which are a good deal more politically radical than their bluffly commonsensical style would suggest. For all his dyspepsia about shock-headed Marxists, not to speak of his apparent willingness to shop Communists to the state, Orwell's politics are much more far-reaching than his conventionally-minded prose would suggest. With much post-colonial writing, the situation is just the reverse. Its flamboyant theoretical avant-gardism conceals a rather modest political agenda. Where it ventures political proposals at all, which is rare enough, they hardly have the revolutionary élan of its scandalous speculations on desire or the death of Man or the end of History. This is a feature shared by

Derrida, Foucault and others like them, who veer between a cult of theoretical 'madness' or 'monstrosity' and a more restrained, reformist sort of politics, retreating from the one front to the other depending on the direction of the critical fire.

Derrida—a consecrated figure for this book, about whom hardly a breath of criticism seems permissible—can sometimes make deconstruction sound like such an ordinary, affirmative, innocuous sort of affair that one wonders why Christopher Ricks and Denis Donoghue do not instantly rush to embrace it. At other times, and for other audiences, it becomes a far more menacing, subversive matter: nothing less than a radicalised form of Marxism, a claim which must come as a mighty surprise to most deconstructionists and all Marxists. Deconstruction can indeed be a politically destabilising manoeuvre, but devotees like Gayatri Spivak ought to acknowledge its displacing effect, too. Like much cultural theory, it can allow one to speak darkly of subversion while leaving one's actual politics only slightly to the left of Edward Kennedy's. For some post-colonial theorists, for example, the concept of emancipation is embarrassingly old-hat. For some American feminists, socialism is as alien a territory as Alpha Centauri.

Gayatri Spivak's own politics are as elusive as her thought-processes; but there are signs in this study that she, too, is rather more audacious about epistemology than she is about social reconstruction. At times, she will speak positively about the need for new laws, health and education systems, relations of production; at other times, in familiar post-colonial style, her emphasis is less on transformation than on resistance. Resistance suggests militant action, but also implies that the political buck is always elsewhere. It is a convenient doctrine for those who dislike what the system does while doubting that they will ever be strong enough to bring it down. Marxism, for Spivak if not for its founder, is a speculation rather than a programme, and can only have violent consequences if used for 'predictive social engineering'. Like the thought of strangling your flat-mate, in other words, it is all very well as long as you don't act on it. The current system of power can be ceaselessly 'interrupted', deferred or 'pushed away', but to try to get beyond it altogether is the most credulous form of utopianism.

This may well turn out to be true; but it sounds a little too undeconstructively sure of itself as it stands, just as this book assumes (rather than openly argues) the dogmatic postmodern case that almost all

universalism is reactionary, almost all transgression or disruption positive, and almost all attempts at precise calculation a form of dominative
reason. For Spivak, to propose an 'other' to what we have at present is
to deny one's inevitable complicity with what we have, and so to leave
critics like herself particularly vulnerable. Nobody would imagine that
Stanley Fish was not up to his ears in capitalism, not least Stanley Fish;
but there are a number of gullible souls in US graduate programmes
who might just make the mistake of seeing Gayatri Spivak as some avatar
of pure alterity. She herself is rightly out to scotch this sentimentalism,
reminding these fans of the Black Female that she is also a highly-paid
bourgeoise and the scion of a colonial élite. She would thus rather opt for
the bad faith of refusing the system while proposing no general alternative to it, than the bad faith of denying her collusion with it.

Guilt can be just as disabling as arrogance, however. The political
good which Spivak has done far outweighs the fact that she leads a well-
heeled life in the States. If complicity means living in capitalist society,
then just about everyone but Fidel Castro stands accused of it; if it
means 'buying in' (as the Americans revealingly phrase it) to something
called Western Reason, then only those racist or non-dialectical thinkers for whom such reason is uniformly oppressive need worry about it.
The word 'complicit' has an ominous ring to it, but there is nothing
ominous about being 'complicit' with the Child Poverty Action Group
or the writings of the suffragettes. In any case, Spivak is logically mistaken to suppose that imagining some overall alternative to the current
system means claiming to be unblemished by it. To imagine that it
would be nice to be in Siena is not necessarily to disavow the fact that I
am in Scunthorpe. She contrasts her own critique of metropolitan post-
colonial theory with her Indian colleague Aijaz Ahmad's scorching
assault on it in his book *In Theory*, and describes her own volume as
'more nuanced with a productive acknowledgment of complicity'. But
why exactly should this be thought a virtue, if the result is a less
searching account? Ahmad may dissemble his involvement in what he
attacks, at least in Spivak's view, but this does not automatically make
for a less accurate portrayal of it. In any case, Ahmad arguably is less
'complicit' than Spivak: he has spent far less time teaching in the West,
is more explicitly committed to a socialist alternative to it, and far less
enamoured of recent Western-bred theories. But it does not really
matter: what matters is how well he writes on post-colonial theory, a

body of work which you can dismiss in Delhi just as you can support it in Sacramento. The post-structuralist emphasis on 'subject position' is oddly akin to the existentialist obsession with authenticity: what matters is less what you say than the fact that *you* are saying it. Liberalism, rather similarly, tends to believe that what is chosen is less important than the fact that I choose it, and is thus an ethic peculiarly fit for adolescents. But it is post-colonialism we are interested in, not the bad faith or psychic hang-ups of its academic practitioners. Spivak is a resolute anti-intentionalist when it comes to other people's works, but constantly anecdotal and autobiographical when it comes to her own. If this is an admirable attempt to introduce a spot of subjectivity into the impersonal debates of the patriarchs, it also betrays rather too much concern with one subjectivity in particular.

When it comes to the idea of resistance, one must surely as a stout Derridean take 'a certain caution, a vigilance, a persistent taking of distance', to quote Spivak's own words on a different matter. Quite a few people in the Soviet bloc in the mid-1980s were convinced that their political system could be resisted but not transformed; but this opinion turned out in the end to be a little too rigid, even if what that system changed into was hardly a just society. One might add that, when the time to sweep away this power structure arrived, collective agency proved not such an essentialising fiction, or precise calculation such a liability, as the post-structuralists seem to imagine.

Harold Bloom

Harold Bloom was once an interesting critic. In the 1970s, he developed an extravagant theory of literary creation for which all authors were locked in Oedipal combat with some mighty predecessor. Literature was the upshot of rivalry and resentment, as poets beset by what Bloom called the 'anxiety of influence' sought to triumph over some 'strong' precursor by rewriting his or her text as their own. All literary works were a kind of plagiarism, a creative misreading of earlier efforts. Wordsworth tried to kill off Milton and Shelley had it in for Shakespeare. The meaning of a poem was another poem.

This theory, as Henry Fielding observed of the belief that the good will get their reward in this world, had only one drawback, namely that it was not true. But it was original, audacious and exciting, and a spot of wild implausibility did it no harm at all. It was also remarkably cunning. What it did was to blend a traditional idea of literature with a modern one, thus winning itself the best of both worlds. Literature was still a matter of great traditions and lonely giants bestriding history, as it had been for early Oxbridge aesthetes like Sir Arthur Quiller-Couch; but these mighty patriarchs were now pitched into a very Freudian antagonism. Bloom was an embattled Romantic, speaking up for genius, inspiration and the creative imagination in a cynically postmodern world. Yet the message would get through to that world only if it was given a suitably bleak, up-to-date twist. You still had literary heroes, masters and disciples; it was just that what they did now was deconstruct each other.

Then, as now, Bloom was deeply scornful of historical criticism. Great

First published as 'The Crack of Bloom' (a review of *How to Read and Why* by Harold Bloom) in the *Observer*, 20 August 2000.

writers needed no historical context any more than a gentleman needed to buy in his own marmalade. But it was always clear how socially conditioned Bloom's criticism was. These poetic warriors locked in virile combat were good old American entrepreneurs in literary clothing, Davy Crocketts and Donald Trumps of the spirit who shaped the world to their imperious will. Bloom spoke up for universal humanity in a New York accent. Poetry had become a kind of Wall Street of the soul, full of pushy young brokers intent on sweeping the old guard into the gutter. His rage against material limit, his pioneering belief in the indomitable will, was as American as cherry pie. It was just that he mistook this for some universal truth.

The critical wheel, however, has come full circle. Aghast at the theoretical excesses to which he so robustly contributed, Bloom, on the threshold of his seventieth birthday, has reverted to the quote-and-dote school of criticism. Indeed, he has fallen back to a level of critical banality which might even have embarrassed Quiller-Couch.

How to Read and Why takes us on a Cook's tour of some of its author's favourite poems, plays and novels, boring the reader with plodding plot summaries or ludicrously long quotations and then adding a few amateurish, undemanding comments. Thus, Maupassant is 'marvellously readable', the pleasures of great poetry are 'many and varied', while 'Shelley and Keats were very different poets, and were not quite friends'. We are exhorted to chant a particular poem out loud repeatedly, and advised in an arresting flash of moral insight that 'in Raskolnikov's Petersburg, as in Macbeth's bewitched Scotland, we, too, might commit murders'. We are also instructed that 'irony broadly means saying one thing and meaning another' and is much to be commended, though this portentously self-important book would collapse at the faintest whiff of it.

It would be charitable to think that Bloom writes as slackly and cackhandedly as he does because he is out to attract the general reader. He is admirably intent on rescuing literature from the arcane rituals of US academia and restoring it to a wider audience. Even so, you cannot help suspecting that this rambling, platitudinous stuff is about the best he can now muster. As with all his work, a certain desperation runs beneath the heroism. Literature is the last surviving source of value in a degraded world, the only antidote to an academia obsessed with crossdressing and multiculturalism.

Bloom is right to criticise US academia as sexually obsessed; but if literature is all that stands between us and suicide, then we might as well commit suicide. He comments after a reading of Browning's poem 'Childe Roland' that 'we have renewed and augmented the self, despite its despair, and its suicidal courting of failure'. Reading is a kind of confidence-boosting or spiritual muscle-building, a familiar enough American fetish from a man who claims to detest ideology.

His criticism is all about the success ethic and the terrors of being a loser. 'The creator of Sir John Falstaff, of Hamlet, and of Rosalind', he tells us, 'also makes me wish I could be more myself.' There are those malicious souls for whom Bloom is quite enough himself without there being even more of him, but the notion of reading as a kind of self-entrepreneurship is plain enough.

Why does Bloom need to augment the self? 'We read', he suggests, 'not only because we cannot know enough people, but because friendship is so vulnerable, so likely to diminish or disappear, overcome by space, time, imperfect sympathies and all the sorrows of familial and passional life.' It sounds as though Harold is a bit short of mates and reads to make up for it. Perhaps he alienates them by his repeated chanting of excessively long poems.

But there are other reasons for reading besides 'alleviating loneliness'. If there is Bloom the self-therapist, there is also Bloom the American TV evangelist, full of windy moralistic rhetoric about how to 'apprehend and recognise the possibility of the good, help it to endure, give it space in your life'. Bloom may idolise Shakespeare with all the sticky sentiment of a teenage groupie, but his own language can be as cheap and threadbare as Jimmy Swaggart's. This book provides us with a number of reasons to read great literature, but none at all to read Harold Bloom.

Stanley Fish

It is one of the minor symptoms of the mental decline of the United
States that Stanley Fish is thought to be on the Left. By some of his
compatriots, anyway, and no doubt by himself. In a nation so politically
addled that 'liberal' can mean 'state interventionist' and 'libertarian-
ism' letting the poor die on the streets, this is perhaps not wholly
unpredictable.

Stanley Fish, lawyer and literary critic, is in truth about as left-wing as
Donald Trump. Indeed, he is the Donald Trump of American academia, a brash, noisy entrepreneur of the intellect who pushes his ideas in
the conceptual marketplace with all the fervour with which others
peddle second-hand Hoovers. Unlike today's corporate executive,
however, who has scrupulously acquired the rhetoric of consensus and
multiculturalism, Fish is an old-style, free-booting captain of industry
who has no intention of clasping both of your hands earnestly in his
and asking whether you feel comfortable with being fired. He fancies
himself as an intellectual boot-boy, the scourge of wimpish pluralists
and Nancy-boy liberals, and that ominous bulge in his jacket is not to be
mistaken for a volume of Milton.

What Fish has in fact done is to hijack an apparently radical epistemology for tamely conservative ends. Epistemologically speaking, he is a
full-blooded anti-foundationalist for whom everything comes down to
contingent cultural beliefs. These beliefs now occupy the loftily transcendental place vacated by previous candidates for the job, such as God,
Geist or Reason. They are transcendental a prioris in the sense that you
can't ask where they come from, or whether they are valid or reason-

First published as 'The Estate Agent' (a review of *The Trouble with Principle* by
Stanley Fish) in the *London Review of Books*, 2 March 2000.

able, since the answers to such questions will be shaped from within your own belief system. You are thus forced back on an old-fashioned fideism: nothing in the world could count as evidence for your beliefs, since what we gullibly call the world is simply a construct of them. And since you do not relate to your convictions as you relate to your socks, selecting a sombre or stylish brand as the fancy takes you, you are as lumbered with them as you are with the size of your feet. Beliefs are constitutive of the self, and so cannot be critically questioned by it. While I am believing I cannot stop believing, just as I cannot not be yawning as long as I am yawning. Convictions are more like influenza than intellectual acts. For Fish, a man has no more control over his beliefs than some ideologues believe he has over his penis. If everyone in the United States must nowadays be a victim of something, Fish is a self-confessed victim of his own assumptions, which exert their mindless tyranny over him as ruthlessly as Stalin held sway over the kulaks.

In a series of audacious bounds, then, we have argued our way from a 'radical' anti-foundationalism to a defence of the Free World. This leaves Fish in the enviable position of accruing cultural capital to himself by engaging in avant-garde theory while continuing to defend the world of Dan Quayle. A superficially historicist, materialist case— our beliefs and assumptions are embedded in our practical forms of life—leads not only to a kind of epistemological idealism, but to the deeply convenient doctrine that our way of life cannot be criticised as a whole. For who would be doing the criticising? Not us, since we cannot leap out of our local cultural skins to survey ourselves from some Olympian viewpoint; and not them either, since they inhabit a different culture which is incommensurable with our own. *They* may think that we are raiding their raw materials and exploiting their labour power, but that is just because they have never heard of the civilising mission of the West. The felicitous upshot is that nobody can ever criticise Fish, since if their criticisms are intelligible to him, they belong to his cultural game and are thus not really criticisms at all; and if they are not intelligible, they belong to some other set of conventions entirely and are therefore irrelevant.

This whole discreditable epistemology rests on a number of errors. In its credulous assumption that any thoroughgoing critique would need to be launched from some metaphysical outer space, it shares the delusion of the liberalism it detests. The only difference is that whereas some liberals used to think that there was such a vantage-point, pragmatists like Fish think that there isn't. Nothing has otherwise altered. To imagine that we are either the helpless prisoners of our beliefs or their supremely disinterested critic is to pose the problem in an absurdly polarised form. Here as usual, Fish's rather stagey relish for the melodramatic theoretical gesture leads him astray. It prevents him from seeing that a certain capacity for critical self-distancing is actually part of the way we are bound up with the world, not some chimerical alternative to it. His case fudges the question of how people come to change their minds, just as it adopts an untenably monistic view of the relations between a specific belief system and particular bits of evidence. It also suggests that we cannot ask where our beliefs come from because any answer to this question would be predetermined by our beliefs.

But the belief that our beliefs are bound up with a historical form of life is itself a belief bound up with a historical form of life. Fish's penchant for the local and partisan, his aversion to human rights and abstract principles, his contempt for what he calls 'mutual co-operation and egalitarian justice', his macho scorn for tolerance and impartiality—all this belongs to a very definite advanced capitalist culture, although Fish, in ironic violation of his own tenets, appears to regard such doctrines as universally valid. Perhaps it is Fish, rather than some universalist abstraction called humanity, who is unable to distance his own beliefs and place them in a broader historical context.

Like most of his compatriots, Fish is not the most cosmopolitan of creatures. The essays in *The Trouble with Principle* deal with racism, pornography, abortion, free speech, religion, sexual discrimination, in fact most of the stock-in-trade of enlightened US academia. This, on any estimate, is a pressing agenda; but it does not betray the slightest sense that there is anything else in the political universe worth discussing. With typical American parochialism and self-obsession, Fish's book is silent about famine, forced migration, revolutionary nationalism, military aggression, the depredations of capital, the inequities of world trade, the disintegration of whole communities. Yet these have been the consequences of the system of which the United States is the linchpin for many perched on the unmetaphysical outside of it. Being unable to leap out of your own cultural skin seems to mean in Fish's case having no grasp of how your country is helping to wreak havoc in that inscrutable place known as abroad. One has the indelible impression that Fish does not think a great deal of abroad, and would be quite happy to see it abolished. He is strenuously opposed to hate speech, but appears utterly ignorant of the structural conditions in his own backyard which give rise to such ethnic conflict. Indeed, he champions the social and economic order which helps to breed the effects he deplores. He is rightly concerned about anti-abortion fanatics, but not, as far as one can judge, about the military, ecological and economic threat which his country represents for so much of the world. For him as for many of his 'leftist' colleagues, a good deal of morality seems to come down to sex, just as it always has for the puritanical Right.

The Trouble with Principle is a series of polemics against liberalism, and scores some splendid points against the creed. Being something of a bruiser, and furnished with the ferociously competitive instinct of a small boy, Fish is almost pathologically allergic to cosy pluralism, and sees shrewdly how it can spring from there being nothing much at stake in the first place. He understands how the procedural formalism of liberal doctrine can trivialise the actual content of passionately held positions, and how its tenderly sentimental equalising of all viewpoints can mask a callous indifference. Like a traditional 'virtue' moralist, he holds that what is at stake in political ethics is the substance of a way of life, not just who gets to determine it. He is alert to the bogus impartiality of a liberalism which has decided in advance what is to count as a viewpoint to be tolerated, and is agreeably scathing about what he calls 'boutique multiculturalism'. Unlike many liberals, he does not make the mistake of seeing zero-sum conflict as necessarily destructive. On the contrary, he refuses to varnish the truth that there are a good many important contentions which someone is going to have to win and someone else to lose. Nor does he indulge in the liberal hypocrisy that power is ipso facto a bad thing, an opinion usually maintained only by those who have it. It is true that he might profit from relishing power a little less flamboyantly, but at least he seems to see that whether it is good or bad depends on who is doing what with it in which situation.

On the other hand, as the good liberals tend to say, Fish cannot for the life of him understand how someone can be tolerant and committed at the same time. If one cannot sit loose to one's own convictions, then tolerance can only be a sham. Fish thus detests liberalism rather as a hill-billy might detest the rococo self-qualifyings of a Jamesian New Yorker too pussyfooting and polite to say what he means. For Fish, liberals really have no balls, and his aversion to them seems quite as temperamental as it is theoretical. But tolerance is not just a question of style, and it is perfectly compatible with passionate partisanship. Fish does not see this because he too often thinks of tolerance as a psychological affair rather than a political one. If I am tolerant, however, this does not necessarily mean that I hold my own opinions lukewarmly; it means that I allow you to hold yours as fervently as I hold mine. Indeed, I am quite as passionate about this as you are about your desire to have your own view prevail at all costs. It is not, as Fish tends to suspect, that liberals are eunuchs whereas the *engagé* like himself are real men. Not all liberals are Laodiceans, and how zealously one holds one's own beliefs will not in itself tell us whether opposing opinions should be censored. Given the strength of my own convictions, I may find it inconceivable that others can hold the views they do, but this does not necessarily mean that I clamour for their suppression. Why she thinks Bill Clinton is a saint is a mystery, but she can broadcast the opinion from the rooftops for all I care. On the other hand, I may have quite a good understanding of what brings some people to be racists, and may well imagine myself feeling the same in similar circumstances, while firmly agreeing with Fish that racists should not be permitted to express their prejudices in public.

Phenomenologically speaking, I cannot imagine what it would be like not to believe that Bill Gates has a somewhat anaemic sense of the human soul. But I can imagine the kinds of condition which would compel me to abandon this prejudice, such as his suddenly publishing a novel of such metaphysical magnificence as to put *The Magic Mountain* in the shade. The opposite of tolerance in this respect is not conviction but dogmatism; and since dogmatism means among other things refusing to elucidate the grounds on which one holds one's beliefs, Fish, for whom beliefs would seem as mysteriously given as the planet Venus, is guilty of the offence. When A.J.P. Taylor remarked that he had extreme views but held them moderately, he may have meant, as Fish would be bound to claim, that he did not really hold them at all. He was, after all, being interviewed for a Magdalen College fellowship at the time. But he may have meant that, though he indeed believed what he believed, he did not believe in pushing his opinions down people's throats, or hanging others bound and gagged from the rafters while he hectored them. Fish, by contrast, sees all conviction as necessarily authoritarian, since he imagines that the political institution of tolerance is just a fancy way of not having the courage of one's convictions. And this is the rather sinister side of his sometimes bracing critique of liberalism.

The Trouble with Principle is quite right to insist that there are views which should not be tolerated, and that free speech is thus in any absolute sense an illusion. It is salutary that no one in Britain for quite some time has been able to utter certain sorts of insult in public without running the risk of criminal prosecution. But Fish, with his usual eye for theatrical effect, enlists this for a swingeing assault on the principles of tolerance, impartiality and mutual respect, as though the fact that they, like any principles, have to allow for important exceptions must necessarily invalidate them altogether. Nor is it anything but sophistry to claim that, since all speech acts are socially conditioned, no speech is really free. This is rather like claiming that since swanning around the Savoy all day is quite as shaped by social convention as labouring in a salt mine, guests at the Savoy are no freer than miners.

Fish dislikes principles because they are abstract, universal, neutral, formalistic and inflexible. By defining all principle in such sublimely Kantian terms, he engages in his usual custom of straw-targeting his antagonist in order to ensure himself a Pyrrhic victory. Everyone is against this kind of principle, just as everyone is opposed to sin. But without certain general principles we would not even be able to identify concrete situations; and when Fish tells us, as though he were telling us news, that abstractions such as justice or equality must be further specified, he is maintaining that it is these abstractions which must be thickened up, rather than, say, the principle that all children under six should be tortured. To that extent, at least, he is committing himself to the language of liberalism. On his own view of things, how could he not, since he is a historical product of it?

In any case, once one begins to spell out why one wants to promote certain partisan interests, it becomes notoriously hard to avoid the language of generality altogether. Even Fish's opposition to hate speech must presumably include, somewhere along the line, the fact that the vilified group is a collection of humans rather than a bunch of hollyhocks, if one may employ a term ('human') which some pragmatists find rather distasteful. *The Trouble with Principle* veers accordingly between a tough but implausible case (all general principles are bogus) and a mild but boring one (all principles must be concretely specified, and will alter in the process) to which hardly anyone, least of all Hegel, would take exception. Like almost all diatribes against univesalism, it has its own rigid universals: in this case, the priority at all times and places of sectoral interests, the permanence of conflict, the a priori status of belief systems, the rhetorical character of truth, the fact that all apparent openness is secretly closure, and the like.

Fish's appeals to history are almost always gestural. He means by history something like what Henry Kissinger means by it—that is, as far back as he can remember. This is a pity, since if he had a rather richer sense of the past he might recognise that the universalist liberal principles he abhors were once the last word in iconoclasm. In the age of Enlightenment, appeals to difference, specificity and local interests were often enough reactionary, and claims to universality could topple princes from their thrones. For a true pragmatist, general principles are as general principles do; at some times and places they may be a lot more subversive or emancipatory than at others. And if lots of local cultures find universal principles useful things to adhere to from time to time, as they plainly do, why should a pragmatist like Fish be so universally dismissive of them?

What these essays do, in effect, is what so much postmodern thought does when confronted with a 'bad' universality—which is to say, set up a 'bad' particularism in its place. They fail to grasp that such militant particularism is just the flipside of the vacuous universalism it deplores, rather than a genuine alternative to it. Stanley Fish is the flipside of John Rawls rather as tribalism is the terrible twin of globalism, or the view from nowhere is inevitably countered by the view from us alone. In this respect, Fish is a fully paid-up tribalist who like Slobodan Milosevic, champions a unique people moulded by its own peculiar customs and traditions. It is just that to Milosevic these people are known as Serbs, and to Fish as academics. One might even dub him something of a communitarian (several of his objections to liberalism, such as his view of the relations between belief and selfhood, are of this kind), were it not for the fact that he despises all such gooey human togetherness for much the same reasons that one imagines Clint Eastwood does.

In the teeth of all such soppy consensus, Fish is a Hobbesian and Machiavellian who enjoys conflict, believes only in what he can taste and handle, and likes to win. He sees his dislike of universal essences as anti-Platonic, though much of the time this is just a high-toned way of saying that he has the outlook on life of an estate agent. It is unclear how winning and intolerance go together, since you cannot be said to have beaten a rival whom you have tethered to the starting blocks; but it is clear enough how this philosophy, which Fish implicitly recommends as universally valid, fits rather better with being the dean of a US university at the turn of the millennium than it does with being a sixth-century Scottish hermit.

To refer to Fish the Dean, however, is to reveal the fact that there are two Fishes, Little and Big. Little Fish is a sabre-rattling polemicist given to scandalously provocative pronouncements: truth is rhetoric, free speech is an illusion, unprincipled behaviour is best. Big Fish is the respectable academic who will instantly undercut the force of these utterances by insisting that they are descriptive rather than normative. Far from being radical recommendations, they simply describe what we do anyway without always knowing it, and 'theory', the Trumps of this world will be relieved to learn, thus has no effect whatsoever on practice. Anti-foundationalism is therefore unlikely to alienate the New York Foundations, and Fish can buy his reputation as an iconoclast on the cheap.

Little Fish is in hot pursuit of a case which will succeed in alienating absolutely everyone; he is the cross-grained outsider who speaks up for minorities, and himself Jewish, comes from one such cultural margin. Big Fish, by contrast, has a consensual, good-boy disdain for rebels, whose behaviour is in his eyes just as convention-bound as those they lambast. It is fortunate for this schizoid character that there is a place where aggression and consensus go together. It is known as the US corporation, of which the campus is a microcosm. In academia, you can hammer your colleagues, safe in the knowledge that, since you all subscribe to the same professional rules, it doesn't really mean a thing.

There is an evident contradiction between the self-interested behaviour of advanced capitalism, and the consensual character of its liberal ideologies. Into this embarrassing gap, *The Trouble with Principle* inserts its mischievous, sub-Nietzschean thesis that we should acknowledge that the God of consensuality is dead and come clean about the self-interest. So far, the system has always resisted this seductive solution to its contradiction, in the belief that hypocrisy was a price worth paying for a few rags of ideological respectability. Fish's work may be one straw in the wind turning an increasingly self-discrediting social order towards this more insolently up-front self-apologia. And if Fish is Nietzschean enough in this, so is he in the eternal recurrence of his writing. He now seems to have written the same book several times over—after you have stated that everything comes down to cultural beliefs, it is hard to know what to do next but to say it again, this time with a few different examples. Perhaps, in order to break new ground, Fish will just have to wait for his beliefs to change, as a man might await the moment when his cell door swings open.

George Steiner

Most of George Steiner's books have mildly sensationalist titles. *The Death of Tragedy, After Babel, In Bluebeard's Castle*—these are the works of a man for whom ideas still have the power to shock and exhilarate, scandalise or enthral. Steiner may be one of the last of the great breed of European humanists; but he is also an intellectual showman with a canny sense of theatre, a flamboyant conjurer who pulls author after author out of the apparently bottomless hat of his erudition.

A book by Steiner is as instantly recognisable as a sculpture by Henry Moore. There is the polymathic range, the burnished, high-pitched rhetoric, the elegaic mood, the magisterial tone. Steiner's favourite mode is the interrogative, which sometimes means posing impossible questions to which neither he or anyone else could conceivably know the answers. 'What was the average lexical capacity of a Castilian peasant of the early 15th century?' would be a (semi-fictitious) example. 'Who, today, reads Statius?' he asks at one point in this dense, strange study. To which the only honest answer is: Who? But Steiner knows who Statius is, as he seems to know about everything from music to mathematics, nuclear physics to negative theology.

'Knows', however, is a chequered term. There are times in his work when Steiner seems to be coruscating on thin ice, and patches of his formidable learning, which he wears heavily enough, might not bear too persistent a probing. The philosopher Wittgenstein did not say that the unwritten *half* of his celebrated *Tractatus* was the most important part, nor does the New Testament have Jesus announcing 'When Abraham was, I am'. Neither is most of what Jesus says in the future

First published as 'Patches of Learning' (a review of *Grammars of Creation* by George Steiner) in the *Independent on Sunday*, 18 March 2001.

tense. But these, like other minor errors in this book, are not the point. One does not go to George Steiner, any more than one goes to the *National Enquirer*, for the facts. One turns to this great hedonist of ideas to renew one's sense of the mighty roller-coastering adventures of the intellect, as well as to savour the distinctive aroma of a European humanism now almost exhausted.

Steiner's range of cultural reference is extraordinary. On a single, randomly selected page of this book, about 350 words in all, he alludes oracularly to Homer, Flaubert, Mozart, Cervantes, La Fontaine, Aeschylus, Dickens, Thomas Mann, Proust, Chaucer and Molière. He is one of the most imaginatively audacious thinkers of our time, though usually more provocative than precise: 'The issue is that of the nature of being', he grandiloquently opens a paragraph. Others may write of Camus or cauliflowers; Steiner writes of creation. The Steinerian tone is liturgical, rhapsodic, and his reverence for the life of the mind is well-nigh religious. He is, indeed, a reluctant rabbi, one of those wounded refugees from the ruins of classical European culture who sets up home with art because—however much he may yearn to do so—he cannot find shelter with God.

Poetry, music, mathematics, speculative metaphysics: these, Steiner announces, are the great domains of human creation. One might notice, less euphorically, that they are also all refuges from the torture-chamber of history for the aloof, unhoused, abstract mind. Without the arts, Steiner tells us in a typical flourish, 'the human psyche would stand naked in the face of personal extinction', as though all of those countless millions without the benefit of his own expensive aesthetic education are a prey to madness and despair. His patrician disdain for the products of modernity is implacable. At one point in this book, he refers quaintly to 'a provincial omnibus', as someone might still speak of the wireless or the electrical telephone.

But this contempt for the modern has its darker roots in his Judaic sense of tragedy. *Grammars of Creation* opens by evoking a 20th century so steeped in blood that the political death toll from 1914 to Bosnia might well number 70 million. It is against this ominous background that the book poses its typically searching questions: What is it to make a beginning? What is the act of creation? Is innovation possible at all? Do we ever really invent, or do we simply discover what was there in the first place?

Steiner, as the priest of high modernism, would still like to believe in pure creativity, as against those postmodernists for whom everything is a quotation, a derivative, a recycled version of something else. What more shop-soiled quotation is there than 'I love you', even when passionately meant? But this book is also gripped by the notion that to create is to tear a kind of wound in some primordial nothingness. In the beginning there was nothing, and to create is thus inevitably to blemish that purity. Since he quotes more or less everyone else on the topic, Steiner might also have quoted here the German dramatist Georg Büchner, in his play *Danton's Death*: 'Nothingness has killed itself, and creation is its wound'. And as Laurence Sterne reminds us, in a venerable Irish tradition, there is much to be said for nothing, considering some of the other things that are in the world.

The work of art is plagued by the sense of its own gratuitous nature—by the thought that it might just as well never have been, that nothing legitimates its existence beyond itself. But Steiner misses an important theological insight here. To say of the world that it is 'created' is for classical theology to say that it is pointless. Like God, and like humanity, it exists purely for its own delight. God created the world just for the hell of it, as a quick look round will doubtless confirm. Creation is a scandal to the sharp-faced stockbrokers for whom everything must have a point.

Like almost all Steiner's works, *Grammars of Creation* is a *tour de force*, a dazzlingly virtuoso performance. It also takes itself very seriously indeed, and would collapse in ruins at the slightest breath of humour, vulnerability or earthy irreverence. It is a brooding, haunted study, full of dark forebodings and apocalyptic rumblings. All that holds out against the abyss, in the end, is art—and nothing could be more abysmal a reflection than that. But what also fends off the demons is Steiner's style—all those rich, rhapsodic metaphors by which he maintains a precarious edge over darkness.

Steven Lukes

Most astrophysicists could write a bad novel, whereas few novelists could rise to being even poor astrophysicists. Those who live in the world of letters have to suffer the humiliation of knowing that, like courting or clog dancing, writing fiction is something that almost anyone can do indifferently. There is a nasty piece of work inside most of us. The author of a study of Durkheim would not seem the most obvious candidate for literary creation, but Steven Lukes's novel is as enjoyable as it is because, not in spite of, the fact that he is a political philosopher. Political theorists, after all, concern themselves with human conduct, as astrophysicists do not; and Anglo-Saxon philosophers are notable for their penchant for jokes, satiric gibes, homespun examples, dotty anecdotes, as German Neo-Hegelians on the whole are not. One would not rush to open a novel by Jürgen Habermas, but Richard Rorty no doubt has a few suave short stories inside him. There are philosophical idioms which are inherently anti-fictional—positivism, for instance —and those which lend themselves naturally to literature. It is no accident that Sartre, whose philosophical thought turns on angst and nausea, should have been the novelist and playwright that one suspects Frege or Husserl could never have been. For many Anglo-Saxon philosophers, this is more or less equivalent to confessing that Sartre wasn't doing philosophy at all, even though one of the texts they most revere, Wittgenstein's *Philosophical Investigations*, is a ragbag of fictional devices. The style of philosophising of the *Investigations* is that of a man who valued art above philosophy, and who dreamed of writing a philoso-

First published as 'Love thy neighbourhood' (a review of *The Curious Enlightenment of Professor Caritat* by Stephen Lukes) in the *London Review of Books*, 16 November 1995.

phical treatise consisting of nothing but jokes.

Steven Lukes's moral fable is in the tradition of tall travellers' tales from Swift and Voltaire to Lewis Carroll and Samuel Butler. Professor Nicholas Caritat, unworldly scholar of the Enlightenment, is forced out of Militaria, his savagely autocratic homeland, and sent off by an improbable plot device in pursuit of the best of all possible societies. His first port of call is Utilitaria, a lethally rational state whose Houyhnhnm-like inhabitants ride roughshod over individual freedom and justice in the name of the general happiness. They run an efficient welfare service but have no fear of death, sense of gratitude or conception of human rights, and (since Utilitarians are ethical consequentialists) they spurn the past and fetishise the future. They are also toying with the idea of putting Frustricide into the water supply, to eliminate desires which can't be satisfied. A thinly disguised version of the Birmingham Six case exposes Lord Denning's judgments on the matter (better to imprison the innocent than bring the law into disrepute) as a classic example of Utilitarian callousness.

From this anodyne utopia, Caritat beats a retreat to Communitaria, a country which works in Gadamerian vein through 'unspoken understandings, unexamined traditions and slowly evolving customs', and whose motto is 'Love Thy Neighbourhood as Thy Self'. Ethnically obsessed and stiflingly conformist, Communitaria is North American identity politics at its most Stalinistic; all cultures deserve equal respect, none can be criticised by another, and the self is rigorously defined by its communal allegiances. There are Acute Akimboists and Loose Akimboists, Stalagmites who see life as upward progress and Stalactites who view it as progressive decline. A list of these groups is available at the airport and enrolment is compulsory. The most grievous crime here is to slight another's cultural identity, and a young artist hounded for blasphemy, for supposedly satirising his own people, sounds dimly familiar. He hadn't actually meant his rock opera to be satirical—indeed Communitaria has no such concept—but the poststructuralist law court has judged that meaning is socially constructed rather than authorially intended.

Besieged by furious feminists from Polygopolis Unidiversity, the hapless professor flees to Libertaria, dreaming briefly en route of being shown round another country by two guides, Karl and Fred. In Proletaria, the state, law, money and markets have withered away, the division of labour has been abolished and there is material abundance for all. Libertaria turns out to be more or less the opposite: a glittering wasteland of social despair and neo-liberal greed, ruled over by the formidable Hilda Juggernaut, where they are selling off shares in the National Library and turning schizophrenics into the street. Forced to survive as a hospital porter, Caritat, accompanied by a garrulous owl of Minerva, finally makes his escape over the border in search of Egalitaria, a land which may prove either a heuristic fiction or a historical possibility. On this wistfully suspended note, the novel shifts out of its satirical register into a genuinely moving conclusion.

Caritat, who holds imaginary conversations with Kant and Condorcet, is a liberal rationalist much in the mould of his creator. There is a smack of such rationalism about the very form of the 18th-century moral fable, which subdues the contingencies of experience to a diagrammatic whole; and this artistic shape is in tension with Lukes's liberalism, which seeks to redeem human freedom and complexity from the tyranny of a single doctrine. What the novel says, and what it does, are thus intriguingly at odds: its allegorical, universalising narrative at once defends and undercuts the particular, just as its disillusioned substance runs counter to its light-hearted style. ('A Pessimist says: "Things could not be worse." An Optimist says: "Oh yes, they could." ') Like all anti-Utilitarian exhortations, it cannot avoid falling prey to a certain didactic utility itself, just as *Tom Jones* tries paradoxically to teach us that virtue is for the most part spontaneous.

Eighteenth-century satirists like Swift and Fielding commonly operate a kind of double optic, using some unworldly innocent to lay bare human degeneracy while deploying the fact of vice to deflate the idealist illusions of the innocent. How can virtue look out for itself, be worldly-wise, and still be virtue? So it is that Swift can round brutally on the boneheaded Gulliver just as we are tempted to take him for our window on the world, a temptation encouraged by the very form of the traveller's tale. Readers understandably identify with fictional travellers, however morally dubious they may be, since they provide the one constant factor in a fleeting succession of locales, and so seem more real than their environs. To undercut one's own protagonist is a neat way of frustrating readerly expectations; and it is to Lukes's credit that he is a good enough liberal to be open-minded about his own liberalism. In a scene reminiscent of the metaphysical encounters between

Naphta and Settembrini in *The Magic Mountain*, Caritat's Enlightenment faith is put to the test by a priest who, with impressive eloquence, rubs his nose in the nightmare of history. Yet one cannot help detecting something of a shuffle here. For Caritat is in fact a somewhat muted Enlightenment apologist, more of a mild reformist than a full-blooded progressivist; and this means that the novel can allow itself to send up grandiose rationalist notions of universal progress while covertly rescuing its own more qualified liberal principles. Those principles are not allowed to be challenged by having the professor actually drop in on a liberal society. The Enlightenment is upbraided for its academicist idealism; but ineffectiveness is not the same thing as error, and the novel does not always draw the line or grasp the relation between the two. Nor is the Enlightenment fundamentally criticised for being itself one of the sources of places like Utilitaria, Libertaria and even—by strident over-reaction—Communitaria. It remains a utopian alternative to these dismal regimes, which indeed it is, rather than being also, in its less savoury aspects, a fetishism of Reason and suppression of the particular which helped to produce them. The novel is thus not quite as even-handed about its own informing beliefs as it would wish to appear.

As for the belief-systems which Caritat encounters, the story is, one might claim, at once too even-handed and not even-handed enough. Lukes has some wonderful fun at the expense of his monstrous doctrinaires, but the mischievous partisanship of satire is at odds with his own liberal values. The treatment of Utilitaria contains some rich reflections, but it is for the most part crudely caricatural; everyone carries a calculator around and jabbers about productivity, and while it is funny to have a family called the Maximands it is cartoonish to have a character called Stella Yardstick. For Lukes, as for the equally glib Dickens of *Hard Times*, Utilitarianism seems to come down to a cold-hearted obsession with statistics, a straw target which is hardly in line with the subtle ethics examined by James Griffin in his study *Well-Being*. Communitaria is a brilliant comic riot but lamentably skewed: not all feminists are moral fascists, and respecting other people's cultures, as opposed to treating them as holy writ, is a necessary if not sufficient condition for the just society. Here, Lukes risks playing straight into the hands of the *Daily Mail*. It is part of the self-assurance of *Gulliver's Travels*, as well as part of its deviousness, that it can occasionally find something of value in the social orders it lampoons: the Brobdingnagians are a fairly commendable species, and even the Yahoos have their finer points.

In the end, however, Lukes is too judicious. Caritat's final judgment on his various ports of call is that each of them pursues one admirable ideal—order, freedom, happiness, community and so on—but in doing so loses sight of the others. The political enemy is not really callousness or greed or bigotry but fanaticism. This is an impeccably liberal claim; but it is stated rather than shown, and one wonders to what extent the text itself subverts it. Libertaria, for example, is a hell-hole not because it fails to combine its inherently admirable idea of freedom with the demands of community or stable identity, but because its idea of freedom is a grisly parody of the genuine article. Communitaria does not enjoy a rich conception of community which is fatally flawed by what it excludes, but practises a form of collectivism which is intrinsically oppressive. It is not just a matter of seeing things steadily and seeing them whole. In any case, the novel advances that doctrine with understandable unease—for how is one to distinguish between a liberalism which aims to mediate all points of view from yet another tyrannical totality? As Will Ladislaw remarks in *Middlemarch*, there can be a 'fanaticism of sympathy' too, and a synthesis is not easily demarcated from a monolith.

The novel's most 'symptomatic' moment, in the Freudian sense of the term, is its Proletaria episode—a fantasy within a fiction. The curious brevity and dreamlike status of this chapter are not the only indications that the author does not know quite what to think about his own creation. There are satirical markers in plenty, but few substantive criticisms of a Communist land of Cockaigne which has long since left its dogmatic phase behind. Perhaps the novel feels able to indulge this pastoral idyll precisely because of its unreality; or perhaps it is Marxism which is objectionably tunnel-visioned rather than the pluralistic Communism to which it might lead, in which case the novel's distaste for monistic views is interestingly complicated. Whatever the reason, the odd faltering of tonal consistency here shows up, by contrast, what is over-achieved elsewhere. The suppleness of Swift's satire means that we are sometimes unnervingly unsure of what exactly is under assault, which is hardly ever the case with this latter-day reinvention. Lukes's allegory, while deftly sustained, is rather too instantly decodable, in need of a little more opacity and obliquity. In good rationalist mode, it is somewhat too transparent: a truly effective allegory generates ambiguous relations between its manifest and latent meanings. On the other hand, although it sacrifices the pleasures of the enigmatic, it is replete with the delights of recognition, at once estranging and reinforcing the familiar. And it manages for the most part to tread a hair-thin line between esoteric in-jokes and laborious explication. The trick isn't always successfully turned; the force of a verbal slip in Utilitaria between 'Pushkin' and 'pushpin' is blunted by a dutiful citation of Bentham's notorious levelling of poetry and pushpin. But this is just an instance of the author's enlightened democratic impulse getting the better of Enlightenment élitism, and so a microcosm of the vexed relations between abstract ideas and political power which this novel so satisfyingly explores.

David Harvey

From the Romantics to the modernists, time was a fertile concept and space a sterile one. Space was static, empty, what you had between your ears or needed to eradicate by bridging; time—or perhaps history—was fluid, burgeoning, open-ended. For a modernist writer like Bertolt Brecht change in itself is a good, just as for Samuel Johnson change was in itself an evil. Bad things were reified products; good things were dynamically evolving processes.

This piece of Romantic banality never went entirely unchallenged. If Pascal was still able to glimpse in space an unsettling sublimity, Marx found in capitalism a system which was claustrophobic exactly because it never stopped evolving. As some modernist artists came to arrest and disorder time, some of their hemmed-in urban audiences began to appreciate the virtues of space. Space became something we needed to give each other, no longer flat but curved, constructed by the mind or by the mutual pressures of the planets. In a post-Einsteinian epoch it began to take on some of time's more alluring qualities: mobile, heterogeneous, multi-layered, no longer sheer void but dynamic force, mutating like a living organism. In the guise of environment, it became something to be nurtured and revered; as the medium carved out by the interplay of our bodies, it was enticingly eroticised. 'Stasis' gave way to the rather more appealing 'structure', and Pascal's sense of sublimity returned in the pleasantly spooky sense that there was something out there in outer space. Spaces were now pregnant with possibility, and

First published as 'Spaced Out' (a review of *Justice, Nature and the Geography of Difference* by David Harvey) in the *London Review of Books*, 24 April 1997.

intellectual life was a matter of terrains of discourse and continents of enquiry. To be spaced-out was no longer to be depleted.

We had, in short, had enough of historicism. The Romantic dream of some infinite temporal unfolding of our creative powers had been aimed at a sternly repressive God, but had ended up as a humanist mirror-image of His omnipotence. There was something unpleasantly self-promoting about this generous-sounding humanism, which in its haste to praise human uniqueness ignored what we had in common with slugs. Historicism needed to be humbled by the biological and the geographical; we had to be recalled to our creatureliness, whipped back inside our material limits, and space—not least because we had all too little of it—was one mode of that self-chastening.

Space is nowadays not only catching up with time but pulling ahead of it. In the shape of the untheorisable uniqueness of place, it has come for some postmodern minds to figure as the joker in the conceptual pack, that which resists abstraction and disrupts all metanarrative. It is now time which is drearily homogeneous, just the same damn thing over again, a phallic trajectory in contrast to the teeming womb of spatiality. And while space has been busy wreaking its revenge on time, nature has been asserting its rights over human history, which is now viewed by the more sinister sort of ecologist as a cancerous growth on the world's body. Hence the paradox of a postmodernist age which insists that everything comes down to culture while turning contemptuously from culture to nature. Both ecology and cultural relativism are ways of dethroning the sovereignty of universal man.

In an age when the traditional boundaries between intellectual disciplines are rapidly blurring, geography shares with literary studies the signal advantage of never having had much idea of what it was about in the first place. Just as literary studies covers everything from dactyls to death, geography spans everything from sand dunes to marriage rituals. David Harvey, the doyen of radical geographers, writes of material limits in a language which disdains all bounds, crossing from Spinoza to scallop fishing, the architecture of Baltimore to the circulation of capital. *Justice, Nature and the Geography of Difference*, which argues the case for a materialist, relational concept of time and space, is a buckled, ramshackle, almost comically ambitious book, which manages to combine modernity and postmodernity, ethics and ethnicity, nature and culture, universality and uniqueness, in its very title. Just as David

Lodge's fictitious literary critic Morris Zapp hoped to bring criticism to a halt by writing on every conceivable author from every imaginable approach, so Harvey has more than a touch of Life, the Universe and Everything about him, pushing the fuzzy boundaries of his academic discipline to cosmic proportions.

In an age which has fetishised the fragment, Harvey's dialectical concern with whole systems and their internal contradictions is bravely unfashionable. In a methodological Introduction on the nature of dialectical thought, he has much of value to say about the priority of relations over things, the mutual constitution of part and whole, the way that forces both resist and collude with one another. But to deny the very distinctions between mind and matter, fact and value, thought and action, as Harvey tends to do, is to sound more like a monist than a dialectician; and though he is well aware of the vacuousness of claiming that everything is related to everything else—that the Pentagon and my left armpit are subtly interconnected—his extension of dialectics from history to nature courts precisely this danger. *Othello* may be said to be internally contradictory, but in what sense is an onion? What of the case that contradictions apply to the realm of meaning rather than of matter, and can be used of badgers and bananas only in some far-fetched metaphorical sense? Both history and nature are matters of process, to be sure; but to over-emphasise this is to risk eliding the distinctions between them in positivist or idealist style. A river does not flow as a sonnet does, nor does time fly like a goose.

As a radical, Harvey believes that change and instability are the norm; but that this is not always politically true is one reason for being a radical in the first place. History from a socialist viewpoint has been at least as much tedious continuity as giddy change. Nor is it persuasive to suggest, as he does, that the stable features of our world are just 'reifications of free-flowing processes', another piece of old-style Romantic vitalism. Objects are not just snarl-ups in the onward flow of nature. If it is illuminating to show that capital is a process rather than a thing, it is not especially eye-opening to show that a banjo is. To dissolve human beings to nexuses of processes may be useful if you had previously thought of them as solitary atoms, but unhelpful when you want to insist on their moral autonomy. Identities are not just Platonic illusions thrown up by a processual reality.

Much of this rather arid Introduction, which oddly discovers dialectical thought in the implacably anti-Hegelian Foucault, could have been profitably slimmed. Part Two of the book turns to nature and ecology, kicking off with a comment by a group of Baltimore blacks some years ago that their main environmental problem was known as President Nixon. Among more important things, the remark serves to illustrate the emptiness of the term 'environment', and Harvey himself is far from some tremulous tree-hugger. Reminding us that the first radical environmentalists in charge of a state were known as Nazis, he claims that there is almost always an authoritarian edge to ecological politics, and with brusque impiety regards New York as an 'ecosystem' which is no more remote from nature than Moreton-in-Marsh. Native peoples are not always ecological angels, and doomsday scenarios ignore the fact that the conditions of human life are better today than they have ever been. 'It is materially impossible for us to destroy the planet earth', Harvey asserts with what some will read as cool realism and others as scandalous complacency. He also rightly considers, against the more Neanderthal type of environmentalist, that controlling nature and dominating it are far from synonymous.

For Harvey, there can be no question of relating society to the eco-system: the very distinction is fraudulent. Money flows and commodity movements are as central to the environment as whales and waterfalls, and debates about preserving nature are really arguments about pre-serving particular social orders. Space and time are social products, and different societies produce qualitatively different conceptions of them. New notions of space-time have been imposed by imperial conquest or colonial domination, and contemporary capitalism has dramatically compacted both time and space with its instant decision-making and dismantling of distances. The more global space becomes homo-genised, however, the more fine differences between places come to matter, since multinational capital is better able to exploit them. And the more somewhere becomes everywhere, the more these somewheres need to attract investment by demonstrating that they are not just anywhere. A relentless levelling of space thus finds its counterpart in various clamorous cults of difference, all the way from nationalism and post-structuralism to the exotic tourist resort, the uniquely hospitable city and the proliferation of jelly bean flavours.

Yet place, in Harvey's dialectical vision, can be a resistance to capital accumulation as well as a form of complicity with it. Place is space, but also in a way its opposite: as a locus of human longings and desires, a site of memories and affections, it represents all that the commodity form finds it hardest to squash. The problem is how a viable sense of place is to be disentangled from mystified Heideggerian mumblings about authentic in-dwelling, just as some genuine meaning of 'community' has to be salvaged from those American communitarians for whom it seems to mean beating up your neighbours if you catch them smoking on the street. Place can be seen as a 'closed terrain of social control', or as an apparent 'permanency' which is in fact always a social process. Some of Harvey's most compelling chapters are about space and time as social artefacts—the way, for example, in which the female-controlled space of the household comes to be disrupted by the insertion of that privatised male space known as the study, sign of a lofty intellect beyond sexuality and domestic labour.

There is something challengingly counter-intuitive about such claims for us heirs of the Enlightenment, since it is well-nigh impossible for us not to see space and time as containers within which things happen, stable frameworks of social action rather than constitutive structures of it. It is hard not to feel that a caterpillar was three inches long even before we came to invent such measurements, or that if it is Tuesday on earth then it must also be Tuesday on Saturn. We can quite easily imagine that there was a space of a certain size which someone then walled off, or catch ourselves marvelling at the exquisitely exact way in which Bradford fits into the area provided for it. In fact, we are busy fashioning the nothing we call space all the time. But there are puzzles even so, which Harvey does not adequately examine. To produce space we need already to be standing in space, just as a new conception of time must have emerged at some particular time. And if colonialists really can reorganise the space and time of their colonial subjects, on what spatio-temporal plane do the initial encounters between them take place?

The dialectic at the heart of Harvey's book is one between difference and universality, which he rightly takes to lie also at the root of the idea of justice. How are we to avoid at once a fetish of the particular and a universalism cruelly indifferent to difference? If old-fashioned Left internationalism was callously cavalier about the pieties of place, sex, body, the postmodern politics which have followed have too often been unable to raise their eyes above their bellies. As Harvey reminds us, the dialectic is delivered to us every morning along with the Rice Krispies: we continue to enjoy a self-contained relation to our breakfast, even though it took millions of people to place it before us. The postmodern vision is at once too parochial and too cosmopolitan, delighting in disconnection while for the most part blandly endorsing an increasingly regimented world order. Harvey is out to provide us with a more dia-lectical relationship of part and whole, a universality which works through difference rather than against it. This is as true of the form of his book as of its content, shifting as it does from Leibniz to workplace safety regulations, Bakhtin and Whitehead to the hazardous waste sites of Mississippi. This is not the kind of geographical discourse we learnt at school, where geography was about maps as history was about chaps. But the book accumulates this prodigal wealth of insights only at the risk of a compulsive relating of everything to everything else which leaves it shapeless. Harvey too often sounds as though he is thinking relaxedly out loud, with a touch too much assurance that nobody will shut him up. His rapid shifts from philosophy to the high street are an admirably bold instance of dialectical thought, yet succeed more than once in showing up the yawning gap between the two. 'One of the viruses of a dialectical/relational approach', he writes, 'is that it opens up all sorts of possibilities which might otherwise appear foreclosed.' Though 'viruses' is presumably a misprint for 'virtues', its suggestion of both scrambling and uncontrolled proliferation is none the less appropriate.

This is, however, symptomatic of a general political condition, not just a compositional failing. If *Justice, Nature and the Geography of Differ-ence* veers somewhat unsteadily between the universal space of theory and the specific places of politics, it is partly because it knows that the problems it broaches could only be resolved by a change in what we do, not just in how we think. Harvey believes that if we pursue only those ecological projects compatible with democracy and equality, we will find ourselves with precious few options. He also agrees with some postmodern critiques of universalist notions of justice, while believing that we can't get on politically without such ideas. Like Walter Benja-min, he is a compulsive collector of theoretical odds and ends, since in our current confused conditions you can never know which of them is going to come in handy. His book is too much a compendium of other people's work, too doggedly encyclopedic in method; but hardly any other Western academic has such an assured command of so many intellectual idioms, or such devotion to that in human life which is not, in the end, a question of intellect at all.

Slavoj Žižek

Schopenhauer saw us all as permanently pregnant with monsters, bearing at the very core of our being something implacably alien to it. He called this the Will, which was the stuff out of which we were made and yet was utterly indifferent to us, lending us an illusion of purpose but itself aimless and senseless. Freud, who was much taken with Schopenhauer, offered us a non-metaphysical version of this monstrosity in the notion of desire, a profoundly inhuman process which is deaf to meaning, which has its own sweet way with us and secretly cares for nothing but itself. Desire is nothing personal: it is an affliction that was lying in wait for us from the outset, a perversion in which we get involuntarily swept up, a refractory medium into which we are plunged at birth. For Freud, what makes us human subjects is this foreign body lodged inside us, which invades our flesh like a lethal virus and yet, like the Almighty for Thomas Aquinas, is closer to us than we are to ourselves.

This 'Thing', as the psychoanalyst Jacques Lacan calls it, with horror movies archly in mind, is otherwise known as the Real, in the Lacanian Holy Trinity of the Real, the Imaginary and the Symbolic. It is also the chief protagonist of the work of the Slovenian philosopher Slavoj Žižek, who by drawing our attention to this most underprivileged of Lacan's three categories, challenges his fashionable image as a 'post-structuralist' thinker. Žižek's Lacan is not the philosopher of the floating signifier but a much tougher, alarming, uncanny sort of theorist altogether, who teaches that the Real which makes us what we are is not

First published as 'Enjoy!' (a review of *The Indivisible Remainder: An Essay on Schelling and Related Matters* by Slavoj Žižek; *The Abyss of Freedom/Ages of the World* by Slavoj Žižek/F.W.J. von Schelling; *The Plague of Fantasies* by Slavoj Žižek) in the *London Review of Books*, 27 November 1997.

only traumatic and impenetrable but cruel, obscene, vacuous, mean-
ingless and horrifically enjoyable. Žižek himself is both dauntingly
prolific and dazzlingly versatile, able to leap in a paragraph from Hegel
to *Jurassic Park*, Kafka to the Ku Klux Klan; but just as Lacan's fantasy-
ridden world of everyday reality conceals an immutable kernel of the
Real, so Žižek's flamboyant parade of topics recircles, in book after
book, to this very same subject. The almost comic versatility of his
interests masks a compulsive repetition of the same. His books, as in
Freud's notion of the uncanny, are both familiar and unfamiliar,
breathtakingly innovative yet *déjà lu*, crammed with original insights yet
perpetual recyclings of one another. If he reads Lacan as 'a succession
of attempts to seize the same persistent traumatic kernel', much the
same can be said of his own writing, which continually bursts out anew
with Schelling or Hitchcock or the war in Bosnia but never shifts its gaze
from the same fearful, fascinating psychical scene.

As Žižek sees it, the Real for Lacan is almost the opposite of reality,
reality being for Lacan just a low-grade place of fantasy in which we
shelter from the terrors of the Real, a Soho of the psyche. The natural
state of the human animal is to live a phantasmal lie. Fantasy is not the
opposite of reality: it is what plugs the void in our being so that the set
of fictions we call reality are able to emerge. The Real is rather the
primordial wound we incurred by our fall from the pre-Oedipal Eden,
the gash in our being where we were torn loose from Nature, and from
which desire flows unstaunchably. Though we repress this trauma, it
persists within us as the hard core of the self. Something is missing
inside us which makes us what we are, a muteness which resists being
signified but which shows up negatively as the outer limit of our discourse, the point at which our representations crumble and fail.

Lacan's infamous 'transcendental signifier' is just the signifier which
represents this failure of representation, rather as the phallus for psychoanalysis represents the fact that it can always be cut off. The Real is
what cannot be included within any of our symbolic systems, but whose
very absence skews them out of shape, as a kind of vortex around which
they are bent out of true. It is the factor which ensures that as human
subjects we never quite add up, which throws us subtly out of kilter so
that we can never be identical with ourselves. It is a version of Kant's
unknowable thing-in-itself, and what is ultimately unknowable is Man
himself.

The Real is desire, but for Lacan, so Žižek argues, more specifically *jouissance* or 'obscene enjoyment'. This enjoyment, which sounds rather less suburban in French, is a sublimely terrifying affair. It is the lethal pleasure of what Freud calls primary masochism, in which we reap delight from the way that the Law or super-ego unleashes its demented sadism on us. Enjoyment, Lacan maintains, is the only substance which psychoanalysis recognises, and it is also Žižek's unwavering obsession. Like Schopenhauer's Will, it is a brute, self-serving affair, as devoid of meaning as the American waiter's mechanical injunction: 'Enjoy!' Like the waiter, the Law instructs us to enjoy, but does so in curiously intransitive mood: we are just to reap gratification for its own sake from the super-ego's crazed, pointless dictats. In *The Sublime Object of Ideology*, Žižek sees ideological power as resting finally on the libidinal rather than the conceptual, on the way we hug our chains rather than the way we entertain beliefs. At the root of meaning, for both Freud and Lacan, there is always a sustaining residue of non-sense.

The Real is the 'inruption' of that nonsense into our signifying systems, and so a much crasser affair than language. But because it can never be signified, seen head-on, it is also a sort of nothing, detectable only through its effects, constructed backward after the event. We know it only from the way it acts as a drag on our discourse, as astronomers may identify a heavenly body only because of its warping effect on the space around it. For the Real to take on tangible embodiment, to crop up in the shape of voices or visions, is for us to become psychotic. The Real is the McGuffin, the joker in the pack, the sign that means nothing but itself. Every signifying system, so Žižek claims, contains a kind of super-signifier whose function is just to point to the fact that the system can't be totalised. It is that system's point of internal fracture, marking the space where it doesn't quite gel. But this absence is what organises the whole system, and so is also a kind of presence within it. You can call this constitutive lack the human subject itself, which is necessary for any set of signs to work, yet which can never be fully encapsulated by them. But this, for Lacan, is also the function of the Real, whose very absence from consciousness is the cause of our carrying on trying to signify it there and always failing. If we failed to keep failing and trying again, if the repression was lifted and the Real burst to the surface, history would instantly cease. In this sense, the sheer impossibility of desire, the fact that we can only ever plug our lack with one poor fantasy object after another, is also what keeps us up and running. That fissure or hindrance in our being which is the Real is also what props up our identity.

This, one might claim, is a classically post-structuralist sort of doctrine. Post-structuralists have almost patented the paradox that what makes something impossible is also what makes it possible. As every first-year English student now knows, what makes a sign a sign is its difference from other signs; but this means that the difference which lends a sign its identity also makes it impossible for a sign to be complete in itself. Difference, as Jacques Derrida playfully puts it, both 'broaches and breaches' meaning. Or take the idea, much touted by Žižek, that blindness is the condition of insight, truth the upshot of misrecognition. For Nietzsche, it is only a blessed state of amnesia that enables us to act, since otherwise we would simply be paralysed by the nightmare of history. For Freud, we are shaped into human subjects only by a shattering repression of much that went into our making. It is this crippling forgetfulness which allows us to thrive. The roots of our conscious life must be absent from it if we are to function as subjects at all, rather as the law, if it is to maintain its august authority, must erase the fact that it was originally imposed by an arbitrary act of violence. The law cannot have been established legally, since there was no law before the law.

Žižek's favourite philosopher, after Lacan, is Hegel, who can also be used to illustrate this paradox. For Hegel, truth is not so much the opposite of error as the result of it. The cunning of Reason lies in the fact that our blunders and oversights, did we but know it, have already been reckoned into account by truth itself, as the very process by which it is achieved. Truth looks like an end-product, but turns out to encompass the whole process of trial and error which led up to it. When we are able to look back and understand that those misrecognitions were essential to the whole enterprise, this is, according to Žižek's rather heterodox view, the moment of truth or Absolute Idea. Similarly, when the analysand is able to free herself from the illusion that there is some truth quite separate from the business of transference, some transcendental knowledge of which the analyst has possession, then for the Lacanians she is en route to a cure. Žižek illustrates the point with the story of a man faking insanity in order to escape conscription, whose 'psychosis' takes the form of rummaging obsessively through a pile of documents saying, 'That's not it, that's not it!' When the doctors, convinced by this frenetic performance, finally present him with a certificate of exemption, he exclaims: 'That's it!' What looked like the result of his behaviour was actually the cause of it, and this reversal of cause and effect is a staple of psychoanalytic theory which Žižek expounds—as he expounds everything else—with extraordinary brio and élan.

He is, in fact, the most formidably brilliant exponent of psycho-analysis, indeed of cultural theory in general, to have emerged in Europe for some decades. The fact that he hails from a former Com-munist society is probably not accidental in this respect, since there was always a certain market for French theory in the Eastern bloc. If the secret police do not take kindly to talk of political resistance, you can always recode it as deconstructing totalities, subverting the Master-Sig-nifier, opening up to the Other. Jacques Derrida had a following in Communist Poland and was arrested for trading on the philosophical black market in former Czechoslovakia. Beijing today boasts an Institute of postmodern Studies, where you can talk of difference and desire without unduly alarming the authorities. Žižek himself is one of a high-powered circle of Ljubljana Lacanians, a man with active political interests in the new Slovenia.

This background is also perhaps relevant to his passion for the Real. Lacan, as we have seen, is not for Žižek a post-structuralist in the popular, packaged sense of the word ('spaghetti structuralism', as Žižek scornfully dubs it), which means dissolving everything into discourse. On the contrary, the whole point of the Real is to give language the slip, block it from the inside, bend the signifier out of true. For Lacan, language is forced up against the wall of the Real and made to turn out its empty pockets. Žižek, who enjoys finding arcane meanings in bits of cliché, would doubtless bark 'Get Real!' to those for whom language is all there is. But this concern for what defeats totality, for the way desire gets thwarted, for how an autocratic authority sadistically enjoins us to enjoy that condition: all of this can surely be read against the back-ground of that mass blockage of desire, along with a cynical invitation to the masses to hug their chains, which was bureaucratic Communism.

There is a parallel here with that other Eastern European heretic, Milan Kundera. In *The Unbearable Lightness of Being*, Kundera speaks of a contrast between the 'angelic' and the 'demonic', the former signifying too much meaning and the latter too little. Totalitarian states are angelic, fearful of obscurity, dragging everything into luminous significance and instant legibility; the demonic, by contrast, is marked by a cynical cackle which revolts against the tidy sense-making of tyranny by revelling in the brute meaninglessness of things. It is not hard to spot Lacan's Symbolic Order in the former and his Real in the latter, or to understand why the sheer contingency of the Real, its trick of disrupting closed symbolic systems with a reminder of unsatisfied desire, should have an appeal to an Eastern European intellectual. What one might call Lacan's ethical imperative—his injunction to the patient not to give up on his desire even while acknowledging its impossibility—sounds rather like the position of Polish Solidarity in its darkest days.

Indeed, for Lacan, the psychoanalytic cure is a little like the achievement of political independence. What troubles us most deeply in Lacan's view is the fact that, though our desire is always the desire of the Other (i.e. drawn from the Other, as well as directed to it), we can never be entirely sure what it is that the Other is demanding of us, since any demand has to be interpreted, and so to be garbled by the duplicitous signifier. 'What do they want of me, what am I expected to be?' is the insistent query which for Lacan hollows our being into desire. The cured patient is the one who has given up on this unanswerable question, acknowledged that her desire is entirely self-grounding, embraced the utter contingency of her own being and relinquished the futile quest of having it confirmed from the outside. If this has a faint resemblance to getting out from under a political oppressor, it also, as Žižek reminds us, has more than a smack of the saint. The image of the cured patient, one might claim, is Samuel Richardson's raped Clarissa, who by the end of his novel has turned her face to the wall, renounced the claims of others and embraced her death by withdrawing her body from libidinal circulation. To be cured of your psychic ailments, you really need to be a saint, which is perhaps one reason why psychoanalysis is such a lengthy, precarious affair.

There is another sense in which Žižek's Marxist background is relevant. No acolyte of Lacan from Paris or Pittsburgh would have anything like Žižek's political nous, a faculty you develop spontaneously in a place where the political is the colour of everyday life. Lacan himself, who advances an essentially tragic philosophy of life, had a lofty contempt for politics, indeed for history as such; whereas Žižek, who fails for the

most part to comment on his mentor's dandyish megalomania, is a
post-Marxist who applies his psychoanalytic insights to racism, nationalism, anti-semitism, totalitarianism, the commodity form. It is hardly
surprising that a psychoanalytic theorist of such virtuosity should have
emerged from the ethnic conflicts of former Yugoslavia, just as Europe's previous most fruitful encounter between Marx and Freud was
the product of a Frankfurt School on the run from Nazi anti-semitism.

Racism, nationalism, anti-semitism are where the abstruse categories
of psychoanalysis are brought home to everyday political life. And Žižek,
who was writing at one point with the Bosnian war on his doorstep, has
a sense of the Realpolitik of the psyche quite foreign to the gentrified,
consumerist, post-ideological Western world for which he has such
proper contempt. If he is more unabashedly theoretical than the typical
Anglo-Saxon intellectual, he is also a lot more practical. He is even
getting a little restive these days with his own post-Marxism, chiding its
neglect of the economic in traditional Marxist style. He is startlingly
casual—indeed, for such a profoundly sophisticated thinker, almost
naive—in the way that he moves so directly from the psychoanalytic to
the political, a frontier along which many a fellow theorist has preferred
to pussyfoot. Fetishism, scapegoating, splitting, foreclosure, disavowal,
idealising, projection: if these are the familiar mechanisms of the
Freudian psyche, they are also mass movements, political strategies,
military campaigns. Writing during the Bosnian war in *Metastases of
Enjoyment* (1994) of a New Zealand tribe who invented a grotesque war
dance for the delectation of some visiting anthropologists, he notes that
'David Owen and companions are today's version of the expedition to
the New Zealand tribe: they act and react exactly in the same way,
overlooking how the entire spectacle of "old hatreds suddenly erupting
in their primordial cruelty" is a dance staged for their eyes, a dance for
which the West is thoroughly responsible.'

'I am convinced of my proper grasp of some Lacanian concept', Žižek
writes, 'only when I can translate it successfully into the inherent
imbecility of popular culture.' His works are awash with allusions to
detective fiction and David Lynch, movies and musicals. A particularly
tricky aspect of Schelling's notion of freedom is illuminated by the
Flintstones, while Kant's doctrine of the transcendental unity of apper-
ception is exemplified by vampire novels. An aesthetic distinction
between classical and avant-garde music is illustrated by whether or not

the audience cough and shuffle at the end of a movement. Commentaries on the films of Hitchcock—Žižek's King Charles's Head, one might say—almost outnumber his analyses of Hegel. In a fine essay on *Psycho* in *Everything You Always Wanted to Know about Lacan (But Were Afraid to Ask Hitchcock)*, a collection of Hitchcock essays by various hands, he treats us to a Lacanian analysis of the moment when the camera first looks down from above on the private eye being attacked by the disguised Anthony Perkins, then cuts to a shot of the stabbed detective hurtling backwards down the staircase. The bird's-eye shot, so Žižek informs us, lays bare an apparently transparent reality, into which the opaque 'Thing' or enigmatic murderer suddenly intrudes; what follows, shockingly, is a shot of the murder victim from the 'impossible' viewpoint of the Thing itself.

The striking feature of Žižek's use of popular culture is its lack of coyness. Unlike his wilfully hermetic Parisian *maître*, his writing is splendidly crisp and lucid, even if his books can be fearsomely difficult. The difficulties belong to the ideas, not to the expression, a distinction between signified and signifier at which the wilder kind of post-structuralist would doubtless baulk. There is no sense that he is strenuously popularising—or of some contrived postmodern pastiche; soap operas and Disney cartoons are just part of his intellectual furniture, objects of his promiscuous inquiries as familiar as God, Kant or consumerism. His style is deep and light simultaneously, shot through with an intense political seriousness but never at all portentous. His prose resonates with the feel of a markedly idiosyncratic personality, but is curiously without self-display. The fact that he is so compulsively obsessional about both Lacan and Hitchcock is a kind of tacit running joke, something so embarrassingly obtrusive that it would be boring for either author or reader even to mention it.

Indeed, jokes form some of Žižek's primary philosophical examples. He has a good line in sardonic East European political humour, as when he remarks that the difference between the Soviet Union and Yugoslavia was that whereas in the former the people walked while their elected representatives drove cars, in the latter, more liberalised version of Communism, the people themselves drove cars through their elected representatives. To illustrate the dialectic of presence and absence, he recounts the story of a guide conducting some visitors round an East European art gallery and halting before a painting entitled *Lenin in*

Warsaw. There is no sign of Lenin in the picture; instead, it depicts Lenin's wife in bed with a handsome young member of the Central Committee. 'But where is Lenin?' inquire the bemused visitors, to which the guide gravely replies: 'Lenin is in Warsaw.'

Žižek thinks Hegel and Lacan entirely compatible, partly because he reads the former through the latter in a heretical deconstruction of Hegel's supposed holism. Indeed the flavour of his mind is thoroughly Hegelian, continually on the prowl for antitheses inverting themselves into identities, in a set of dialectical guerrilla raids on common sense. Some random examples: it is not that order and disorder are opposites, but that the imposition of a (purely contingent) order on chaos is itself the highest mode of disorder. The Lacanian Other—the Symbolic Order, or language as a whole—can have no Other to itself, which is to say that there can be no ultimate guarantee of the field of meaning. Multiculturalism is just a kind of racism in reverse, respecting another's culture from the distancing, unchallenged vantage-point of one's own. The law must be irrational, since if there were reasons for obeying it it would lose its absolute authority. The unconscious is not the opposite of consciousness, but the founding act of repression by which consciousness is established in the first place.

The following captures something of his characteristic intellectual style: 'At first glance it would seem that the sausage in the hot dog wedges apart the two pieces of roll. But the roll itself is nothing but a "space" which the sausage creates around it, the phantasmal "frame" or support of the sausage without which it would vanish to nothing. On the other hand, the sausage itself can be seen as no more than an embodied gap between the two pieces of bread, the mere pretext or occasion which prevents them from ever uniting.' This is my parody rather than Žižek's own words, but much odder passages are to be found in his work.

Žižek is especially deft-fingered when it comes to dismantling the opposition between the universal and the particular. The universal, he points out, must exclude particularity, and so can't really be as universal as it supposes. We have access to universals only because we are situated within a specific culture, a point which both rationalists and relativists might do well to ponder. Cultural relativism, Žižek notes, is much vexed by our supposed inability to gain access to the 'other'; but what if this other were inherently incomplete, and so in any case unknowable as a whole? What if what I share most deeply with the other is just the fact that I, too, am never self-transparent, never complete, never wholly bound to my own cultural context but always to some degree out of joint with it? What I and the other have in common is the fact that there is always something which eludes our grasp (Lacan's 'big Other'), and it is in the overlapping of these twin absences that we can meet. It is when we are able to discern the blindspot of another culture, its point of failure, that we are most at one with it, since it is just such an internal limit which constitutes our own forms of life, too.

In his latest two books, Žižek has turned to the study of the German philosopher F.W.J. Schelling, who over the past few years has been shot from Teutonic obscurity to something like philosophical stardom. Žižek, naturally, finds a lot of Lacan in Schelling, as he finds him in everything; but he also makes some rather extravagant claims for Schelling as a precursor of 'the entire post-Hegelian constellation', from Marxism and existentialism to deconstruction and New Age obscurantism. He is especially fascinated by Schelling's highly esoteric theology—unsurprisingly in a way, for what is the Real, this kink or deviation at the heart of things without which they would not work, but the fortunate Fall or *felix culpa*? The Real is a psychoanalytic version of Original Sin, and Schelling boldly applies this notion to God as well, who like us is never fully himself, plagued by a foreign body at the core of his being which is (one should have guessed it) precisely what allows him to be the Almighty. That the Creator is also afflicted by the Real is perhaps some small comfort to his creatures. It is curious that conservative pessimists who find no problem with the doctrine of Original Sin would doubtless dismiss both Lacan and Žižek as theoretical nihilists.

'If we were able to penetrate the exterior of things,' Schelling comments, 'we would see that the true stuff of all life and existence is the horrible.' One can see, then, why he is Žižek's sort of thinker. But Žižek never really takes time off from his explorations to reflect on just what a hideous view of human life he is delivering us, or on how this is compatible with the political dissent which he clearly still embraces. How is 'Lacanian radical' not to be as oxymoronic a phrase as 'military intelligence'? The view from the Real is admittedly no more horrible than what Anglican vicars are supposed to believe, but then Anglican vicars are not noted for their political radicalism. Just as human existence for Lacan is the fantasy by which we plug the terrifying void of the Real, so Žižek's chirpy wit and anecdotal relish serve in part to mask the obscene vision of humanity he offers.

If the only topic psychoanalysis recognises is enjoyment, the same might finally be said of Žižek the writer. His books have an enviable knack of making Kant or Kierkegaard sound riotously exciting; his writing bristles with difficulties but never serves up a turgid sentence. The demotic companionability of his style is an implicit rebuke to the high-minded terrorism of so much French theory. Lacan may insist that the analyst is an empty signifier, that he holds no secret key to the patient's unhappiness, but his posturing rhetoric belies any such disavowal. 'Enjoy!' is Žižek's implicit injunction to the reader, as he shifts within a single chapter from Mozart to time travel, hysteria to Judaism, Marx to Marlboro ads, while managing somehow to sustain a coherent argument. In his case too, however, form and content are subtly at variance. The mercurial sparkle of his work is at odds with its bleak, mechanically recurrent content, for which enjoyment, in the Real, is where we encounter the least delectable truths of all.

Stuart Hall

Anyone writing a novel about the British intellectual Left, who began by looking around for some exemplary fictional figure to link its various trends and phases, would find themselves spontaneously reinventing Stuart Hall. Since he arrived in Britain from Jamaica in 1951, Hall has been the sort of radical they might have despatched from Central Casting. Charming, charismatic, formidably bright and probably the most electrifying public speaker in the country, he is a kind of walking chronicle of everything from the New Left to New Times, Leavis to Lyotard, Aldermaston to ethnicity. He is also a Marxian version of Dorian Gray, a preternaturally youthful character whose personal style evokes a range of faded American epithets: hip, neat, cool, right-on.

There are two ways to recount his story, one less charitable than the other. The more jaundiced narrative is one of a relentless modishness. If you want to tune in to the latest style of leftspeak, find out what Stuart Hall is up to. Under his aegis, the Centre for Contemporary Cultural Studies at Birmingham University moved in the '70s from left-Leavisism to ethnomethodology, flirted half-heartedly with phenomenological sociology, emerged from a brief affair with Lévi-Straussian structuralism into the glacial grip of Louis Althusser, moved straight through Gramsci to post-Marxism, dived into discourse theory and teetered on the brink of postmodernism. Hall himself, having left the Centre in 1979 for the Chair of Sociology at the Open University, became a leading analyst of Thatcherism, coining the phrase 'authoritarian populism' for that

First published as 'The Hippest' (a review of *Stuart Hall: Critical Dialogues* edited by David Morley and Kuan-Hsing Chen) in the *London Review of Books*, 7 March 1996.

regime, and surfaced as a major architect of so-called New Times, a revisionist current close to the Communist Party which scandalised traditional socialists with its heretical relish for markets, mobility and shopping malls. Hall was now an enthusiast for the 'new movements' around race and feminism, an apologist for the decentred and diffuse, an ageing avantgardist who had been hopping from one cultural cutting-edge to another for almost half a century.

There are three things wrong with this tale of eclectic opportunism. To begin with, Hall helped to fashion many of the trends he conformed to. If he had the air of a camp-follower, he had usually pitched a fair bit of the camp himself. For another thing, his political surfing was not always smooth. A convinced pro-feminist, he was targeted as patriarch-to-hand by his feminist students at the Birmingham Centre, and escaped to the Open University from what sounds like a climate of ugly sectarianism. Charlotte Brunsdon deals with the episode in diplomatic retrospect in this volume of essays on his work. But in any case, Hall's chameleon-like career can be read just as plausibly in terms of consistency as of fashionability. Where he is now, proclaiming the virtues of a pluralist politics which thrusts culture to the fore, is pretty much where he kicked off in the days of the old New Left. It is not so much that he has come full circle as that he has hardly shifted. Or as though, after a long detour through rebarbative theories and revolutionary politics, the age has now finally caught up with him. As Colin Sparks reminds us, Hall was writing of such postmodern matters as the dissolution of the industrial working class as early as 1958.

Indeed, it is more than a glib piece of wordplay to claim that what has been unchanging about Hall is precisely his open-endedness. This is no doubt partly a matter of temperament and conviction, but also perhaps a question of his colonial origins. The move from the Caribbean to the Cowley Road was one between clashing cultural frames, whose partial, perspectival nature he was thus more likely to spot than, say, a Briton like Richard Hoggart, reared within a working-class milieu which seemed to be wall-to-wall. Hall was pitched between conceptual systems as well as countries, alert to the rough edges of any single doctrinal system, as heterodox in theory as he was hybrid in culture. It is no accident that he started on a postgraduate thesis at Oxford on Henry James, hardly the most congenial of topics for an English literary leftist, but with an obvious appeal for a student of intercultural relations.

His suspicion of fully-fledged systems is also, ironically enough, characteristically English. The most obviously alluring creed for Hall, Marxism, was one with a notoriously vexed relation to the conditions of the colonised, so that he was bound to come at it left-handedly. He never reneged on revolutionary Marxism, since—apart from a brief mid-'70s interlude in which 'Marxist' and 'cultural theorist' were as synonymous as Ivana Trump and liposuction—he was never much of a Marxist in the first place. In (post-) colonial conditions, culture is a vital medium of power, and culture, not least in the Stalinist '50s when Hall set out, had never exactly been Marxism's strongest point.

If culture is integral to colonial power, however, it is equally central to advanced capitalism, so that Hall was able to transport his 'culturalism' from colonial periphery to metropolitan centre. The colonial background which set him askew to classical industrial capitalism—he has never been much involved with proletarian politics in Britain, and sprang from a conservative middle-class family back home—was also, paradoxically, what lent power to his elbow as a commentator on a media-ridden, consumerist, post-imperial West for which culture was increasingly a significant political and economic issue, and which was now undergoing in its own way the kind of identity crisis it had once induced in its colonials. With fabular coincidence, Hall's emigration to Oxford as a Rhodes Scholar coincided with the first waves of Commonwealth immigrants to these shores in the '50s, rather as Oscar Wilde's earlier translation from Dublin to Magdalen represented a 'higher' enactment of one of the most common Irish experiences of his day. Nothing is more native to the colonies than getting out of them.

Commonwealth immigration was to throw up problems of culture and identity in the metropolitan heartlands which Hall, as an intellectual as well as an émigré, was peculiarly well placed to dissect—so that in this sense, too, the margins shifted with him to the centre. His in-betweenness meant a heightened awareness of cultural questions, which put him at odds with a reductionist Marxism; but it gave him also a feel for the relativity of particular cultures, which set him against the cultural absolutism of the literary establishment of the day. In time, that contradictory gesture of at once overrating the cultural, and sceptically patrolling the limits of any specific culture, was to lead him into the arms of the postmodernists. Reading the world in terms of culture is a familiar habit of the colonial subject; but it is also an occupational hazard of the metropolitan literary intellectual, and Hall happened to be both.

He was also, however, to blossom into a different species of intellectual altogether, as the various densely packed interviews with him in this collection testify well enough. Far more than Raymond Williams or Perry Anderson, and more persistently than E.P. Thompson, Hall has been the Left's finest instance of the strategic intellectual, the theorist as mediator and interventionist, broker and communicator, bringing the more arcane flights of Frankfurtian or post-structuralist theory to bear on questions of voting patterns and televisual imagery, racism and youth culture. Nimble, mercurial and timelessly up-to-date, he has nipped from one burningly topical issue to another, turning up wherever the action is, like a cross between a father figure and a Mr Fixit. Compared with Williams or Anderson, he is not an intellectual heavy-weight, and Jorge Larrain, in a strenuously analytic essay, has little trouble in spotlighting the flaws in his notion of ideology. In some forty years of ceaseless intellectual production, Hall has never authored a monograph. His elective genre is the essay, that most supple, tactical of literary forms, and he fashions it with a rare blend of metaphorical flourish and polemical punch. In contrast to the identikit style of many of his acolytes, exemplified here by the arthritic jargonising of the American sociologist Lawrence Grossberg's 'History, Politics and Post-modernism', Hall pitches his tone somewhere between heavy-duty theory and zesty journalism, at once quick-footed and high-minded, showman and specialist. He is less an original thinker than a brilliant *bricoleur*, an imaginative reinventor of other people's ideas, as his essay on 'The Problem of Ideology' in this volume well reveals.

Indeed, he shares with his New Left confrères Thompson and Williams a certain impatience with abstract notions, in which one can detect both the political activist and the residual Leavisite. His concrete, contextualising style of thought marks yet another fortunate conjuncture between what seems psychologically native to him, and what the age demands. If he theorises himself, he gives off the air of doing so on the hoof, en route from one meeting or motif to another, a prodigious improviser who can effortlessly churn out a sort of intellectual equivalent of rap. If he is sometimes a bit thin on the ground, with the odd bald patch peeping through his densely tressed conceptualisations, he compensates for this with a striking versatility, leaping from discourse to the diaspora, Rastafarianism to post-Fordism, with all the disdain for traditional academic demarcations of the classical left-wing intellectual. This intellectual range is reflected in his personal serenity of being, which seems to contain multitudes; but if he resembles Raymond Williams in this apparent equipoise, he combines it with something of the prophetic zeal of an Edward Thompson, and so appears eirenic and engagé together.

The frenetic recycling of theories in the realm of culture belongs to the very commodity fetishism it seeks to analyse. As a socialist, Stuart Hall is thus plainly sincere when he remarks in an interview in this book that 'I don't believe in the endless, trendy recycling of one fashionable theorist after another, as if you can wear new theories like t-shirts.' There is a kind of good sense or moral soundness about Hall, again ironically English in quality, which resists the more extravagant excesses of the postmodernism with which he fellow-travels. He would not, one suspects, be much enthralled by the card-carrying, right-on variety of the creed celebrated by Iain Chambers in a rhapsodic piece entitled 'Waiting on the End of the World?' This is partly a question of age: despite his generational cross-dressing, Hall, unlike any other contributor to this collection, is a veteran of Suez and Hungary, of the New Left clubs and early CND, and there is a world of difference between the subdued wisdom of the scarred veteran and the brittle cynicism of theorists bred in the discos. Chambers is all for disruption and destabilisation, in a cerebral sort of way; Hall, one imagines, has lived through quite enough of that to resist romanticising it.

But there are affinities between the generations, too, by which Hall must rightly feel rattled: if he has given up on revolutionary politics, they never even got to the starting line. If he is post-Marxist in the sense that Oasis come after the Beatles, they are post-Marxist in the sense that the Internet comes after the Somme. Hall may dislike trendy theories, but this is a bit like Jeffrey Bernard campaigning against drinking clubs. Whatever his reservations, he does stand for all the Right Things in the arena of cultural studies, impeccably anti-essentialist, anti-totalising, anti-reductionist, anti-naturalist and anti-teleological. In a furiously busy essay, Dick Hebdige delivers a convincing thumbnail sketch of postmodernism in just these terms; and if Hall really wants to put some daylight between himself and these banal pieties of the cultural Left, he might stop to consider whether essentialism, totality, teleology, human nature and the rest, defined in a less bugbearish way than the post-modernists conveniently insist on, might not be in some sense a good deal more radical than their modish opposites. For the moment, however, for all his open-mindedness, he is far too deeply mortgaged to this orthodoxy to countenance any such full-blooded challenge.

Even so, he is determined not to be its prisoner either. In an interview reprinted here, he castigates some postmodern notions as 'wildly exaggerated and ideological', rejects the fantasy that social life is nothing but discourse, reminds us that we are natural as well as cultural beings, and recalls those grim material constraints which the more callow forms of postmodernism would dissolve into a haze of signifiers. Not all of this would be music to the ears of, say, John Fiske, whose essay 'Opening the Hallway' upbraids the maestro for coming down too hard on Michel Foucault. Hall has been engaged for some time in a precarious balancing-act between socialism and postmodernism, class and race, epistemic realism and epistemic constructivism, and one name presiding over this trade-off in our times has been that of Antonio Gramsci. This ardent Leninist has come by a devious process of editing to stand for a Marxism soft-focused enough to suit a post-radical age. The real-life Gramsci helped to arm the Italian workers in 1920 and organise Red Guards and factory councils; he was a Communist Party boss who held out against a united front to defeat Fascism and for a while supported the line of the Soviet Stalinists. The fictional Gramsci constructed by cultural studies is a kind of Sardinian version of a London polytechnic lecturer in discourse theory, complete with enlightened opinions and pluralist politics, more interested in organising signifiers than auto-workers. He stands, in one of Hall's own slogans, for a 'Marxism without guarantees', which suggests a sort of liberal-Anglican brand of historical materialism, not too fussed about dogma and tradition.

More promisingly, Gramsci stands for a non-reductive style of Marxism which takes cultural meanings seriously without denying their material determinants, and it is this *via media* which Hall seeks to patrol. (Althusser also might stand for such a middle road, but his otherwise fairly orthodox Marxism is still disturbingly fresh in the post-Marxist mind, whereas Gramsci's even more orthodox Marxism has happily faded from memory. It also helps that Gramsci did not murder his wife.) Reductionism must be rejected, but not in the name of society as a completely open discursive field. The reality of representations must be acknowledged, but not at the price of denying that they do, after all, represent something beyond themselves. Discourse is of vital importance, but so are the historical forces which shape it. Language may never capture absolute truth, but this is not to see it as sheerly indeterminate. Identity politics must be affirmed, but not in a way which throws class struggle and material production onto the junk heap of history.

What seems problematic about all of these positions is how plainly true they are. There is something faintly ridiculous about Hall, or anyone else for that matter, having to argue with jaw-jutting defensiveness that there is more to the world than metaphor, that social class has not just evaporated, that a representation of a plum pudding cannot be eaten, that the fact there are no iron laws of history does not mean that we could slip back into feudalism next Wednesday. It is a sign of the portentous absurdity of so much postmodern thought that such glaringly self-evident positions need to be so loudly affirmed. And it is a mark of how much Stuart Hall is in thrall to this theoretical camp that he needs so defiantly to re-emphasise them.

The re-emphasis, for all that, is much to be welcomed. Hall, sensibly enough, wants the new without relinquishing the best of the old, and like all such straddlers is vulnerable to assault from both camps. If he is not quite Marxist enough for Colin Sparks's taste, in an essay which examines the New Left's oblique relation to the creed, one suspects there are others in the volume for whom he is rather too shamefaced a postmodernist. It is as though he has turned postmodernism's own sceptical open-endedness against itself, outflanking it with its own logic; and if he can accomplish this so adroitly, it is because as far as sinuous, provisional, non-monistic thinking goes, he was there a good thirty years before it. Yet he wants to ride this particular tiger as well as rein it in, as his enthusiasm for New Times—referring to the transformed nature of contemporary capitalism—suggests. Hall believes that this new kind of consumerist capitalism can, for all its faults, liberate the individual in valuable ways, and reacts angrily to the 'élitist' idea that consumption or the media are just ways of duping the masses.

It is here that his most persistent political strength—a deep-seated belief in popular democracy—collides headlong with that compulsion to be *au courant* which is one of his basic flaws. He was never, to be sure, quite the starry-eyed advocate of consumerist freedoms which his critics made him out to be. It is unlikely that he would rush to endorse Angela McRobbie's heady claims for the participatory value of Japanese team-based work practices. Hall, typically more Janus-faced, sees much late-capitalist culture as 'commodified consumption', but also as a chance for popular choice and control. What the traditional Left has ignored are 'the landscapes of popular pleasure', which is true and important enough. It is just that it is more a sign of the problem than the solution that this seems to boil down for the moment to media, shopping and lifestyle, and that those who look for forms of individual self-development other than choosing between fancy brand-names should be slurred as both sexist and élitist.

Stuart Hall's impatience with out-of-touch left theorists springs from his genuinely demotic dimension, from the man who co-authored an early book about jazz and film long before cultural studies proper were up and running. But it is also the impatience of one who, just as much as Tony Benn, came to traditional working-class values from the outside. To romanticise those values, or write them off as drearily passé, are sides of the same coin. There is a difference between being *au fait* and being *à la mode*, which Hall has not always respected. Driven by nothing but democratic motives, and chock-full of reservations, he has never-theless lent some of his formidable authority to a designer socialism which was born less out of a courageous break with the antiquated than out of aimless desperation. No movement or individual is ever exactly abreast of the times; we are always either premature or belated, either oldies or yuppies, too far in advance of the army or hobbling to catch up with it. It is not a question of being up-to-date, just a matter of choosing between being too archaic and too voguish. Of the New Left's founding fathers, Raymond Williams went the first way, Stuart Hall opted for the second, and Edward Thompson solved the problem ele-gantly by dividing his time between Blake and the Bomb.

But it is not for New Times that Stuart Hall will be remembered. He will be honoured as the man who helped to pioneer cultural studies in this country, as a tireless political activist and as a rhetorician of great splendour. Like Joe Hill, he pops up wherever there is something politically urgent to be done, an extraordinarily present figure who can turn his hand to any of half-a-dozen academic disciplines. He is one of those rare male leftists who have been genuinely rather than notionally transformed by feminism; and as the final section of this absorbing book suggests, his has been one of the most significant voices in the discourses of Britishness, ethnicity and multiculturalism of our post-imperial twilight. Once more, with the emergence of these intensely topical concerns, the age has finally caught up with where, at some level, he was all along. In this sense, it is more than a pious flourish to claim that, by virtue of his personal history and political experience, he is better placed than almost anyone to reflect on the future destiny of this nation. That personal narrative, and the public history of Britain in the second part of the 20th century, have been strangely intertwined, at once deeply symbiotic and sharply at odds. It is among Hall's major achievements that he has moved among the British middle classes for the past forty-four years while shedding nothing of his warmth and geniality.

Peter Ackroyd

In this extraordinary study, the abiding passion of Peter Ackroyd's previous works now speaks its name directly. *Hawksmoor, Blake* and *Dickens, English Music, The Life of Thomas More* and *London: The Biography* were all aspects of Ackroyd's enduring love-affair with a certain idea of Englishness, an idea that runs as deep in his writing as property in Jane Austen or memory in Proust. Even cross-dressing, the subject of his earlier study *Dressing Up*, crops up here as a typical instance of English comedy.

Albion is the consummation of Ackroyd's previous work in more senses than one. It combines the exuberance of Blake with the erudition of T.S. Eliot, the spiritual ardour of Thomas More with the grotesquerie of Dickens. It is a dilapidated treasure-house, full of cluttered nooks, twisting corridors and rambling outhouses, like the English architecture its author admires. Its broken-backed structure reflects the irregularity which Ackroyd sees as a virtue of English culture, in contrast to the formal artifice of less favoured nations. As with Sir Thomas Browne's genially ambling prose, Robert Burton's eccentric *The Anatomy of Melancholy* or Laurence Sterne's *Tristram Shandy*, all works which Ackroyd finds quintessentially English, you can dip in and out of this volume without missing out on the storyline, since there is none. England is about muddle rather than metaphysics, amiable anecdotes rather than grand narratives. The culture is cross-grained, eclectic and mongrelised, and its enemies are purity and abstraction. When Ackroyd speaks of 'the haunted, shambling melancholic figure of [Samuel]

First published as 'Irregular Virtue' (a review of *Albion: The Origins of the English Imagination* by Peter Ackroyd) in the *Times Literary Supplement*, 20 September 2002.

Johnson', who 'swallowed great draughts of recondite learning in the attempt to sublimate his own disturbed genius', it is not hard to read a self-reference into this admiring cameo. *Recondite* knowledge, being quirky, charming and gloriously pointless, is characteristically English, whereas rational, purposive knowledge is unnervingly Continental.

The English, then, do not go in much for fancy ideas, and neither does *Albion*. The book's feel for English culture is intuitive rather than conceptual, less a matter of common law or political economy than the sudden delight of spotting in Wells Cathedral the small carved figure of a man with toothache holding open his mouth in pain. *Albion* is profuse in such wayward, miniature, anecdotal odds and ends, representing as they do the English response to Continental rationality. It pauses to note a carving in Beverley, Humberside, of a man carrying his scolding wife in a wheelbarrow, and in Blackburn of a fox preaching to a congregation of hens. Ackroyd's imagination is sensuous and materialist, more Catholic than Protestant, fascinated by Turner's gusts of turbulent light or the way medieval monks tanned and scraped their illuminated parchments, smoothed them with a pumice-stone, then whitened them with fine particles of chalk. He is seized by the Gothic and grotesque, the intricate and offbeat, the phantasmal but also the fleshly. He is not much drawn to the high roads of history or to what obtrusively catches the eye.

The study begins, idiosyncratically enough, with a section on trees: Druidic oaks, hawthorn trees as Anglo-Saxon boundary markers, Gainsborough's forested landscapes, John Clare's hallowed elm and ash, Tolkien's legend of moving trees, Thomas Hardy's reflections on the 'runic obscurity' of their murmured language. As with all the book's portraitures, the method is cumulative and empirical, and the final effect one of fitting glittering shards into a stained-glass window or weaving multi-coloured strands into a complex tapestry. *Albion* is English in method as well as motif. From *Beowulf* to Tennyson, it traces a bleak, stony, swampy English landscape in which it seems always to be winter. No investigation of Englishness could fail to mention the weather. The book lingers affectionately over individual figures—Julian of Norwich, Spenser, Hogarth, Johnson, Blake—but has its favourite topics as well: the 'mixed and motley' character of English culture, its broad sexual humour, its preference for an art of the surface, its susceptibility to embarrassment, its passion for biography, its eye for the decorative and elaborate, the melancholia of its sensibility. The sea whispers through *Albion* as it does through the history of the nation, and the English imagination is seen to quicken and flourish in the great Platonic idea of the garden: intricate, small-scale, earthy but civilised, a cherished patch of privacy.

There are times when the book risks lapsing into potted cultural history. Its chapter on Shakespeare is high-minded but uninspired, and its musings on Romanticism curiously flat for such an extravagantly Romantic study. The book is at its most dutiful and perfunctory when it threatens to sag into a history of English literature, and at its most ebullient when it abandons the literary canon for cultural and spiritual byways. The English admire the heretic as well as the traditionalist, love a character as much as they love a lord, and *Albion* balances the two with enviable aplomb. In fact, it is unrivalled in its ability to have it both ways. The English who emerge from this loyal portrait are both visionary and pragmatic, sacred and profane, united and diverse, orthodox and individualist, sombre and grandiloquent, epic and understated, mystical and materialist. They have, in brief, triumphantly swept the board.

'Beginnings', Ackroyd announces in his introduction, 'will be granted more importance than endings.' He can say that again. *Albion* comes to a halt before the Industrial Revolution, and it is hard to see how it could have done otherwise. Its image of the English nation is not one which can accommodate disruption, brutality or discontinuity. The book, to be sure, is a symbolic rather than social history of England; but it is remarkable how that symbolism reflects one social version of the nation rather than another. Ackroyd's England is a Chestertonian realm of monks, mystics and morris dancers, not of slave traders, colonial adventurers and industrial manufacturers. Despite his praise for the tolerant, adaptive, all-inclusive nature of English culture, there is no suggestion that it ever did anything for which it might be criticised. (There is also, despite this inclusiveness, a strange absence of Geoffrey Hill, in some ways Ackroyd's poetic and ideological counterpart.) *Albion* is *Othello* without Iago, a race whose imagination is untainted by racism, bread riots, hand looms, wars and massacres. English culture over the centuries indeed proved remarkably absorptive: India, Africa, Asia, Ireland, North America. But Ackroyd's proud claim that 'England is the principle of diversity itself' might come as something of a surprise to the parents of Stephen Lawrence.

As always, 'unity' is the word which must follow as soon as one has breathed 'diversity'. Ackroyd's Englishness, like the classical work of art it secretly is, is both infinitely plastic and utterly self-identical. This is not a history of the English imagination, since for Ackroyd the English imagination has no history. Like heaven, England is a land unafflicted by mutability. From the Mystery Plays to Miss Marple, all of its mighty works are eternally co-present. The melancholic note of Anglo-Saxon poetry is sounded again in Gray's 'Elegy', to resound once more in the pathos of Sterne and the music of Delius. The rich surface display of Wells Cathedral anticipates the ornamental coverings of Victorian upholstery and the flatness of Pre-Raphaelite painting, not to speak of Richard Rogers's Pompidou Centre. There is indeed a beast called Englishness, whose habits hardly vary from the Druids to Dickens. And if the English were God's chosen race for the Venerable Bede, so are they for the venerating Ackroyd. Even more so, perhaps, since the nation has always been a handy surrogate for those who find God hard to swallow.

There are, of course, vital historical affinities at work in any culture, which the postmodern cult of the discontinuous damagingly ignores. Even so, it is hard to discern quite as intimate a bond between Durham Cathedral and the Lloyds Building as Ackroyd does. From this view-point, there would seem little to choose between Jonathan Swift and Graham Swift. Both are manifestations of the archetypally English, even if the former Swift was actually Irish. (Laurence Sterne, another of Ackroyd's totemic Englishmen, inconveniently hailed from Tipperary, and his non-Englishness shows in his writing.) Ackroyd's imagination, like Seamus Heaney's, has always been possessed by the notion of the past as a depth to be excavated within the present, as vertical or geo-logical rather than horizontal and historical. The present is a kind of palimpsest through which the spectral lineaments of the long-buried are dimly visible, awaiting their disinterment by the redemptive rites of the literary imagination.

If Ackroyd's fiction has turned this conception to some magnificent uses, *Albion* discloses something of its more sinister face. The book is a hymn to blood and soil, even if of an angelic rather than demonic kind. It is true, *pace* the more callow kind of globaliser, that men and women need the local as much as the universal, a sense of belonging as much as the experience of mobility. Even so, Ackroyd fails to see that the other

face of his idealised England—the domain of Britannia rather than of
hobgoblins and priapic jesters—has uprooted a good many people in
its day, destroying their dwelling places and riding roughshod over
their local pieties. In fact, Ackroyd's English nationalism is, among
other things, a response to the global forces which are today laying
siege from every quarter to the semi-mythical land he loves. And the
actual rather than the mythical England has played a key role in fos-
tering those forces.

It is not out of the question that Albion might stir and Arthur rise
again, to save us from the euro. In traditional English life, so the book
informs us, 'there was no wholesale adoption of continental modes',
which might always provide us with some useful ammunition against
Brussels. Ackroyd is sceptical of the distinction between historian and
mythologiser, and well he might be: this is not history but poetic special
pleading, summoning an England which never really existed to do
battle on behalf of one which might cease to exist altogether. For all its
Romantic disdain for politics, it is, in typical postmodernist style, history
as political invention.

The English imagination, Ackroyd writes, 'takes the form of a ring or
a circle. It is endless because it has no beginning and no end ...' The
verbal infelicity of a circle being endless because it has no end betrays
the shoddy sentimentalism of the thought. Like all nationalist mythology, *Albion* needs violently to erase actual history from the nation's
narcissistic self-imaging. If the race's origins and ends are to be at
one—if history, in T.S. Eliot's phrase, is to be now and England—then
nothing as degradingly secular as process or temporality can be allowed
to squeeze between them. One can imagine a companion volume to
this study entitled *Erin*, the ancient name for Ireland, which spoke
fondly of shamrock, Queen Maeve and shillelaghs while affirming the
imperishable spirit of the Irish race. Its author would be more likely to
be investigated by the Special Branch than nominated for a prize.

The case of Ireland is relevant here in more senses than one. Ackroyd
concedes nervously in his introduction that some of what he sees as
peculiarly English may well not be so. Indeed it is not, though he offers
no real defence against this disconcerting truth. If much English art is
decorative, elaborate and of the surface, so is much Irish; indeed, the
preference for detail over structure which Ackroyd regards as peculiarly
English is ascribed by Matthew Arnold to the Celts. If the English

sensibility is mournful, the lugubrious Irish brooding over runes and ruins is equally legendary. If there is a rich lineage of dream poetry in England, so is there in Ireland. If Catholicism shaped English culture as deeply as Ackroyd believes (he numbers Shakespeare among its adherents), then it scarcely needs pointing out that there would be little Irish culture without it.

Albion, however, is not interested in Abroad. Diversity ends at Dover. Apart from a quick glance at Renaissance Italy, England here is a culture quarantined from foreign contamination. If it interacts with other nations, it does so only to assimilate what it finds useful for its own ends. It has been a closed, self-regarding, morally rather smug society, rattled by the idea of otherness. Ackroyd does not seem to realise that the sense of being *sui generis* is just what the English share with most other peoples. That they are a provincial species is hardly a novel insight; it is just that not many writers these days actually go so far as to celebrate the fact. So it is that *Albion*'s lucid, serviceable prose is marred by lyrical outbursts of breathless hyperbole: 'The English imagination is forever green' (a hard case to peddle in Doncaster); it takes the form of 'an endless enchanted circle or shining ring'; 'Shakespeare may be compared to the air we breathe.' This is English Heritage prattle, not the prose of the author of *Hawksmoor*.

Indeed, for all its splendid fascination with the whimsical and perverse, the book is in some ways depressingly conventional. Shakespeare turns out predictably to have been an unpredictable child of Nature, while everything authentically English happens by warm-hearted spontaneity rather than coldly calculating design. England is organic, Europe is mechanical. The Continentals blueprinted themselves into existence in their robotically self-conscious style, whereas we English just grew. Some aspects of English society—industrialism, for example —did indeed just grow, though rather more like cancer than Topsy. It is true that the English felt free at times to dispense with big ideas like justice and liberty, but some of their subalterns were not quite so fortunate in this respect. For all its prodigal insight and intelligence, *Albion* suffers in the end from a certain naivety. It reads like the work of a man who has been too deep in Aelfric and Jane Austen ever to bother buying a newspaper.

Seamus Heaney

Writing in 1887 of the proposal to establish an Anglo-Saxon-based school of English at Oxford, the moral philosopher Thomas Case protested that 'an English School will grow up, nourishing our language not from the humanity of the Greeks and Romans, but from the savagery of the Goths and Anglo-Saxons. We are about to reverse the Renaissance.' Not for the first time, an Oxford don had mistaken his university for the spiritual heart of humanity. A century later, a move against Old English in Oxford provoked one apocalyptically minded medievalist to warn of the 'worldwide demoralisation' that would inevitably ensue.

Far from barbarously undermining liberal civilisation, pre-modern literary studies at Oxford lent it a new lease of life. What was needed, as an increasingly godless century wore on, was a set of myths and archetypes which might recall us to the neglected questions of good and evil, hierarchy and tradition, and provide an alternative symbolic universe to the levelling technological present. The result was the fiction of the Anglo-Saxonist J.R.R. Tolkien and the medievalist C.S. Lewis, both of whom raided the heroic resources of early literature for contemporary ideological ends. The blend of whimsy, escapism, reaction, regression and erudition was quintessentially Oxfordian.

Anglo-Saxon, as Cambridge calls the stuff, or Old English, as Oxford prefers to label it (the choice of name is itself politically significant), has for long been a cockpit of ideological contentions over national origins, pedigrees and continuities. Seamus Heaney, for example, refers casually to *Beowulf* as being 'in English', as though there were some

First published as 'Hasped and Hooped and Hirpling' (a review of *Beowulf* translated by Seamus Heaney) in the *London Review of Books*, 11 November 1999.

unbroken thread from the speech of Hrothgar to the idiom of William Hague. Oxford's dilemma was that you needed a philologically based English school if you were to have something substantial to examine, this being seen as the mark of a kosher academic subject; but since much of the influential work in this area was German, this also meant throwing in your hand with a bunch of Teutonic barbarians who, come 1914, were marauding at the gate in a more than merely intellectual sense. The Oxford English professor Sir Walter Ralegh, with a fine flash of the humanism to which he was devoted, remarked that he 'should like to get up a team of 100 Professors and challenge 100 Boche professors. Their deaths would be a benefit to the human race.' Only Oxford professors, it appeared, were to be granted the dignity of the upper case.

Yet it helped, in battling the Boche, to know that you hailed from an ancient race with bluff, manly vowels and a handy way with a sword, and this gave the Anglo-Saxonists a belated boost at their most perilous historical hour. Perhaps some of the Germans' own uncouth virility could be hijacked for the struggle against their dominion. Not long afterwards, by the time an English school at Cambridge was up and running, this view of English and Englishness had evolved into a full-dress cultural ideology in the hands of F.R. Leavis and his collaborators. Unlike Oxford, Cambridge had sought to solve the Anglo-Saxon problem by ensconcing it in a separate faculty from English. Spiritually, however, what would eventually become known as Cambridge English adopted just the opposite strategy, boldly redefining the essence of English language and literature in vaguely Anglo-Saxonist terms. If the subject itself was academically sequestered, its colonising spirit was everywhere apparent. Authentic English was gnarled, racy, muscular, robust, richly specified and concretely realised, and the literary canon would be drastically reconstructed as one continuous laying bare of its nerve and sinew. In the process, poetry, that most cissy of all activities, would be repossessed for the male species. Unlike cerebral, anaemic languages such as French, English words had the good fortune sensuously to enact their own meanings, so that the archetypal English poem sounded rather like the rumbling of a sack of potatoes being emptied. Not even the thinnest blade could be slid between signifier and signified. What Freud had seen as a characteristic mark of schizophrenia—the confusion of words and things—was raised to a sign of ethnic distinction. For this quasi-sacramental poetics, 'Où sont les neiges d'antan?' palely alluded to something, whereas 'mossed cottages trees' was a matter of real presence. Once again, in the long history of English nationalism, Englishness was everything that the abstract, frivolous, revolutionary French were not.

There is a geographical as well as a theological poetics at work here. Roughly speaking, the nearer you approach the Arctic Circle, the more authentic your language grows. Northern poems—from *Beowulf* and Ted Hughes's *The Hawk in the Rain* to Seamus Heaney's *Death of a Naturalist*—are craggy and brawny, whereas southern ones are more devious and deliquescent. The Northern Irish poet Tom Paulin, with his penchant for words which sound like the squelching of a leaky boot, raises this doctrine to the point of self-parody. In poetry like Heaney's, you can hear the pluck and slop of brackish water as the signs button down snugly on their referents, whereas Donald Davie's words stand at a chaster distance from his meanings. This, needless to say, is linguistic nonsense. Basil Bunting's words are no closer to his material objects than Thomas Hardy's, for all that the former came from the North-East and the latter from the South-West. The relationship between language and the world is not a spatial one, any more than the relation between a spade and the act of digging with it. The celebrated 'materiality' of a poet like Heaney is really a linguistic trompe l'oeil, a psychological rather than ontological affair, a matter of association rather than incarnation. The density of his discourse does not 'embody' material process, as we post-Romantics are prone to think; it is just that the one phenomenon brings the other to mind. Poetry is a sort of trick, whereby an awareness of the textures of signs puts us in mind of the textures of actual things. But the relation between the two remains quite as arbitrary as in any other use of language; it is just that some poetry tries to 'iconicise' that relation, make it appear somehow inevitable. This— what Paul de Man referred to as the 'phenomenalisation of language'—is the mark of ideology, and it is ironic that poets should typically regard themselves as the antidote to ideologists, giving us the feel and pith of things rather than the delusory abstraction. It is hard to imagine, however, that de Man is bedside reading for the theory-allergic Heaney.

Words may not be things, but the poet, like the small child making its first sounds, is one who invests them as though they were. There is thus something regressively infantile as well as dauntingly mature about poetry, rather as the grandeur of the imagination is embarrassingly close to libidinal fantasy. Does language transport the writer to the heart of reality, or does messing about with the stuff substitute for that reality like a child's Plasticine? How can the erotic mouth-music of the babbling toddler become somehow cognitive?

If the poem salvages the use value of words from their tarnished exchange value, then it becomes an organic society all in itself. It is thus not surprising that the Cambridge English version of language should go hand-in-hand with a nostalgia for a non-alienated community, in which objects had yet to lapse into the degraded condition of commodities. Hence, perhaps, the rural-born Heaney's affection for *Beowulf*'s burnished helmets and four-square, honest-to-goodness idiom, its Ulster-like bluffness and blood-spattered benches. He likes the poem's blend of directness, ornateness and obliquity, unsurprisingly for an Ulsterman who is given to verbal opulence and is notoriously elusive in some of his opinions. He is also attracted to the way it floats somewhere between formulaic oral tradition and self-conscious artistry, a metaphor for his own in-betweenness as an intellectual sprung from the common people.

In terms of Irish stereotypes, *Beowulf* seems like a Gaelic rather than Celtic piece of art—canny, virile and earth-bound rather than dreamy, spiritual and involuted. Heaney evidently began translating the piece at the same time as he was first exposed to the 'unmoored speech' of contemporary American poetry, and saw in it a kind of 'aural antidote' to that verse—a way of ensuring, as he puts it in his extravagantly figurative prose, that 'my linguistic anchor would stay lodged on the Anglo-Saxon sea-floor'. But it would be more accurate to see the materialist, melancholic *Beowulf* as an extraordinary fusion of both registers, which brings us closer to the source of its fascination for our leading English-language poet.

Within Heaney's writing, the civic and the chthonic have always slogged it out, and this magnificent translation is no exception. Scattered among *Beowulf*'s desolate moors and marshes are a few besieged centres of human culture, ceremony and solidarity—the lords' lighted halls which hold out against the encroaching dark. Torn between light and darkness, air and earth, Heaney himself is an enlightened cosmopolitan liberal born into an Ulster whose allegiances are to some degree cultic, parochial, pre-modern. Unlike most liberal intellectuals, however, he is aware that the tug of roots and communal loyalties cannot be briskly disowned as so much surplus historical baggage. Even so, there has been a ferocious tension between the elemental and the educated in his work. If he is allured by the bleak seascapes of the Norsemen, he is even more seduced by the mellow Hellenistic warmth of more southerly Europe. There is a similar tension between the Derry nationalist culturally alien to literary London, and the Heaney who can sometimes sound, politically speaking, as if he might have been raised in Dorking.

Beowulf, a poem both subtle and savage, is thus an obvious target for his talents, which are in any case so formidable that he needs a big-time author (Sophocles, Virgil, Dante) who will give him a run for his money. In his introduction, in a typical piece of lushly over-fanciful Heaneyspeak, he writes of the poem as having its keel 'deeply set in the element of sensation while the mind's lookout sways metrically and far-sightedly in the element of pure comprehension—which is to say that the elevation of *Beowulf* is always, paradoxically, buoyantly down-to-earth'. The dragon of the text he sees as having both a 'foundedness' and a 'lambency' about him, 'at once a stratum of the earth and a streamer in the air'. This great coiled beast, in short, turns out to be none other than a certain Nobel Prize-winning Irish poet, who has spent a lifetime struggling to reconcile the earth of local affinities with the air of uncommitted freedom, the foundedness of Armagh with the lambency of Athens.

What reconciles these things for Heaney is the redressing activity of poetry itself, an occupation as utopian in form as it is demystified in content. But *Beowulf* allows him to relish a more precise kind of resolution, since it accommodates conflicting realities, pagan and Christian, within a single order. It is written by a Christian poet about the pre-Christian past of his people, and thus combines historical detachment and imaginative inwardness. Like Heaney and Northern Ireland, the *Beowulf* poet metaphorically connives in these tribal warrings while being spiritually out of joint with them, holding his own people critically at arm's length. If he is a bit of a historical revisionist, chiding his forebears for their barbaric ways, he is also one of the gang. Like Northern Ireland, this is a community caught up in a cycle of violence, bound by its death-dealing codes of honour and loyalty; but as a poem written near the millennium it also has a broader political resonance. 'A world is passing away,' Heaney writes of these bickering Danes, 'the Swedes and others are massing on the borders to attack and there is no lord or hero to rally the defence.' The poem, like the millennium, closes on a note of sombre foreboding.

Earth and air were equally complicit in this translation's origin. As a Catholic nationalist student in Belfast, Heaney informs us, he felt dispossessed of his own language, until the tentacular roots of certain words, the complex crossings between the Irish and Scots Gaelic *uisce* and the English 'whiskey' (in an extra twist, Heaney spells the word in Hiberno-English style), made him imagine a kind of 'riverrun of Finnegans Wakespeak pouring out of the cleft rock of some prepolitical, prelapsarian, urphilological Big Rock Candy Mountain'. It is a typically brash, subtle Heaney trope, but one rather more slippery than he suspects. This epiphanic moment hoists him out of earth into air, out of his sullen politico-linguistic resentment into a 'sweetening' awareness of verbal hybridity. The polarities of Irish and English, Celtic and Saxon, are momentarily collapsed, in what Heaney, borrowing a phrase from his poetic compatriot John Montague, describes as an escape from the 'partitioned intellect' into some larger-spirited, unsectarian country of the mind.

It seems a pity to sour this eirenic liberal pluralism. But the 'partitioned intellect' in Ireland is not in fact one which sees Irish and British culture as rigidly adversarial. On the contrary, it is one which sees them as intimately interwoven. It is liberal Unionism, not nationalism, which holds to a unity of Irish and British culture in order to rationalise British rule of part of the island. Cultural hybridity is here in the service of political division. Heaney rather typically fails to notice this, intent as he is on his own spiritual liberation. Even so, it was this revelation that made him see *Beowulf* as part of his own 'voice-right', and recognise as a politically aggrieved late adolescent that he was born into its language and its language was born into him. Translating the poem is thus the final, triumphant reversal of his cultural dispossession. Just as this most 'authentic' of artworks is also profoundly alien—we have no idea who wrote it, or exactly when or where—so Heaney's own idiom can be seen as both askew to metropolitan English and somehow closer to the bone of the language. Much the same is true of the poet who, so he tells us, first formed his ear, Gerard Manley Hopkins.

The erstwhile outsider, then, has now placed himself boldly at the *fons et origo*, claiming the tongue as always-already his own from the outset. It is hard to know quite how *Beowulf* is the origin of Arthur Hugh Clough or Simon Armitage, but in any case Heaney has dug down with his pen to 'the first stratum of the language' and appropriated his birthright. As Harold Bloom might less decorously put it, the belated bastard off-spring has now installed himself as the founding patriarch. It might be argued that Heaney's anxious need for this move to be legitimated is a sign of the cultural colonisation it aims to overcome. Yet, having reversed his cultural dispossession, he then reverses the reversal. In searching for the pitch or enabling note of the work, he finds it in the weighty, 'big-voiced' utterance of some family relatives. Having kicked free of Ulster soil into the upper air, he now has the confidence to touch down on it again.

The result is a marvellously sturdy, intricate reinvention, which betrays its author's poetic dabs less in its earthiness than in its airiness. It is the canny colloquialisms ('in fine fettle', 'under a cloud', 'blather', 'big talk', 'gave as good as I got') which are most Heaneyesque, not the smell of the soil. If the stark subject-matter is redolent of *North*, the treatment has the mild touch of insouciance of a more recent collection like *Seeing Things*. This poet is so superbly in command that he can risk threadbare, throwaway, matter-of-fact phrases like 'of no small impor-tance' or 'the best part of a day'. He has a casual way with the alliterative pattern of the original, which helps to strip its craft of portentous self-consciousness and frees up its syntax to move more nimbly. Lines like 'He is hasped and hooped and hirpling with pain, limping and looped with it', which the young Heaney might well have written in earnest, are really an ironic postmodern quotation, a self-parodic hint of the racket the whole poem might make if you bound yourself too grimly to its form.

The epic poem, as Marx once observed, requires historical conditions which the steam-engine and the telegraph put paid to. Mechanically reproduced commodities have lost the aura of ancient objects, just as the self-conscious fictions of modernity have lost what Heaney calls the 'hand-built, rock-sure feel' of a poem like this. But modern objects, typified for Georg Lukács by Charles Bovary's extraordinarily con-voluted, visually unrepresentable hat, have also shed what seems to us the unalienated candour of material things in *Beowulf*, which exist more as narrative elements than as literary enigmas. In any case, we no longer believe in heroism, or that the world itself is story-shaped, and we ask of literature a phenomenological inwardness which is of fairly recent historical vintage. All of this is a signal misfortune for Seamus Heaney, an artist so exquisitely gifted and imaginatively capacious that only a work of such mighty scale would answer to his abilities.

Roy Foster

Roy Foster's genius as an Irish historian is in one sense all his own, in another sense a quality of his class. In his supple, civilised intelligence, stylish wit and sceptical cast of mind, he is one of the most distinguished modern heirs of the great tradition of Anglo-Irish liberalism, which flows through Wolfe Tone and Charles Stewart Parnell to W.B. Yeats (of whom Foster is the official biographer), and on to such latter-day luminaries as the essayist Hubert Butler and the historian Leland Lyons. There are four characteristically erudite, illuminating chapters on Yeats in this new collection of essays, along with a probing, remarkably pious piece on Butler (clearly a walking-on-water figure for Foster), and a graceful chapter on Lyons.

The Anglo-Irish liberal tradition has been a roll-call of free spirits, bracingly agnostic, courageously nonconformist and keenly suspicious of tribal loyalties. In its free-thinking individualism, it has played an honourable role in Ireland in resisting a brutal Gaelic triumphalism. It has given the country some of its most imaginative political leaders, along with some of the finest blooms of its artistic culture. One such piece of artistry is the fiction of Elizabeth Bowen, 'freighted with sensuous language, baroque humour, oblique psychological insights, penetrating moral issues and overall strangeness', as Foster remarks of it here in an essay of exceptional insight and delicacy.

Throughout this Anglo-Irish lineage runs a vein of coolly sardonic wit thinly concealing a covert irascibility, part of both the class's assurance and its insecurity, which Foster mines to the full. He is enjoyably

First published as 'Welcome to Blarneyworld' (a review of *The Irish Story: Telling Tales and Making It Up in Ireland* by Roy Foster) in the *Guardian*, 27 October 2001.

devastating about the fact that Ireland these days is basically one enormous historical theme park, and mordantly satirical about the prolier-than-thou sentimentalism of Frank McCourt's *Angela's Ashes*. He is refreshingly brisk about those Irish who fall off their bar stools unable to stay sober because of the English victory at Kinsale in 1601. He has the superciliousness of his class along with its suggestively off-centre vision. He also combines its worldly-wiseness with its creative brio, as a blend of tough-minded historian and superb literary stylist.

Foster shares the prejudices of his class as well. In an image quite as wincingly sentimental as anything out of *Angela's Ashes*, he writes of the patrician Hubert Butler's house 'commanding' the surrounding countryside but 'in its gentle way'. The fact that he does not see what thousands of Irish men and women would find darkly amusing about that image is very revealing. If the Anglo-Irish liberals bravely championed the people in the teeth of Gaelic-Irish accusations of bad faith, they were also a rather dotty élite paternalistically intent on spreading sweetness and light among the obtusely mythological masses, partly to buttress their own declining power.

Foster, the great demythologiser of Ireland, perpetuates this practice today, though like most demythologisers he remains trapped in a few myths of his own. He cannot, for example, free himself of the old-fashioned liberal prejudice that political commitment must be inevitably reductive. Though *The Irish Story* is needlingly partisan, its author tends to believe that partisanship is always the property of one's antagonist. Foster never ceases to harp on the complex, ambiguous nature of Irish history, which would make taking sides seem positively crass. (One wonders whether he feels the same about sexism and white supremacism.) Whenever an outright conflict emerges, he is usually to be found standing dauntlessly in the middle.

It is a pity that he feels the need to carry so much anti-ideological baggage, not least because he does indeed have a vigorous case to promote. It is just that, like all the best brands of ideology, it fails to recognise itself as such. His intellectual suavity thus conceals an extraordinary ideological naivety; and this, too, is a feature of the spuriously as well as admirably disinterested tradition he inherits.

A few instances of this non-partisan partisanship may suffice. *The Irish Story* uncritically celebrates posh Irish Protestants, while reserving most of its flak for nationalist Gaels. It is withering for the most part about

Irish anti-colonialism, but much more reticent in rebuking the Unionists. The only form of colonial exploitation it will admit to is non-Irish writers muscling in on the Irish studies—and this from a cosmo-politan spirit supposed to abhor parochialism. Those in the outer darkness who muscle in on Foster's own political side, oddly enough, are rather more welcome to the club.

By the end of the volume, Foster's liberal inclusiveness has managed to exclude journalists, republicans, post-colonialists, post-structuralists, left-wingers, theorists, polemicists, 'born again newly Irish Eng.Lit. academics' (that's me), anyone who holds the eminently plausible case that Bloody Sunday was probably planned by the British army, and anyone in Ireland nostalgic for anything apart from the heyday of Anglo-Irish liberalism. (Another of Foster's briskly modernising myths, incidentally, is that nostalgia for the past is always morbid, and this in an age of Chris Evans, nuclear missiles and the IMF. Conversely, he seems to think embracing the new is likely to be a positive move, and this in a world ruled by Kodak and Coca Cola.)

Irish nationalists in these essays tend to have 'pieties' rather than convictions, while post-colonial thinkers are 'addicted' to their theories rather than simply holding them. There is an absorbing essay on the novelist Anthony Trollope, who lived in Ireland for a while, and who believed that the Great Famine was an act of divine providence sent to lick the feckless Micks into shape. He also objected to rural agitators partly because they interfered with fox hunting. Yet Trollope, as an upper-middle-class English Protestant-cum-honorary Irishman, clearly qualifies for the club, and Foster's treatment of this racist bigot is far more affectionate than his lip-curling comments on the much less noxious sentimentalism of Frank McCourt. Trollope's idealising of Ireland is fondly indulged, whereas no such big-hearted concession is extended to the romantic strains in Gerry Adams's autobiography.

Foster assumes in a rather jeering tone that any of his compatriots who feel serious hostility to the British state are simply the deluded victims of demonology. There must be a fair few Satanists with scars from plastic bullets. He rightly assails the culture of victimage in Ire-land, even though his own class sometimes did their bit to deepen the misery. His earlier study *Modern Ireland* overreacted to nationalist bleating and whingeing with some unpleasantly hard-faced apologias for, say, the shabby British handling of the Famine relief campaign.

The Anglo-Irish tradition, so Foster claims, could sometimes raise unsettling questions and subvert complacent orthodoxies. So it could; but though its wit, insight and coruscating intelligence live on in these lucid essays, the dissent is now pretty much a dead duck. The latest inheritors of the lineage, like Foster himself, understand much about liberty and next to nothing about liberation. Foster's constant nationalist-knocking, far from representing some daring dissidence, is now the purest platitude in these islands. In fact it would be hard these days to get an academic job in Irish history without a certificate of proficiency in the pursuit. Foster is a supremely talented analyst of Ireland, an impeccable establishment figure who tells the chattering classes just what they want to hear about the place.

Alan Ayckbourn and Dario Fo

Dario Fo is probably the most frequently performed living playwright
on the planet, while Alan Ayckbourn, author of thirty-six new plays in
London in as many years, is the most popular dramatist in this country.
(A survey has shown that Ayckbourn and Shakespeare are now staged in
Britain with roughly equal frequency.) There, however, the affinities
between the two writers would seem to end. Fo is a political gadfly who
has been arrested, vilified and threatened with death, a devout former
Maoist whose plays have been staged in converted cinemas and occu-
pied steel factories. Bombs have been placed in his theatres, and his
partner Franca Rame, one of Italy's most admired actors, was once
raped and razor-slashed by right-wing thugs.

Ayckbourn, whose name probably means 'oak by a stream', has a
very English distaste for extremism, and the sedate continuity of his
Scarborough theatre over the years contrasts sharply with the Italian's
hand-to-mouth, on-the-hoof melodrama of a career. With his dogged
provincialism, shyly introspective temperament and harrowing ontology
of the commonplace, Ayckbourn might seem to be the Philip Larkin of
the English theatre. His plays are enjoyed by the Queen and the Queen
Mother, neither of whom, one imagines, are fervent devotees of *Accidental Death of an Anarchist.*

Born in London in 1939, Ayckbourn launched his theatrical career as
an assistant to Donald Wolfit, ensuring that his supplies of Guinness
and gin were steadily maintained, before being taken on as an actor by
Stephen Joseph's repertory company at Scarborough. He himself was to

First published as 'Harlequin and the housewife' (a review of *Alan Ayckbourn:
Grinning at the Edge* by Paul Allen and *Dario Fo and Franca Rame: Harlequins of the
Revolution* by Joseph Farrell) in the *Times Literary Supplement*, 11 January 2002.

become leader of the outfit in the early 1970s. It was under Joseph's flamboyant tutelage that he turned to writing in the early 1960s, scoring an early hit with *Relatively Speaking*, and following it up over the years with such bleakly comic investigations of human mismatching as *How the Other Half Loves*, *Absurd Person Singular*, *The Norman Conquests* and *Intimate Exchanges*. Sex, class and power have been his abiding obsessions. In *Gosforth's Fête*, a wimpish scoutmaster hears of his wife's infidelity over an erratically functioning tannoy at a church fête; in *Season's Greetings*, a bored housewife tries to have sex with a guest and ends up setting off the elaborate *son et lumière* that her husband has rigged up on the Christmas tree.

Dario Fo, born in an Italian village thirteen years earlier than Ayckbourn, was a gifted painter before turning to the theatre. Success in radio, cabaret and satirical revues led him in 1951 to set up the Piccolo drama company in Milan, and his first full-length play, *Archangels Don't Play Pinball*, was to herald such later tours de force as *Toss the Lady Out*, *Mistero huffo*, *Can't Pay? Won't Pay!* and *Accidental Death of an Anarchist*. In 1968, he and Franca Rame set up Nuova Scena, a theatre company dedicated to the cause of proletarian revolution, which staged works with such immoderate titles as *Chain Me Up And I'll Still Smash Everything*. Nuova Scena was followed in 1970 by a new group, La Commune, which fell foul of censorship, police harassment and legal prosecution in the urban-terrorist-ridden Italy of the 1970s. Fo then ensconced himself and his comrades in a disused Milanese fruit market, the Palazzina Liberty, and persisted in his lifelong mission of enraging the Vatican, the Christian Democrats and the Italian bourgeoisie. At the centre of *Accidental Death of an Anarchist* is a crazed modern-dress Harlequin, originally played by Fo himself, who, in a world of crooked judges, corrupt bureaucrats and bent policemen, is the sole arbiter of reason and decency.

Fo is an exuberant extrovert, a clown and jester in satiric medieval style, whereas the intensely private Ayckbourn once bit a circus clown when he was a child, and has been wary of audience participation ever since. Ayckbourn is a spectacular commercial success, while Fo defiantly spurned the commercial theatre in 1968. The Italian's work is in a Brechtian style largely indifferent to the intimate or psychological, while the Englishman is a virtuoso of marital misery. Fo is a cosmopolitan artist, whereas Ayckbourn has never seen a Brecht play, couldn't be bothered to take in *Look Back In Anger* when it first opened, and once dropped off to sleep during his own performance in *Waiting for Godot*. For a long time, his plays were regarded as not literary enough for publication. The contrast between European avant-gardist and English suburbanite, however, is to some extent deceptive. As far as cosmopolitanism goes, Fo doesn't speak English, whereas Ayckbourn is influenced by Ibsen and Chekhov. Beckett may have put him to sleep, but he has infiltrated his art through the mediation of Pinter; and the Scarborough company, in which Ayckbourn got his start as a young actor, produced Strindberg, Giroudoux and Pirandello alongside *Dial M For Murder*. In his openness to European influence, as well as in his political temperateness, Ayckbourn, it turns out, is far from being theatre's answer to Larkin.

In any case, Fo, on a closer look, is scarcely more avant-garde than Ayckbourn. It is earthbound popular culture, not rarefied experimentalism, which fuels his rumbustious art. Indeed, as Joseph Farrell points out in his serviceable biography of Fo and Rame (the latter, chivalrically included, grabs rather less of the action), this political revolutionary is in fact a theatrical traditionalist. He may opt to pitch his plays in factory yards or community centres, but only after he has first unloaded a full panoply of stage sets and lighting rigs. His politically conscious touring companies hark back to the peripatetic players who form the backbone of Italian theatrical tradition.

There are further parallels. Both men are theatrical all-rounders as well as writers. Ayckbourn, who can do more or less every job in the theatre, had a spell as a radio drama producer, and is said to have been a remarkably competent actor as long as he was able to hide himself in a role. 'Give him a hump, a limp and he was tremendous', comments a colleague. Fo is an accomplished painter, singer, film-maker and stand-up performer as well as a dramatist. The two playwrights are probably the world's leading *farceurs*, connoisseurs of black humour who can pluck major art out of minor genres such as cabaret, burlesque and domestic drama.

Political commitment would seem to make the difference. Yet Fo, like Brecht, began more as an apolitical iconoclast than a Marxist, and, despite his turbulent political involvements, has always been a maverick of the Left. More Harlequin than Hegel, he never joined the Italian Communist Party (Brecht was refused membership of the Danish party even before he had applied for it), and allied himself instead with mobile, militant political grouplets whose structure, or lack of it, paralleled his own theatrical activities. Despite his lavish praise for the Italian Resistance, he fought in the Second World War in a notorious Fascist parachute division, an aberration which his political enemies have not been slow to exploit. And despite his earlier rejection of commercial theatre, he is now a Broadway hit and a Nobel Prize winner.

Fo's theatre may be allergic to personal emotion, but Ayckbourn's has a similar chariness of spontaneous feeling, fascinated as it is by English emotional repression. And while some of Fo's later work is explicitly feminist, largely under the influence of Rame, the apparently unpolitical Ayckbourn is obsessed by that most luridly power-ridden of human arenas, domestic life. Ayckbourn's drama may inspect the petit-bourgeois suburbs, but it reveals a darkly anarchic subcurrent worthy of Fo's carnivalesque cavortings, along with a deep sympathy for the (mostly female) ill-treated and unhappy. If the middle-aged Ayckbourn has a look of Santa Claus about him, it is with a touch of the satyr. Fo, son of a station master and a peasant, is a man of the people in a way that the Haileybury-educated Ayckbourn is not; yet Ayckbourn's scatty, story-writing mother, a chronic fantasist who fed him gin as a baby and who would grace any Fo stage, put him askew to respectability forever.

Both of these lucid, meticulously researched biographies lapse from time to time into the characteristic biographical vice of providing us with more trees than wood. Paul Allen, in particular, who organises much of his narrative on a play-by-play basis, might have stepped back from the theatrical nuts and bolts to engage in a more reflective commentary on his retiring subject. Even so, his impressively detailed account benefits enormously from long conversations with his protagonist, as well as from a rich inside knowledge of theatre. Unlike Allen, Farrell is an academic, though his sprightly approach manages successfully to conceal the fact. He is especially strong on Fo's political context, while rather more reticent about the plays themselves. Both studies are adept at capturing the odd blend of comedy, tragedy and grotesquerie of their respective authors. Fo's theatre reflects a tragic political history in puckish, boisterous style, while Ayckbourn is our finest imaginative analyst of the hilarity of human unhappiness.

Nick Groom

Postmodernism awards high marks for non-originality. All literary works are made up of recycled bits and pieces of other works, so that, in the words of Harold Bloom, 'the meaning of a poem is another poem'. This doctrine of intertextuality is not to be confused with good old-fashioned literary influence. Such influences are mostly conscious and generally sporadic, whereas for postmodernism it is impossible to open your mouth without quoting. As Roland Barthes and others have pointed out, the phrase 'I love you' is always a citation, indeed one of the most shop-soiled citations of all, even when it is sincerely meant. For the romantically inclined, this opens up an ominous gap between experience and expression; but if words are what we are made of—if I can know that what I am feeling is love only because I have language in the first place—the romantic view may need to be modified.

In the beginning, then, was the repetition. My signature is authentic only if it is a reproduction of its previous versions. Postmodernism is entranced by imitation but sets itself sternly against mimesis, or the notion of realist representation, so that what copies reproduce is not the world but other copies, in a ceaseless chain of simulacra. If meaning is a matter of difference, then there could have been no primordial word, since one word already implies another. If language can be said to have been born, Lévi-Strauss reflects, then it must have been born 'at a stroke'. In any case, as Wittgenstein muses, it is difficult to imagine an origin without feeling that you could always go back beyond it. As the business of looking things up in the dictionary suggests, all words are

First published as 'Maybe he made it up' (a review of *The Forger's Shadow: How Forgery Changed the Course of Literature* by Nick Groom) in the *London Review of Books*, 6 June 2002.

stand-ins for other words, and all our language is filched and forged, reach-me-down rather than bespoke.

If texts can be translated, then a certain translatability or recycling is constitutive of what they are. And translations can certainly improve on the original, as with the word 'Vienna'. Similarly, we would not call 'literary' a piece of writing which was not somehow portable, more capable than a shout of 'Fire!' in a crowded theatre of being transported from one context to another and interpreted differently each time. In this sense, literary discourse is what it is by virtue of never being quite identical with itself. But the point cuts deeper than literature; we would not call a mark which could happen only once a sign. Language must belong to the Other—to my linguistic community as a whole—before it can belong to me, so that the self comes to its unique articulation in a medium which is always at some level indifferent to it.

Who, then, wrote the first poem? If poetry, like potholing, is a practice governed by certain public conventions, then surely those conventions had to be always already in place for a piece of writing to be identifiable as a poem. I might furtively conceal some dreadful doggerel of mine from public view, but unless it was in principle accessible to others I could not speak of it as a poem at all, even a lousy one. With regard to origins, literary and social conventions are rather like the laws of physics. The mystery of the Universe's origins is not so much how, *pace* King Lear, something could have come of nothing, since a random fluctuation in a quantum field might have popped an inflatable particle into fleeting existence, but rather where the quantum field itself might have come from. Or is to raise such a question merely to confuse different language games, modelling a quantum field on a material entity?

Plagiarism of a sort, then, is our normative condition, and self-parody, as Nick Groom recognises in *The Forger's Shadow*, is the closest we can come to authenticity. (When the dust jacket informs us that the author is a former rock musician and contributor to the *Erotic Review*, who spends his time drinking 'bitter in Devon pubs and red wine in his Soho club', one yearns charitably to read this as deliberate self-parody while darkly suspecting that it is not.) Groom draws a useful distinction between forgery (an original work which is a con but not a copy) and counterfeiting (a fraudulent facsimile copy of an original). But a further distinction between counterfeiting and plagiarism is a touch obscure, and a bit later on we are informed, inconsistently, that counterfeiting has 'no necessary source', which blurs its contrast with forgery.

There is, in fact, a fourth category, known to the Irish (but apparently unknown to Groom) as 'anti-plagiarism'. This little-known genre conflates Groom's forgery with his plagiarism. In 19th-century Ireland, authors like William Maginn, Francis Sylvester Mahony and James Clarence Mangan were in the habit of producing literary texts cunningly modelled on the work of some well-known author like Tennyson or Thomas Moore, which they then coolly claimed to be the lost original that the author had plagiarised. Maginn, who founded *Fraser's Magazine* and died an alcoholic pauper, is said to have been familiar with Hebrew, Syriac, Sanskrit, Basque, Turkish, Assyrian and Magyar (though nobody ever caught him reading), and occasionally penned verses in these languages which some detested rival could then plausibly be accused of having hijacked into English. Mahony, a spoiled priest and fellow imbiber, composed French troubadour ballads of which, so he maintained, Moore's *Irish Melodies* were imitations, and generously acknowledged that some of Moore's 'plagiarisms' were almost as fine as the originals. Moore's poem *Lalla Rookh* (or 'Larry O'Rourke', as one Englishwoman misheard the title), originally appeared in the Mogul language in the audience chamber of the King of Delhi, so Mahony earnestly claimed. Mahony's anti-plagiarist pursuits were themselves, he confessed, plagiarised from a French Jesuit who insisted that Horace's *Odes* were written by a 12th-century Benedictine monk. In a similar way, Maginn's compatriot Laurence Sterne, who was born and reared in Tipperary, includes in *Tristram Shandy* an indignant denunciation of plagiarism which is itself plagiarised.

The Irish poet James Clarence Mangan, who produced 'translations' from exotic languages of which he was entirely ignorant, was a political nationalist, as his anti-plagiarising might well suggest. For anti-plagiarism mischievously reverses the relationship between source and derivation, the authentic and the bogus, rather as Irish nationalism seeks to put an end to the colony's enforced mimicry of its British proprietors so as to become self-originating. Anti-plagiarism, which inverts the relation between host and parasite texts by throwing the passage of time into reverse, is an Oedipal attempt to turn one's own belatedness into priority, thus refuting the charge that the Irish are a mere botched pastiche of their colonial masters. In stealing and defacing the work of others, you can cheekily expose their own usurpation. Nationalism reverts to the primordial origins of the nation, an origin it then endlessly repeats. Some of the leading advocates of non-originality in our own time—Derrida, Kristeva, Foucault, Althusser, Lyotard—have all had experience of client societies, either in French North Africa or Soviet-ruled Bulgaria, and are out to unmask the Real Thing as a sham. Nick Groom's book is clearly influenced by some of this thought; but like the counterfeiter it is not exactly out to trumpet its indebtedness, thus appearing rather less of a facsimile than it actually is.

The Forger's Shadow, after some suggestive theoretical reflections, settles down to a series of case-studies of celebrated literary forgers, from James Macpherson and Thomas Chatterton to the Shakespearean forger William Henry Ireland and the Victorian con-artist Thomas Griffiths Wainewright. Much of this is illuminating, and impressively wide-ranging: the book pirouettes energetically from poetry and the visual arts to law and economics, dropping erudite allusions and scattering portentous insights at the frenetic pace of a half-hour television documentary on the Renaissance. Indeed, it becomes at one point a kind of scriptive equivalent of such programmes, as Groom portrays himself rambling around Bristol in search of Chatterton's ghost ('I paced about, in the footsteps of Oliver Goldsmith, Samuel Johnson, James Boswell and many others ...'), for all the world like a print version of Simon Schama. One can almost see the make-up and microphone. It is a smart rather than deep study, with more wit than soul.

Groom's rather predictably provocative thesis is that the forged work is actually the truest one—a case which, in rehearsing a familiar move in deconstructive theory (the deviant is the measure of the normative), is itself a compound of the derivative and the original. Forgery is creative rather than contemptible, rather in the way that a sign, according to Umberto Eco, is anything you can use to lie with. Since there can be no talk of authenticity without the concept of a fake, the phoney is the true ground of great art. The forger both buttresses the authority of the canon and is cast out by it, thus becoming Groom's personal contribution to a familiar gallery of glamorised postmodern victims (villain, lunatic, bastard and the like). Just as others have tried to shift Native Americans, the disabled, Mormons and the mad from margins to centre, so Groom seeks derivatively to place non-originality in the spotlight. But this case presupposes that there is indeed a tolerably clear distinction between the sham and the genuine, thus undoing with one hand what it achieves with the other. Rather than dismantling the model of margins and centre, it simply parks a new resident in the latter.

To deconstruct, however, is to transform a conventional wisdom, not just to stand it on its head. When Groom speaks in his jaunty, hit-and-miss way of artistic invention as 'an endorsed form of lying', he misses the point that art dismantles the distinction between truth and fiction rather than simply countering truth with falsehood. Literary propositions are parodies of real-life ones, not versions of real-life lies. Putting the forged artwork in place of the genuine article simply transfers the aura of the latter to the former. But by idealising the inauthentic in this way, Groom can reconcile his postmodern persona with his Romantic one. There are really two texts jostling for precedence within *The Forger's Shadow*: one a sometimes glib, rather modish postmodern discourse, the other a more extravagant, spiritually-minded Romanticism which is fascinated by the mystical and occult, values the traditional doctrine of poetic inspiration, and subscribes to a cult of the great man. The book is cool and oracular by turns.

On one level, these conflicting idioms consort together quite happily. *The Forger's Shadow* is an academic work striving hard to hook a more general audience (it hails from Picador, not Oxford University Press), and few things are more calculated to do this than an agreeably spooky ambience of spectres, hauntings, lunatics, criminals, the demonic, literary mysteries, Promethean heroism, esoteric wisdom and artistic suicides. The book's chapter-headings—'Villain', 'Ghost', 'Lunatic', 'Daemon', 'Bastard' and so on—don't bring to mind the way Dame Helen Gardner organised her materials. (Speaking of organising one's materials, the volume informs us no less than three times that in the 18th century a suicide's corpse was usually buried naked at a crossroads impaled on a stake.) A dash of Gothic sensationalism does no harm in the bookshops, and to this extent Romantic agony and postmodern commercialism are by no means the mutual strangers they might seem. Groom portrays his great men in suitably streetwise journalese, as in the sentence 'In the blue corner is Samuel Johnson, the greatest man of letters of the 18th century: an elderly, elephantine, scrofula-scarred, half-blind manic depressive.' Besides, the Romantic idea of inspiration, suggesting as it does a certain self-alienation, is not hard to reconcile with the postmodern cult of non-identity.

*

A little late in the day, Groom's Romantic humanism puts up a brief, perfunctory fight against his postmodernism. What, he asks himself at the end of the book, if the upshot of all of this juggling of signs and mixing of codes is an estrangement of one's humanity? Buried somewhere in here, then, is a human subject still authentic enough to be capable of estrangement, and thus at odds with the simulacra he seems happy to celebrate elsewhere. As befits a postmodern study, *The Forger's Shadow* is for the most part relaxedly amoral about its central topic. Groom would scarcely allow himself to be drearily unreconstructed enough to champion truth and reality against the frissons of fakery. 'Can forgery be defined', he inquires, 'without a debilitating recourse to words like real, true or authentic?' Such terms may have a debilitating ring to them in Soho clubs, but perhaps rather less so among those families who still want to know where the Bosnian Serbs buried the bodies.

Poets who poach the odd image from other poets may not be villains, but what about academics who lift their postgraduate students' research without acknowledgment, not to speak of those who walk off with someone else's country? Were the people of East Timor simply trapped in nostalgic, haut-bourgeois notions of legitimate possession in their resistance to Indonesia's incursions into their territory? Ideas of authenticity may prove debilitating when it comes to art, but we still need to know whether reports of political torture are true, and whether the police have been forging the evidence again. Groom would surely not disagree; but his fashionable denigration of truth and authenticity leaves his position dangerously unclear. How would he react were I now, finally, to disclose the truth that I have been sitting on for so long: *that I wrote this book on his behalf?* Perhaps he will claim to have no memory of asking me to do so; but then his memory is clearly fragile, as he himself acknowledges when he remarks that he cannot recall from which book of my own a certain passage he quotes comes. Maybe he made it up.

There are problems, too, with the postmodern dismissal of origins. The primordial can indeed be a tiresome fetish; but there are ways of censoring the investigation of origins which play right into the hands of political reaction. Pascal, Hume, Kant and Burke all counsel against any such exploration, for just such reasons. It is, as Hume puts it in his

Treatise of Human Nature, that at the source of every nation we will find violence and usurpation; and if its citizens are now gratifyingly docile and quiescent, it is simply because they have thrust this aboriginal trespass or violation into merciful oblivion. For Burke, the impious uncovering of this original sin, which is what the odious Jacobins are up to, is a kind of sexual indecency akin to the horrific unveiling of the Freudian primal scene. Political origins are not, to be sure, the same as artistic authenticity; but calling the comparison to mind might persuade one to speak a little less cavalierly about origins in general.

In one of the uncanny hauntings of which this study is so fond, Romanticism returns in all its starry-eyed splendour, only this time as the simulacrum rather than the original. In an ironic inversion, it is now the simulacrum which needs to be protected from the contaminations of the authentic. 'The simulacrum', Groom comments in typically hyperbolic style, 'is our reality, but in our being we remain haunted by the chimera of authenticity. We can overcome this authenticity by craft and by making, and in rebellion, and in becoming inspirational.' So it is now the authentic which is the revenant, the unexorcisable shade at the postmodern feast, the virus or disability which must be conquered in an act of self-mastery, a vigorous if vague therapy of making, rebellion and inspiration. The terms have been ritually reversed, but nothing has really changed. Groom the reluctant postmodernist is being constantly dragged back to his closet Romanticism, but must resist this insidious seduction with all the inauthenticity at his command. Being only human, even the most savvy and sophisticated of forgers find themselves backsliding into truth and stumbling into reality in moments of forgivable weakness.

Or—an alternative code for the same slippage—even those critics most intent on appealing to a wide commercial audience find themselves at risk of lapsing into the esoteric life of the intellect. *The Forger's Shadow* is an uneasy compromise between the cerebral and the commercial, the scholarly and the sensationalist. It is a highly intelligent book and a show-off one as well, bristling with energy and enthusiasm yet oddly self-regarding, attractively ambitious in scope but suspiciously thin on the ground. It generously acknowledges the Bodleian Library, along with Jim and Pat, George and Gaye, Cheri and Jamie, Nick, Norman and Jane and a horde of fellow boozers at the author's local pub, not to mention Andrew, Mandana, Bill, Dorcas, Jo, Laura and a host of others at his London club. Some of these people might be a bit surprised to learn that they have helped to shape his thoughts about the etymology of the term plagiarism or Plato's view of poetic inspiration. But that's intertextuality for you.

Alain Badiou

There is a paradox in the idea of transformation. If a transformation is deep-seated enough, it might also transform the very criteria by which we could identify it, thus making it unintelligible to us. But if it is intelligible, it might be because the transformation was not radical enough. If we can talk about the change then it is not full-blooded enough; but if it is full-blooded enough, it threatens to fall outside our comprehension. Change must presuppose continuity—a subject to whom the alteration occurs—if we are not to be left merely with two incommensurable states; but how can such continuity be compatible with revolutionary upheaval?

One might risk the generalisation that French radical thought has, on the whole, plumped for unintelligibility rather than continuity. From Rimbaud's '*Il faut être absolument moderne*' to Jean-François Lyotard's notion of the paralogical innovation which creates its own law, this vein of avant-gardist theory would rather be opaque than old-fashioned. From Sorel and the Surrealists to Jean-Paul Sartre, from Levinas to Lyotard and Derrida, such thought returns incessantly to the break, crisis, disruption or epiphany of otherness that will tear you free of everyday inauthenticity—of *doxa, das Mann*, the consensual, the practico-inert or the *être-en-soi*—and throw open for you instead the portals of truth, freedom and authenticity. It is a current of thought suspicious of the German and dialectical, for which a certain revolutionary continuity would still appear possible.

The result is a series of sharp oppositions between the kingdom of necessity and the realm of freedom: between otherness and identity,

First published as 'Subjects and Truths' (a review of *Ethics: An Essay on the Understanding of Evil* by Alain Badiou) in *New Left Review* 9, May/June 2001.

truth and knowledge, sublimity and beauty, history and Nature, freedom and bad faith, *Vernunft* and *Verstand*; the crisis-ridden truth of the
subject and the stabilities of the symbolic order, the emancipatory
impulse and the positive disposition of objects, the disruptively Dionysian and the smug Apollonian certainties of the civic arena. What is
required is some *acte gratuit*, act of faith, political conversion or existential commitment that will catapult you out of the one realm into the
other, leaving behind the drearily deterministic narrative of tradition,
biology, ethical consensus and political conformity for the heady milieu
of liberty, *engagement* and authentic selfhood. One can lend a deconstructive twist to this born-again narrative by insisting that nothing
simply escapes or is left behind, that each pole of the opposition
inexorably implicates the other, that the metaphysical or identitarian
are not simply to be given the slip. But it is still obvious enough which
pole is most to be valorised.

There is a sense in which Michel Foucault hedged his bets here. On
the one hand, the more positivist Foucault soberly dismissed all talk of
absence, repression, silence and negation in the name of taking
supremely seriously what actually existed, in the shape of given regimes
of objects and discourses. But the more Dionysian Foucault could
always be felt lurking around the edges of these sombre investigations,
bursting out here and there in some extravagant praise of Bataille or
sudden purple poetic flight, giving free rein for a moment to a clen-
ched refusal of all regime and positivity in the name of something
which trembled on the brink of articulation but could not yet speak its
name. Jacques Derrida, by contrast, has always been far more ready to
share with us his thoughts on the unthinkable, and in such works as
Donner la mort has been busy providing us with an extravagant parody of
an ethics of otherness. Ethics, for the later Derrida, is a matter of
absolute decisions, which must be made outside all given norms and
forms of knowledge; decisions which are utterly vital, yet which completely evade conceptualisation. One can only hope that he is not on
the jury when one's case comes up in court. Such ethical choices are at
once necessary and 'impossible', wholly mine yet 'the decision of the
other in me', a kind of implacable destiny for which, like Oedipus, we
are nevertheless entirely to blame. Confronted in our solitude with such
asocial, incommunicable crises of judgment, 'we fear and tremble
before the inaccessible secret of a God who decides for us although we

remain responsible'. It is not quite clear how this bears on such questions as whether to eat meat or strike for better conditions. Gayatri
Spivak repeats the position, leaving us with the spectacle of 'an
impossible social justice glimpsed through remote and secret encounters with singular figures'.

Derrida's view is both fideistic and Kierkegaardian. It is a new-fangled
version of the fideistic heresy that faith is merely some blind leap in the
dark, quite impervious to reason; and it has a remarkable resemblance
to Kierkegaard's conception of faith as an incommunicable holding fast
to an opaque, impossibly paradoxical Otherness that can never be
conceptually formulated but must be lived in fear and trembling. The
ethical thought of Alain Badiou, the former French Maoist who is now a
member of the militant ultra-leftist group *L'Organisation Politique*, might
best be seen as both supporting and subverting this model. On the one
hand, Badiou has no time at all for fashionable postmodern ideas of
otherness, and is splendidly savage in his onslaught on them. His
judgment on this whole Levinasian legacy is terse and scurrilous: 'a
dog's dinner'. Ethics, he believes, have now come to displace politics
(one might say much the same about culture), as a bogus humanitarian
ideology of victimage, otherness and 'human rights' thrusts aside collective political projects.

Denouncing the ideology of Man in deliberately old-fashioned, theoretical anti-humanist terms, and defiantly evoking such anti-humanist
1960s luminaries as Althusser, Lacan and Foucault, Badiou characterises the political situation today as 'the unrestrained pursuit of self-
interest, the disappearance or extreme fragility of emancipatory politics, the multiplication of "ethnic" conflicts, and the universality of
unbridled competition'. If this is scarcely an original portrait, his assault
on the conventional ethical response to this dispiriting condition is
more striking. The ideology of human rights divides the world between
helpless victims and self-satisfied benefactors, and implies a contempt
for those on whose behalf it intervenes. The idiom of difference and
otherness that accompanies it reflects a 'tourist's fascination' for moral
and cultural diversity; it accepts only those others who are 'good'
others—which is to say, those like myself; which is to say, not other at
all. It has no respect for the difference of those who do not respect its
own cherished differences. In an audacious return to the universal,
hardly à la mode among the Parisian intelligentsia, Badiou claims

instead that difference, infinite alterity, is what we actually have, and that the real question is one of achieving sameness. The political problem is one of struggling against the current of dominant, differentiating, unequal, particularist interests, in the name of the revolutionary universal.

The sameness he has in mind is more one of truth than equality. Truths, he insists, are the same for everyone, and anyone at all can proclaim them. This is a timely assault on the post-structuralist fetishism of 'subject-positions', that genetic fallacy or epistemological reductionism which would judge the truth-content of a proposition wholly in the light of its enunciator—a habit common to both post-structuralists and the upper classes. But the kind of truth Badiou is thinking of is not of a propositional kind. If he differs from the Kierkegaards and Derridas in his Kantian universalism, he is at one with them in this. For one thing, truths may—must—be universalised, but in themselves they are stubbornly singular. In fact, there are as many truths for Badiou as there are human subjects. Or rather, there are as many human subjects as there are truths, since a subject, for Badiou, is what is summoned into being by a response of persistent fidelity to an eternally enduring 'truth event', which breaks disruptively, unpredictably, into the given in all of its irreducible, incommunicable singularity, beyond all law, consensus and conventional understanding. And this is the other way in which Badiou's thought runs in the same theoretical grooves as some of the very acolytes of otherness he most scathingly opposes.

Truth events come in various shapes and sizes, from the resurrection of Jesus to Jacobinism, falling in love to making a scientific discovery, the Bolshevik Revolution to Badiou's own personal subject-constituting truth event of May '68. As far as that goes, a dogged fidelity to an originary revelation, a Lacanian 'Keep Going!' or 'Don't give up on your desire!' in spite of losing the thread and feeling the original event fade into obscurity, is clearly a universal ethics derived from a highly specific situation. Indeed, among the various candidates for truth events he throws in the Chinese Cultural Revolution, which might suggest that he is not yet an entirely recovered Maoist. Whether all significant truths are of such a sublime, world-shaking kind is a point worth considering. Badiou, then, wields a quasi-Kantian universalism against the multiculturalists—though a Kantianism shorn of its deontology and normativity, which is hardly much of a Kantianism at all. But he rejoins some of his political and theoretical enemies on the distinctly un-Kantian ground of the non-conceptualisable, revelatory, irreducibly singular, evental, subject-constituting character of truth. In fact, his thought is a curious mixture of Enlightenment universalism and Romantic particularism.

For Badiou, to be sure, ethics is not identical with the revelation of truth; it is rather the business of striving to remain loyal to it, and thus a practical form of life rather than a lonely epiphany. It is a question of 'persevering in the disruption', a phrase which clips together both innovation and continuity, visionary crisis and dogged consistency, or what in Badiou's language would be the 'immortal' and the 'mortal'. The big bang of truth and the steady state of ethics can thus be combined in a single theory. Here, too, Badiou differs from some of his *confrères*, for whom the problem is knowing what to do once the General Strike is finished, the public clocks have been shot at, the Dadaist happening is over, otherness has been duly intuited, the epiphany has faded and the moment of *jouissance* is no more than a fond middle-aged memory. He wants, in short, to insert the eternal into time, negotiate the passage between truth event and everyday life, which is what we know as politics. Though he has produced an avant-gardist ethics, he is aware of the perils of absolutising a truth event, and his language on this topic has much in common with, say, Lyotard's.

But the passage is not easily effected. It is blocked by the fact that Badiou, for all his undoubted political zeal, is as much caught in an élitist sort of antithesis between the ordinary and epiphanic as Derrida. He sees the need for truth and politics to be immanent in the given situation; but what he means by 'immanent' is not simply parachuted in from some transcendent outer space. He does not mean, as Hegel and Marx do, that there are forces which are part of the situation but which also have the power to transform it. He does not trust the quotidian world sufficiently to believe that. At one point, in writing of the ordinary, he puts the word in scare quotes, as though to distance himself demotically from any implication of disdain. Yet the disdain is in fact distinctly present. Commonplace social life, in that most Gallic of motifs, is for Badiou, as much as for Sartre, a zone of inauthenticity. Common knowledge is just idle opinion, and there is as sharp a gap for him between doxa and truth as there is for Plato. Indeed, Badiou characterises everyday life in quasi-biological terms as a realm of appetite, self-interest and dull compulsion. If this is the case, then indeed, little short of a quantum leap out of it into a higher dimension of truth is going to suffice. But if he had a less jaundiced view of the everyday, he might need a less exalted alternative. As it is, his philosophy reads rather like a bizarre conjuncture of Hobbes and St Paul. Are there really no contradictions in this quotidian realm? Is there no selflessness, compassion, extraordinary endurance? Or do we need to resort for such virtues to the numinous sphere of our fidelity to nonnormative, exceptionalist truth events?

Badiou gives short shrift to Aristotelian virtue ethics, partly because they are concerned with happiness or wellbeing rather than truth. He might do well to rethink this prejudice against the notion of happiness, which is certainly central to Marx's own ethico-political thought, as indeed is Aristotle. He might also, through Aristotle and Marx, be less dismissive of the idea of what the latter calls our 'species being' entering into ethical questions. One needs, to be sure, to avoid some naive naturalism here; but so should one avoid Badiou's antithetical error of humanism, enforcing in Sartrian style too rigid an ontological gap between our routine biological being and the death-defying leap into history and freedom. ('Death-defying' is exact for Badiou: it is through this commitment that one becomes an 'immortal' subject rather than a mere death-oriented animal.) Virtue ethics can remind us that the good is a common-or-garden matter, a question of getting proficient at certain social practices, rather than a more imposing, epiphanic affair. For Aristotle, it is more akin to learning how to play the trombone than it is to some beatific vision. Christianity encompasses both registers, finding the signs of *metanoia* or spiritual conversion in such sublunary affairs as whether you feed the hungry and visit the sick.

Badiou shares the banal conviction of the post-structuralists he berates that all social consensus is inherently negative, along with the modernist platitude that truth consists in breaking with such tedious traditionalism. But what if the situation within which one is innovating is already marked by a militant or revolutionary consensus—or is such a phrase simply oxymoronic for those who value disruption per se and despise consensus as such? Yet why should the word be confined to the polite opinion of the suburbs? Badiou remarks at one point that all consensus seeks to avoid divisions, forgetting perhaps the popular solidarity that overthrew apartheid or Communist rule. And is not capitalism the most innovatory mode of production of all, not just some static, dully consensual regime with which one must break, but one which perpetually breaks with itself? Not all innovations, to be sure, constitute truth events; but one must be cautious about admiring the disruptive and boldly inventive, confronted with the transnational corporations.

As for valuing disruption or innovation as such, Badiou has now, perhaps a little late in the day, altered his view on the matter. In this book, he accepts that such phenomena as Nazism may fulfil many of his criteria for truth event, while being in fact mere 'simulacra' of the genuine article. But he must of course produce some criteria by which authentic truth events are to be distinguished from bogus ones, and he does this somewhat implausibly by claiming that a genuine truth event always evokes and names the central 'void' implicit in the situation from which it springs. He maintains, for example, that Marxism is an authentic truth event because Marx designates, under the name 'proletariat', the central void of early bourgeois societies—the proletariat being 'entirely dispossessed and absent from the political stage'. But the proletariat was not always in fact either, and the fact that it was not does not invalidate Marxism. As for the resurrection of Jesus as a valid truth event, Badiou himself, as an atheist, does not give it literal credence. But if he does not, it must be because he is judging it according to a notion of truth rather more humdrum than the French Revolution or the empty tomb. Truth as accuracy cannot be so drastically subordinated to truth as disclosure.

Truth, in short, cannot just be the product of an event. Its procedures must already be in place to determine what is to count as such an event, as well as what is to count as persevering in one's loyalty to it. Badiou speaks of love as though it is a self-evident experience, which may be true for Parisians but not for the rest of us. The question 'What counts as love in this situation?' is, on one view, the whole end of moral discourse. But this is not wholly to endorse Badiou's own 'situation ethics', to give his avant-garde theory an old-fashioned 1960s name (for him, there is no ethics as such, just the ethics of this or that practice or situation). This rather conventional position raises some familiar problems. What is to count as a situation, and who decides? Are there really any 'singular situations', as Badiou seems to imagine? And is there any way of analysing, or even identifying one, which does not implicate general categories?

There are problems, then, with Badiou's ethics, as there are with anyone else's. But scarcely any other moral thinker of our day is as politically clear-sighted and courageously polemical, so prepared to put notions of truth and universality back on the agenda, so swingeingly radical in his assessment of the sorry ideological mess into which ethical thought has lapsed in its haste to confiscate the political. *Ethics* is a ferociously polemical essay, written—of all things!—for schoolchildren, and well served by its English translator, Peter Hallward, who also provides a lengthy interview with the author. Badiou has launched a transformative new intervention, which deserves to evoke a persisting response.

Colin MacCabe and John Springhall

There are four broad types of cultural analysis. One can choose the formalist approach, which lifts a cultural work free of its context in order to examine its internal logic, or alternatively select the historicist method, which returns the work to that context in order to understand it. But though these two modes are generally at daggers drawn, they can also be combined to produce two further perspectives: historical formalism, which detects the stealthy motions of history in the forms of a cultural artefact, rather than just in its raw content; and cultural materialism, which also looks at historical forms, but this time in the sense of the technologies and social institutions that mediate between the particularity of art on the one hand and the generality of 'history' on the other.

Though he might jib at the 'cultural materialist' label, Colin Mac-Cabe is certainly a card-carrying cultural technologist, whose fascination lies less with concrete texts or abstract theory than with media, audiences, pedagogy, censorship, curricula and questions of literacy. His professional career, from spurned Cambridge structuralist to Strathclyde chair, Pittsburgh professor and head of production at the British Film Institute, has involved an extraordinary double-act as don and cultural commissar, academic and apparatchik. As a naturally amphibious creature, the London-Irish MacCabe has been one of the forlornly

First published as 'Cambridge in spite of Cambridge' (a review of *The Eloquence of the the Vulgar: Language, Cinema and the Politics of Culture* by Colin MacCabe and *Youth, Popular Culture and Moral Panics: Penny Gaffs to Gangsta Rap, 1830–1996* by John Spinghall) in the *Times Higher Education Supplement*, 16 July 1999.

few links between radical theory and public policy, equally well-versed as he is in Chomskyan linguistics and film copyright law, floating the signifier and pinning down business sponsorship for the arts. If he wants to test out the truth of the 'author is dead' doctrine, he turns not to Barthes or Foucault but to the messy, hand-to-mouth business of making a movie. An avant-gardist-turned-administrator, his bloodless, briskly instrumental prose smacks more of the CEO's memorandum than the philosopher's meditation; he uses naff phrases like 'crystal clear' and 'to my incredible surprise', and his prose suffers from just a touch of self-importance. But these worldly-wise collected essays also reveal a capacity for sheer intellectual excitement well beyond that of most literary academics. They represent a kind of theorising on the hoof, as one imagines their author dashing from the BBC to the BFI, jotting down his thoughts about Milton or mass literacy on the back of a taxi receipt. Few pieces in this volume travel beyond ten or so pages; like the writings of Stuart Hall, they are the working notes of an intellectual activist rather than the esoteric reflections of the theorist.

They also reveal the obtuseness of any simple-minded contrast between traditional literary pursuits and the world of cultural studies. MacCabe, who can shift easily from Hegel to *Hancock's Half Hour*, is progressively minded precisely because he is in some ways so thoroughly traditional. He springs not from the media studies department of some ex-polytechnic but from Cambridge English, and what led him to Derek Jarman and Jean-Luc Godard was as much in line with that lineage as in revolt against it. Two aspects of Cambridge English—its social and historical sense of literature, and its relative openness to literary modernism—inform these pieces to their roots. The Cambridge-bred film journal *Screen*, of which MacCabe was a co-editor, was in its own leftist way just as self-consciously rigorous, loftily dismissive, militantly vanguardist and coterie-minded as F.R. Leavis's *Scrutiny*. The same excess of moral seriousness disfigured them both. Indeed, MacCabe quotes in this book a statement from Leavis about the nature of literary criticism that might have sprung straight from a contemporary cultural studies brochure. And little in this volume would have been possible without the influence of Raymond Williams, who, like Leavis and MacCabe, both embodied and dissented from Cambridge English values.

Where MacCabe first discovered the importance of the material

forms of culture was not in marketing or video but in that most
venerable of 'Cambridge' inquiries, the history of the English language.
There are essays here on the interrelations between speech, writing,
printing technology and political power, which ask among other things
how what began as a socially despised 'Anglo-Latin creole' ended up as
the official or joint official language of more than seventy states
throughout the world. Other pieces on film, television and popular
culture take their cue from this materialist concern with cultural institutions. Cultural studies, MacCabe claims, must be set in the longest of
historical perspectives, a claim that he illustrates by proposing ancient
Athenian drama, Elizabethan theatre and the advent of television as
comparably momentous moments of cultural history, all of them
straddling 'high' and 'low' culture. He also throws in a perceptive
parallel between the Elizabethan university wits and today's Monty
Python-type satirists.

What finally dismantles the high/low opposition is of course cinema—'properly the postmodern art', as MacCabe comments—which has
managed to chalk up an impressive array of masterpieces while
appealing to almost everyone. But the book is no wide-eyed apologia for
yet another batch of MA theses on *Neighbours*. 'The analysis of contemporary capitalist forms of culture', MacCabe admonishes, 'is almost
always divorced from the analysis of traditional forms with a remarkable
impoverishment of both.' If he has abandoned his former Marxism,
high theory and modernist vanguardism, it is not in the name of some
brittle postmodernist relativism. Latin is a fine language, but not as fine
for science as English; Glaswegian is quite as worthy as standard
English, but not so useful for certain international forms of communication. The isolated study of 'English' should yield ground to the
study of 'the whole range of cultural productions', but literature is after
all a mightily important component of this field, and the point is to
place the new and old media in fruitful commerce, not dogmatically to
privilege one over the other. It is the traffic between new technology
and traditional culture that fires MacCabe's imagination, and he is one
of the few intellectuals who see that where it matters most of all is in the
school classroom. Today's crisis of literacy, he thinks, is a lot more than
the figment of right-wing paranoia; but the truth is that basic literacy
never brought much cultural or political benefit to most of those who
enjoyed it, and the traditional literary values now hotly defended by

some commentators probably never spread to more than 5 or 10 per cent of the population in the first place. On the other hand, each time television serialises a Jane Austen or George Eliot classic, tens of thousands of copies of the books are sold. And if the new media have played their part in a new illiteracy, more and more highly literate types are needed to run these institutions. A postmodern capitalism that lowers cultural standards for some raises them steeply for others. As always, it is not a question of rising or declining standards in general, but of what one might call the social distribution of cultural capital.

For the professional pessimists, however, the only sure thing about cultural standards is that they were once higher. Most conservative critics, from Samuel Johnson to T.S. Eliot, have adopted a 'deteriorationist' case about culture, though Eliot is torn between the view that things are not what they used to be and the belief that they are as bad as they always were. The unspeakably prosaic truth, far too banal to pluck a book out of, is that some things used to be better and some worse. John Springhall's *Youth, Popular Culture and Moral Panics* shows us how today's moral outrage over the insidious effects of the media was prefigured in spasmodic fits of hysteria over such popular Victorian pursuits as the penny theatre and the penny dreadful. So much for Victorian values. Like much popular culture, these demonised forms of entertainment were for the most part morally orthodox and politically conservative, but what the middle class really objects to is the dangerous stimulation of plebeian senses.

The very class in Victorian England that impugned these evils was the one that reaped enormous profits from them, just as some Conservative politicians today praise commercial radio out of one side of their mouths while condemning poems that do not rhyme out of the other. Gripped by the notion that there is something profoundly subversive about people enjoying themselves, the Anglo-Saxon middle classes, so Springhall demonstrates, have continued to indulge in regular spasms of wrath over everything from gangster films to 'gangsta rap'. The book has a particularly fascinating section on the relation between the American fear of mass culture and McCarthyism. One right-wing US polemic alleged that two comic-book companies were staffed entirely by homosexuals, 'operating out of our most phalliform skyscraper'.

It is not true, then, that things are not what they used to be. It is rather that they are as bad as they always were. Just as the modernist demand to break with history has an exceedingly long history, so the complaint that popular culture is degenerating would seem to run back to ancient times. We are by definition always posterior to the golden age in which the Common Man alternated a spot of morris dancing with a snatch of Homer. Even so, the vote-catching brand of academic populism for which mass culture can do little wrong is music to the ears of those who grow rich on the cultural deprivation of others. If high culture tends to fetishise the past, cultural populism tends to erase it; but nostalgia and amnesia are sides of the same coin. It was Williams, our wisest advocate for the eloquence of the vulgar, who pointed out in his *Culture and Society* that a society that had only its contemporary experience to live by was poor indeed. But he also insisted that all tradition is a constant selection and reselection of ancestors, from the inevitably partisan vantage point of the present. There is, after all, an alternative to a conservative veneration of the past on the one hand, and an avant-garde disavowal of it on the other. What puts both cases in question is the idea of a radical tradition. In grasping this truth, Mac-Cabe is an inheritor of that dissenting tradition, from Leavis and Empson to Williams, that was neither dully conformist nor callowly iconoclastic, but that was rather, in Leavis's poignant words, 'Cambridge in spite of Cambridge'.

Iris Murdoch

'What's it all about then, guv?' a London taxi driver is said to have asked when he recognised his passenger as Bertrand Russell. The popular belief that philosophers should reveal the meaning of life, teach us how to live, survives the most arid excesses of logical positivism, and Iris Murdoch's mammoth new book, for better and for worse, is every London taxi driver's idea of what philosophy should be about.

For better, in that *Metaphysics as a Guide to Morals* is driven by a passionate hunger for truth and goodness, courageously prepared to ruffle a few Oxford philosophical feathers by taking the unfashionable Schopenhauer seriously, mixing in mysticism with Kant, Taoism with Wittgenstein, and encircling in its ample girth everything from tragedy to aesthetics, Freud to Krishna, God to Goethe. This, indeed, is philosophy dragged from the cloister, dusted down and made freshly relevant to suffering and egoism, death and religious ecstasy, how we look at pictures and how we feel compassion for others. Iris Murdoch's earliest philosophical enthusiasm was for Sartre, who believed that one could spin philosophy out of the ashtray; and if the novel is her natural medium, it is because the speculative notions which grip her—the good, the true, the beautiful—are there fleshed out in felt experience. It is logical that Sartre and Murdoch should write fiction, and logical that A.J. Ayer should not.

There is, however, a price to be paid for this breathtaking generosity of vision. *Metaphysics as a Guide to Morals* (the title surely parodies *Zen for Business Executives*) is a rambling, repetitive ragbag of a book, the philosophical equivalent of Murdoch's devotion to the loose baggy

First published as 'The good, the true and the beautiful' (a review of *Metaphysics as a Guide to Morals* by Iris Murdoch) in the *Guardian*, 20 October 1992.

monster of a novel. It sacrifices rigour of thought to imaginative scope, and some of its more technical sections have a generalised, second-hand feel about them. For all its sprawling richness, the book revolves around a starkly single antagonism.

In the right corner is Plato, whose vision of the intimate interrelations of truth, virtue and knowledge is one Murdoch endorses. The hardest thing is to transcend our tedious egoism, purify our desires, and look with steadfast selflessness on the luminous reality of others and of the world. Only through such truthful apprehension of the real will we become fully moral beings, and if art matters supremely, it is because it provides us with the finest image of such imaginative self-transcendence. If Murdoch returns as often as she does to Kant, Schopenhauer and the early Wittgenstein, it is partly because she is keen to distinguish such saintliness from mere stoical indifference.

In the left corner is one Jacques Derrida, who has abolished truth, morality and reality and left behind him nothing but an infinite play of language. Derrida stalks like some mischievous Gallic goblin through these pages, a kind of composite bugbear or handy straw target for all Murdoch finds nightmarish about modernity. But she can't be said to have looked with saintly selflessness on the reality of his work. Derrida is called a structuralist, which he is not. Structuralism is confused with deconstruction, and deconstruction with postmodernism, in the kind of slipshod conflation of one's *bêtes noires* which no academic would tolerate in a first-year undergraduate's essay. Murdoch seems to think deconstruction is 'scientific'—it is exactly the opposite—and then, contradictorily, accuses it of sacrificing the facts to its passion for change. It is said to hunt for the deep unconscious meanings of literary works, which is not true either (deconstruction detests depths), and Derrida is charged, in a now drearily familiar litany of conservative grouses, with having done away with experience, truth, meaning and the individual, rather than (as he has always insisted) trying to re-think these entirely indispensable notions. There is no doubt that Jacques Derrida has experiences, believes himself to be an individual, and thinks his Parisian apartment is real. It is just that he has raised some awkward questions about the meaning of such beliefs, questions not best calculated to land one an honorary Cambridge degree.

If the novel matters for Iris Murdoch, it is because it values the sheer contingency of human life, its tragi-comic muddle and incompleteness, against all that would try to systematise it. But post-structuralism values exactly that too; and if Murdoch is so keen to oppose it, it is because it represents her own vision of things pushed to an embarrassingly radical extreme. When the post-structuralists are celebrating contingency, Murdoch reaches for her Plato: beneath the flux of experience lie certain enduring Forms. But when she herself is celebrating contingency, Derrida and his crew are conveniently travestied as soulless white-coated technocrats who seek to wrap everything up in their dogmatic codes. You really can't have it both ways, but Murdochian muddle and incompleteness does its best.

The beauty of Murdoch's Platonic vision of the good is undeniable. This book could only be the product of a virtuous as well as deeply intelligent author. But as with all of us, Murdoch's intelligence is constrained by her unconscious ideological prejudices, so that she seems incapable, unlike William Blake, of seeing the dangers of an ethics of selflessness. To lay aside self-interest, to relinquish selfish desire, is the familiar political advice given by the privileged and powerful to those less fortunate than themselves, and if the less fortunate are to seek justice they would do well to close their ears to such speciously altruistic talk. This book has much to say about how we should relate to the world—whether we should embrace it, relinquish it, see it for what it is. But it never pauses to ask what kind of world, in concrete historical fact, led its philosophers to take up the postures they did. The history of ideas floats here in a luminous void: philosophy may be about real life, but it is in no sense conditioned by it. And this, indeed, is Platonism with a vengeance.

One by one, the long-suffering literary humanists have begun to pick themselves up off the floor and do battle with the theoretical enemy—even if, like Iris Murdoch, they cannot quite get its name right. First there was Dame Helen Gardner, launching an impassioned defence of Literature. Then George Steiner, in his *Real Presences*, took up the cudgels against deconstruction. Frank Kermode, the most liberal-minded of all the literary traditionalists, has been weighing in recently with a series of tirades against fancy French theorising.

Iris Murdoch's book is wholly unpolemical in tone, but it belongs firmly to this genre, even if its sideswipes at Derrida are far less interesting and well informed than its subtle speculations on Kant and Plato. But it is all, alas, far too late. What nobody told these critics was that deconstruction is effectively over. Jacques Derrida has shot his intellectual bolt, and his influence has been for some time on the wane. This doesn't matter much to the traditionalists, since the name Derrida is just shorthand for all they detest about modernity, which for Iris Murdoch includes television, computers, sociology and a good deal else. It is odd to see such finely intelligent men and women arguing such a crude, one-sided case; and *Metaphysics as a Guide to Morals*, like many such works, is a striking mixture of wisdom and short-sightedness.

James Kelman

At the centre of James Kelman's passionate, ill-crafted essays lies the Romantic myth of the artist as fearless truth-teller, besieged on all sides by soulless administrators, mean-minded censors, self-appointed experts. Artists are Dionysian, dangerously subversive types devoted to justice, freedom and telling it like it is, whereas the rest of the world consists largely of abstract dogmatists, fancy theorists and buttoned-down bureaucrats who are out to shut them up.

It would be pleasant if this were true—if, for example, Craig Raine, Penelope Lively and Alan Ayckbourn really were Promethean revolutionaries eager to blow the lid off middle-class society and expose its exploitative depths. But despite Kelman's Romantic delusions, most artists are no more conspicuous for their political rebelliousness than most tax inspectors. Good artists, Kelman considers, are by definition opposed to any form of social discrimination, a view which entails that there was no art worth mentioning from Horace to Housman. In any case, it is hard-won expertise and boring administrative work which tend to make a political difference, not oracular pronouncements from those comfortably ensconced before their computers. One would not put Arthur Rimbaud on the sanitation committee. The political declarations of most artists, including left-wing ones, are usually as piously platitudinous as those of pop stars and UN Secretary-Generals.

In some of his moods, Kelman recalls this sobering truth. But he is not a man for nuanced judgments, and finds swingeing generalisations a lot simpler. 'In our society we are not used to thinking of literature as a form of art that might concern the day-to-day existence of ordinary

First published as 'Down with headbangers' (a review of *And the Judges Said: Essays* by James Kelman) in the *Times Literary Supplement*, 9 August 2002.

men and women.' Which society does he have in mind? Homeric Greece? Seventeenth-century France? Has nobody bothered to tell him what has been afoot from Defoe to Drabble? Has there been no evolution in this respect from Joseph Addison to Martin Amis? It is true that with a few superb exceptions like Kelman himself, working-class writers are almost as dismally thin on the ground today as they were a century ago; but this is because working people are educationally and culturally deprived, not because a lot of publishers would not love to get their hands on a fashionably plebeian piece of writing. Besides, you do not need to be working-class to be ordinary, as any small shopkeeper knows.

With truculent self-indulgence, Kelman writes as though literature were still the home of the personal valet, the imperial sunset and the cucumber sandwich. 'Ninety-nine per cent of traditional English literature', so he irately informs us, 'concerns people who never have to worry about money at all.' From Jane Austen to Evelyn Waugh, English literature, in fact, seems stuffed with people who worry about very little *but* money. They are known (Kelman may just have heard of them) as the property-obsessed middle classes. The patrician literature which Kelman seems to have in mind is as minor a current in modern English letters as the proletarian one. Where, he inquires, is the literary art which takes seriously subjects such as drug addiction, homelessness, alcoholism, racial abuse? The answer can be delivered in five words: everywhere on the London stage.

Several of these essays fulminate against censorship, which Kelman, like the rest of us, must surely endorse. Exactly how much anti-Semitic fiction does he believe should be prescribed at GCSE? He is thinking rather of prissy-minded newspaper editors deleting his four-letter words, but it is typical of his shoot-from-the-hip style that he fails to make such vital distinctions. There is, he believes, a cultural élitism at work which insists on certain stereotypes: fat women must have hearts of gold, Jews are greedy, people on the dole are lazy, and the like. There is indeed a potent cultural élitism in modern society, but it does not for the most part trade in such pathetic clichés, and is all the more resourceful on that account. Those on the dole may not be lazy, but Kelman himself is that most indolent of polemicists, one who luridly caricatures the opposition and thus buys his victories on the cheap.

This is a pity, since the mild paranoia of these essays, like most forms of mild paranoia, has a lot to be said for it. It is indeed the case that working-class writers, or anyone who writes in other than Standard English, have a hard time getting a hearing. Kelman's insistent question—'How could I write from within my own place and time if I was forced to adopt the "received" language of the ruling class?'—is an urgent, entirely valid one, even if he seems to think that everyone around him writes like Noël Coward. 'Ordinary people' may well have won a hearing in English writing a long time ago, but it is true that whole reaches of social experience remain closed to the metropolitan literary establishment. And few have breached those barriers more productively than Kelman himself, even if some of his opinions (he doesn't like left-wing doctrine in fiction, for example) would not be at all out of place in an Oxbridge common room.

The interesting Kelman is not the one who churns out limp clichés about 'the primacy of the world as perceived and experienced by individual human beings', with which all of his cultural antagonists would instantly concur. Nor is it the author who speaks up for literature but can't be bothered to turn a shapely sentence in this expanse of drably utilitarian prose, let alone a funny or ironic one. It is the man who is by no means comfortably ensconced before his computer—the dedicated activist who has played his part in the struggle for freedom of speech in Turkey, as well as lending his voice to the Edinburgh homeless, unemployed steel workers and Glaswegian victims of racial violence.

It is accounts of such campaigns which form the most memorable pieces in this collection, not self-centred rants against the apparatchiks of the Edinburgh Fringe. Kelman is the kind of man whom anyone at the sticky end would want on their side, a writer who combines intense local engagement with generously international perspectives. He has, in short, quite enough courage, integrity and zeal for justice not to need to imply that almost everyone around him is an arty-farty headbanger.

David Beckham

One suspects that David Beckham wrote this book rather in the sense that the Pharaohs built the pyramids. Sentences like 'Some of the things I used to wear a few years ago were horrendous and when I look back, I think what was I doing?' smack more of mutterings to some hired hack over the snooker table than of the tortured stylistic wrestlings of a Flaubert. In fact Beckham's prose is as excruciating as one imagines V.S. Naipaul's shots at goal would be. Reading this aggressively styleless book is a bit like munching your way dutifully through yard upon yard of muslin.

Curiously, though, its very monotone, stream-of-tape-recorded-consciousness style begins after a while to seem like some artful, sub-Pinteresque device. 'I had', he tells us, 'one really, really good friend called John at primary school, but when we moved on, we went to different schools and sort of split up. We were never as good friends again. I had other friends at school and out of school, but no one like him.' There have been livelier narratives. We never encounter John again, or probe deeper into why he meant so much to Beckham. It is just one of those bald, uninterpretable things, like chasing someone with a vacuum cleaner, wearing a sarong or including a close-up photo of your dirty feet in your autobiography. Not that any of this matters much, since the text in this lavish production is far less important than the photographs, and neither can compete with the volume's delicious aroma. There could be no finer reason to buy this book than to sniff it. Readers who buy it but don't inhale are missing out on most of the fun.

Since you can now apparently take a course in David Beckham at the

First published as 'Written on the body' (a review of *My World* by David Beckham) in the *Guardian*, 14 October 2000.

University of Staffordshire, there's no point in his pretending to be an ordinary guy. Ordinary guys don't land up on the syllabus alongside Plato and Pynchon. But this is precisely what this crafty, apparently guileless book is out to counterfeit. Beckham projects himself as a shy, modest, chaste, uxorious, home-loving, extravagantly commonplace type, faintly naive and just a mite boring, not quite as geekish as Gary Lineker but tilting more towards him on the football-star spectrum than to the Dionysiac George Best. He tells us with arch, little-boy winsomeness that he is now 'relaxed enough to be in the same room as [the Spice Girls] and not sweat', but to avoid sounding a complete nerd adds roguishly that he tried to hold his partner's hand on their first date, since 'that's the way I am'.

He is relentlessly devoted to his wife, who seems to be some sort of performer, and records how much he was moved by her legs and short skirt when they first met. 'I see us as the perfect couple', he announces, a phrase which avoids odious self-adulation only because it clearly doesn't know itself to be even more unacceptable than referring to oneself and one's partner as a couple of prize turds. Their wedding ceremony, he remarks, went very well, though at one point he did 'get very hot in the folly'. This sounds an unusually risqué remark for such a doctrinaire New Man, but it turns out to be a reference to a bit of the castle in which they were married, rather than some salacious Cockney slang. For a man who has been regularly 'hit by thongs and knickers', Beckham is upright in a moral rather than libidinal sense. At one point, he observes leeringly that a particular set of bra and panties he received in the post must have come from 'a big girl'. Elsewhere, however, he reveals that he likes to get in touch with the feminine side of himself: hence the celebrated sarong. He even cautiously enjoys a bit of art, and has been known to indulge in a little nature imagery, such as 'over the moon'.

Nor has he any craven changing-room fear of feeling. Throughout the book he runs the whole gamut of emotion from 'chuffed' to 'gutted', while being on the whole (surprisingly, for a fabulously gifted millionaire) more gutted than chuffed, and he cheerfully confesses to a short temper. He is also far more addicted to cool new-age tattoos than to tacky old-style booze; indeed he intends to have the names of his future children etched into his back along with that of Brooklyn—which, given his ferocious domestic affections, might end up taxing even his lithe torso.

The irony is that Beckham is indeed an ordinary guy, even if he is also playing at being one for all he's worth. The counterfeit is true after all. He comes across as attractively—as well as tediously—low-key, and is as quick to praise others as he is to criticise himself: 'I was showboating, hitting flash, stupid balls', he comments of his early days as a player. He also detests racism (he is a quarter Jewish himself), and isn't in the least bothered by being fancied by gay men. He may be a lousy author, but he is clearly a loving father, who has to endure obscene chants from the terraces about his wife and child. But even as an author he has his strong points. A lot of people will read this book as one might read something scribbled by a badger: what matters is the author rather than the content. But football fans will read it for inside information, and there's a good deal of that.

But this regular guy is also a public fetish, and the book can work only by prudishly playing down that whole dimension. 'I have a camera up my backside almost 24 hours a day', Beckham tells us, but it's hard to know whether this is a boast or a whine. He is scrupulously careful not to overdo the moaning, so as to sidestep the obvious riposte: how come he's so averse to cameras when half this book, indeed half his life, consists of images? The camera here may not quite be poking up his backside, but it lingers on his naked torso or splayed thighs, surprises him in the bath or discovers him locked in erotic embrace with his wife or car.

This split down the book's middle, between text and image, is also the fissure known as David Beckham. In the front half, the bashful lad who loves his old mum and prefers curling up with a take-away to showbiz orgies; in the second half, the sultry, self-displaying narcissist, hungry for the admiring gaze. In generously all-inclusive spirit, the first half of the book is for male football fans, the second for female fantasists. The split is most obvious when Beckham opens his mouth and speaks, as the sleek, postmodern body is suddenly converted into the uncertainly articulate working-class boy. There is no old-fashioned attempt at resolving this contradiction. The two personae simply lie incongruously cheek by jowl, with an inexplicable blank between them, as with so much of the culture that Beckham symbolises.

Roy Strong

The history of a nation is no more a story than it is a symphony or a soap opera. You can talk of the story of Pink Floyd or Marks and Spencer, since these things are projects with a shaping intention behind them. But there is no shaping intention behind British history from Hadrian to Heseltine. Nobody deliberately churned out a remarkable achievement called Britain, in the way that someone produced the paperclip or *Mansfield Park*. A nation is not something meant, in the way that each bit of a literary narrative is supposed to slot neatly into the whole. There is no plot to British history, no end or origin, no riveting suspense or astounding denouement. History may be full of rattling good yarns, but it doesn't constitute one in itself.

In this lavishly illustrated volume, designed for those who like easy-on-the-eye history and have the odd free corner on their coffee table, the art critic Roy Strong sets out by speaking of the history of the nation in aesthetic terms, as a 'strong narrative' centred on powerful personalities. Five hundred and sixty-seven pages later, he briskly undercuts his own project by confessing that there is no single unfolding pattern to it all. There is, so he bizarrely claims, a beginning to British history, but no possibility of an ending. (At what exact time of day does he think it started, and why couldn't it grind to a halt in a few years with the break-up of the nation state?) So there is no grand storyline from the Venerable Bede to Tony Blair after all, even though the book behaves exactly as though there was.

The Story of Britain indeed has an epic fable to recount, one in which things are generally found to be in pretty good shape from the ancient

First published as 'Kings, Queens and gardeners' (a review of *The Story of Britain* by Roy Strong) in the *Guardian*, 26 September 1996.

Romans right up to the Rolling Stones, when British history took a nosedive into materialism and amorality. Even here, however, Strong cannot help sounding an upbeat note: at least, he remarks with an audible gritting of teeth, ours is the age of the common man. It is hard to feel that he secretly finds this any more enthralling than knocking a nail through his nose, but it belongs with his relentless cheeriness to affirm it. The irony is that that cheeriness is based on a bland indifference to the actual fate of the British 'common man' throughout the centuries.

Like many such fables, Strong's book is really a history of the British ruling bloc rather than of the people who kept them in hounds and liquor. History for him consists of art, war, religion and high politics, while work, sexuality, material hardship get thrown a perfunctory paragraph here and there. Misery and distress are noted from time to time, but usually as a mere episode of a history steadily on the up. History is really the story of Great Men, in a book which devotes considerably more space to Inigo Jones than to the 17th-century peasantry. Edward I was over six feet tall and majestic in presence; Edward II was 'tall, good-looking, with fair curly hair, muscular in build'; Richard II invented the handkerchief; Henry V had a long oval face and full red lips. What is this, a chronicle or a beauty contest? Elizabeth I's campaign in Ireland is recorded, but not the fact that it was genocidal. The slave trade is passed over discreetly in a sentence or so, and one turns a page to discover that the nation has suddenly, painlessly acquired an empire. Eighteenth-century gardens receive more attention than 18th-century bread riots, suitably enough for the author of *Successful Small Gardens*.

In this 18th-century golden age, Strong rhapsodizes, 'everywhere life assumed a new radiance' (one thinks of all those beaming handloom weavers), even though he also lets slip that over half the population were sunk in poverty. Later, we learn that the Tolpuddle martyrs 'unfortunately' engaged in illegal oaths, which (so it is implied) is why they were transported. A chapter revealing the rigid hierarchies of Victorian England is mysteriously entitled 'Victorian Britain: the Classless Society'.

Things aren't improved by Strong's Ladybird style, rich in emulsive banalities. 'Roman soldiers looked very different from the Celts they defeated'; 'for centuries the church had gone through good and bad periods'; Henry II showed that 'red hair and fits of temper often go together'. There are snatches of newsreel history: 'Everywhere the Romans went they took their civilisation with them.' Since the book is too hard for five-year-olds but too simple-minded for anyone older, and since the author himself admits that there is nothing particularly original in it, one wonders why he did not just give us another batch of successful small gardens.

The answer is broadly political: what is important is not any particular sentence in the book, most of which are stalely familiar, but the act of rehearsing this tale right now. In the teeth of the current leftist 'deconstruction' of Britishness, Strong wants to persuade a 'younger generation of islanders' to contemplate what it is that binds them together as British. What it was for their forebears, so Linda Colley has argued, was a heady brew of Francophobia and anti-Catholicism. Perhaps for the younger generation today it is football or Pakistanis or Britpop or nothing in particular.

Strong himself would not be much enthused by any of these brutally realistic responses, even though his conservatism can be critical enough: he thinks that traditionalism has led to the nation's economic decline and is in some respects a zealous moderniser. But he also believes that the fact that Britain is an island is more important than any other in understanding its history, a claim which provides his very first sentence and which is palpably false. Geography, in short, is destiny: the fact that we are surrounded by water mysteriously accounts for our pragmatism, tolerance, innate conservatism, just as north/south conflicts within the island are basically a matter of highlands versus lowlands. In this crudely determinist perspective, all that sordid wrangling with the Scots comes down to a question of altitude. 'Island claustrophobia', Strong suggests, 'must account for the great geniuses of our history', unaccountably overlooking some of the great idiots too. It is remarkable how the custodians of culture reach for their Nature when under threat. If you cannot beat the deconstructors with ideas, try on a bit of topography.

To ask 'less when and how than why' is how Strong describes his aim here. In fact, nothing could be more ludicrously at odds with his practice. This portrait-gallery brand of history shows no grasp of social causality or structural conflict, so that while what the book says is usually pretty predictable, what it fails to say is resoundingly eloquent. Strong's style of history is like the kind of literary criticism which thinks that its job is just to summarise the plot. It is the historiography of the victors, who unlike their victims do not know that states of emergency are routine rather than untypical.